FORGET THE CAMEL

ELIZABETH MELAMPY

FORGET THE CAMEL

THE MADCAP WORLD OF ANIMAL FESTIVALS AND WHAT THEY SAY ABOUT BEING HUMAN

APOLLO
PUBLISHERS

Forget the Camel: The Madcap World of Animal Festivals and What They Say about
Being Human
Copyright © 2025 by Elizabeth MeLampy

Visit our website at www.apollopublishers.com.

Library of Congress Control Number: 2024933928

Print ISBN: 978-1-954641-43-3
Ebook ISBN: 978-1-054641-44-0

Printed in the United States of America.

FOR BAM AND BEEPA.

CONTENTS

CONTENTS

Our animal origin is the story of our place in the world. It's the basis of how we give meaning to our existence. This is an impossible task without first accepting that humans are animals. This should be straightforward, yet it isn't. In truth, we live inside a paradox: It's blindingly obvious that we're animals and yet some part of us doesn't believe it.

Melanie Challenger

———————

We tell ourselves stories in order to live.

Joan Didion

PREFACE

I never expected to live stream a woolly worm race. But here I am, eyes glued to my computer screen, as seven strangers cup black-and-brown woolly worms tenderly in their hands. On the announcer's mark, the racers set their worms at the bottom of the special track: seven pieces of string hung vertically in a row from a frame-like structure. The first woolly worm to make its way to the top of its string wins.

When the race begins, the racers coach their worms: "You've got it!" "Go, go, go!" Some blow on the worms, while others clap at them. Two human mascots—Misti and Merri Weather—dance around the small stage, dressed as woolly worms in black-and-brown striped onesies, red sneakers, and puffy gloves. A chant emerges from the small audience: "Worm, worm, worm!" But despite all of this encouragement, the stubborn woolly worms don't understand their mission. Many of them head the wrong way, turning around or falling off the string entirely.

"Worm down, worm down!" the announcer exclaims. After a few minutes the race still has no front-runner.

"They've gotta go all the way to the top?" someone's voice off camera asks incredulously as the minutes tick on.

"Oh yeah" comes the answer. The camera focuses in on the worms, allowing me to get a better view. The bodies of these tiny woolly worms ripple as they inch along.

After nearly seven minutes—which is a long time to watch these tiny things crawl—one finally reaches the top, prompting the referee to blow his whistle. The winning worm crawls all over its human's hands while the official "reads" the worm. Folklore suggests that the colors of the woolly worms—which are not worms at all but caterpillars—forecast how bad the coming winter will be. But since every worm found in a given year has a slightly different coloration, it's hard to know which worm's prediction should be trusted. The competition determines which worm will be the official weather predictor. The winning worm being the strongest worm of the year, its prediction for the coming winter is considered the best. Surrounded by a weekend of other activities, this race is the centerpiece of Banner Elk, North Carolina's annual Woolly Worm Festival.

At festivals like this all around the country, communities gather to celebrate their local history, raise money for civic causes, and open their town to visitors. People use events like these to mark time, build their identity, and throw a good party. It's an old instinct. As the author Nancy Meyer (not to be confused with the film director Nancy Meyers) wrote in her history, *Festivals of the West*, "No one knows when men first gathered at an agreed-upon place at an appointed time to celebrate some break in the chain of routine days. But it must have been near the dawn of man."[1] Festivals are unique performances of local identity that exist at the crossroads of our symbolic and practical lives. Their purpose is twofold, looking both inward and outward at once. They are community-centered and localized but are often designed to entertain tourists and other visitors too. At festivals we celebrate tradition, remind ourselves who we are, and evoke common heritage. Then we project that self-image to the world.

Animal festivals have an abiding power to unite communities and raise spirits. Take the Woolly Worm Festival, which had been forced to transition into a virtual "Woolly Worm Webfest" in light of a recent hurricane in the region. When organizers could not host the full-scale event, they decided to live stream a significantly smaller race than usual, taking advantage of the virtual format to ensure the annual ritual went forward. The town still didn't have running water, but the Woolly Worm Festival forged ahead. Animal festivals are that important.

While festivals may be hard to define, they typically include a central theme that informs the music, food, entertainment, and decor. There are dozens of festivals around the United States that use animals as that central theme. This is nothing new or even particularly American. The word "carnival," for instance, derives from the Latin word for "meat," stemming from the centuries-old European tradition of pre-Lenten festivals that centered on feasting before the season of abstinence. We humans do all sorts of things to animals for the sake of tradition and entertainment: kill them, eat them, race them, ride them, or sometimes even adore them.

As someone who has always cared deeply about animals, I am constantly trying to encourage people to think differently about the creatures with whom we share our planet. This is why animal festivals are so deliriously intriguing to me. Each event reveals a slice of how we think about animals and how, in many ways, we disregard them even as we host events seemingly in their honor. These festivals perform a piece of local history, but they also solidify and reaffirm our relationship with animals, relying on symbolism to teach visitors, children, and each other what really matters: ourselves. They offer normalcy in trying times, and opportunity in good ones. They are part of how we connect with the past, and they help us construct our identity for the future. These festivals tell stories about animals—which, ultimately, are also stories about us.

IDITAROD TRAIL SLED DOG RACE

ANCHORAGE, AK

"These dogs are born to run, and these mushers let them do it all the way to Nome!" The announcer's voice echoed over the loudspeakers as we fidgeted on the side of Fourth Avenue, trying to keep our toes warm. It was negative six degrees Fahrenheit when we left our hotel that morning, and it had warmed up to a balmy two degrees by the time the dogs were set for the ceremonial start of the Iditarod Trail Sled Dog Race in downtown Anchorage at 10:00 a.m. The snow that had been plowed out of the city streets all winter long had been pushed back onto Fourth Avenue the night before to prepare a path for the dogsleds, and now people crowded the street waiting. Kids around us tugged at their parents' jackets, asking where the dogs were. The excitement was palpable.

The street was packed with vendors, tourists, and mushing enthusiasts. Everyone was dressed warmly, bundled in snow pants, scarves, and hats. Some people wore full fur coats—one man even wore a full bearskin, head and all. The stores along Fourth Avenue bustled as people bought hand and foot warmers and dog-themed souvenirs. Volunteers handed out foam husky ears, which hundreds of spectators wore on top of their winter hats. Behind the start line the dogs and mushers were staged in their mobile kennels. Many dogs were barking, seemingly eager to be strapped to the sled. Tourists like us milled about and jostled for a spot to watch the race.

We counted down the minutes—our toes were now officially numb—until the ceremonial start. Just before 10:00 a.m., a couple of "iron dogs," or snowmobiles, roared down the path. The national anthem played, along with the Alaskan anthem, and Senator Lisa Murkowski spoke about the importance of this event in Alaskan heritage. People cheered, clapped their gloved hands, and raised handmade signs to cheer for their favorite competitors.

Then the first musher was off, running down the man-made snowy trail in the middle of the street. This was the first time I ever saw sled dogs in action. They were surprisingly small, somewhere between forty and sixty pounds, and wore little booties over their paws. They were attached to the sled by elongated harnesses linked to a central towline. When the first sled rushed past us, the dogs were already panting and their tongues were lolling side to side. They moved at a clip between a trot and a run, and they looked energetic and excited. The musher waved and smiled as he passed us. Every few minutes, another dog team barreled down the track.

Billed as "The Last Great Race on Earth," the Iditarod is an iconic dogsled race that spans over a thousand miles through rural Alaska. The real race would begin tomorrow, about seventy miles northwest of Anchorage. The mushers would then follow the Iditarod Trail northwest to the old, off-the-grid mining town of Nome. It is an incredibly grueling journey, for both human and dog athletes. Fewer than nine hundred humans have ever made it to Nome to complete the race, where the famed Burled Arch awaits finishers. To put that number in perspective, more than seven times as many people have climbed Mount Everest. But today, the mushers would take only a festive, eleven-mile jaunt around downtown Anchorage as part of a ceremonial start. Today was about showing off to the city and to the spectators, letting people meet the dogs, and celebrating the long history of the event. Today was about community, not the race.

Tomorrow, the hard work would begin.

The Iditarod race was established to honor and celebrate Alaskan frontier history. Throughout the Alaskan gold rush of the late 1800s, the Iditarod Trail served as a path of camps and trading posts.[2] At that time, traveling around Alaska required a variety of transportation systems, including boats, railroads, wagons, and, of course, dogsleds. Dogsleds were especially useful for travel during the territory's long winters, when any roads that existed became impassable and water-ways grew solid with ice.

In 1925 a diphtheria epidemic broke out in Nome in the depths of winter. The rural outpost was accessible only by boat or dogsled, but the harbor had frozen over and become impassable; the town could not receive more supplies until spring thawed the water. When the local doctor discovered his stock of diphtheria antitoxin was both too small and expired, options for finding a way to get more to the town were slim. As children began dying, gray film closing over their throats, the entire nation learned of the plight of the tiny arctic community and followed, rapt, as a plan to relay the antitoxin to Nome by dogsled teams came into fruition. Some officials advocated for using then-nascent arctic air travel, which would have been faster; but because airplanes were open-air, winter air travel was at best dangerous and at worst practically impossible.[3]

Instead, dogsled teams carried the serum from Nenana to Nome in a relay that took five and a half days. Twenty mushers and more than one hundred and fifty dogs took part in that run, which encountered blizzards and traversed the treacherous Norton Sound. Four dogs died from exposure in that serum relay, and others were forced to retire from injuries. But the antitoxin arrived safely in Nome and spared the town of fourteen hundred residents the worst possible outcome of such an outbreak. Three weeks later, the town doctor lifted the quarantine, ending the ordeal.[4]

The nation was captivated by the novelty of Alaskan sled dog travel, the underdog story of overcoming all odds, and the personalities of the mushers and lead dogs. Balto, the lead dog on the final stretch of the relay to Nome, became a national celebrity and went on a tour around the country, as did Togo, another lead dog who ran the longest stretch of the relay.[5] A statue of Balto was erected in Central Park in New York City that same year.[6] In 1995, proving the longevity of the story and the powerful mythology of the arctic frontier, the actor Kevin Bacon voiced the hero in the animated film *Balto*, which loosely recounted the serum run.

But the heroic and lifesaving actions of the serum relay are not directly tied to the founding of the Iditarod race. In the 1960s, a committee was formed to research historical events in Alaska over the past century. Dorothy Page and Joe Redington Sr. worked together to dream up a long-distance dogsled race over the historic Iditarod Trail. In 1973, the thousand-mile Iditarod race was run for the first time. Joe Redington Sr., known as the "father of the Iditarod," raced the course nineteen times and was buried in his favorite dogsled after he died in 1999. While the race is often associated with the original diphtheria serum relay in 1925, the race route is, in fact, a reconstruction of the historical trail and freight route.[7]

The Iditarod nevertheless capitalizes on that founding myth, continuously invoking the fantastic tale of overcoming the elements to save children's lives. The Iditarod website itself explains, "it's important to channel the grit and determination that allowed teams of mushers to complete this herculean effort and deliver diphtheria serum that saved countless children's lives. That spirit lives on in Alaska today, and should be celebrated!"[8] That history turned mythology of the lifesaving dogsled run undergirds the entire event. Alaskans identify with that unflinching and selfless ethos, channeling the strength and stalwart effort required to live and thrive in such forbidding land. To establish their identity today, Alaskans look back, using sled dogs as a bridge to the past.

The past is what brought me to Anchorage too. When my grandmother died, she had just started working on what would have been an academic anthology of animal festivals around the world, exploring animal symbolism and the human rituals that have sprung up because of it. My grandmother—Elizabeth Atwood Lawrence—became one of the first woman veterinarians in the 1950s, and by the time I was born, she had gone back to school to earn a PhD in anthropology from Brown University. She wrote books about the complicated relationships between humans and animals, mainly in the American West. She was a pioneer in the burgeoning field. I grew up hearing about trips my grandparents took to animal festivals for her research: wren hunting in the United Kingdom, weather predicting on Groundhog Day, and snake wrangling in Texas. Throughout my life, her unfinished work has hung heavy over my family, a sad reminder of my grandmother's death anytime it came up. My parents—in an act borne out of some combination of aching nostalgia and guileless hope—saved my grandmother's files in their attic, where they stayed until the day I pulled a dusty box from its shelf.

Like my grandmother, I have always had a fondness for animals. Part of this came directly from her. I remember, for example, shrieking at a small beetle when visiting my grandparents' farm as a child. The next time I saw my grandmother, she gave me a book describing the pixelated worldview of insects so I could learn about them, not fear them. I remember begging to borrow her stethoscope with my sister so we could listen to our dog's heartbeat, and then our own, comparing the pumps of blood coursing through our mammalian bodies. I remember receiving a letter from my grandmother when my cat died, in which she wrote that animals, just like people, go on living after they're gone, both with God and in our hearts.

I've carried those lessons through to adulthood. In law school, my generalized care about animals sharpened into advocacy when I learned about what befalls animals every day in perfectly legal situations. I read about wild animals kept in tiny enclosures with only fetid water and moldy food in roadside zoos. I watched videos of farmed animals suffering on an immense scale, and I studied slaughter reports that turned my stomach. I read about animal abuse at the circus and rodeos, at hunting contests and horse races. The more I learned about how we treat animals, the more I was appalled at the injustice of it. I simply couldn't believe all of it was legal.

One day a colleague mentioned an animal welfare controversy at an annual rattlesnake hunting event in Texas. It reignited a long-dormant memory—my grandmother had attended this event for her research before she died. I called my mom and asked her if she still had my grandmother's boxes, then jumped in my car when she said yes. I was curious to know how far she had gotten into this project and what remained of her work.

There was an overwhelming amount of material in these boxes, and flipping through the pages felt like a glimpse into my grandmother's overflowing mind. Folders with simple labels like "frogs" or "butterflies" burst with material from nearly a dozen animal-themed festivals. Tucked between pages and falling out of folders were dozens of small, handwritten notes-to-self containing sources to track down, quotes she liked, or sometimes just a single word or two. It felt like I had a lot of puzzle pieces but didn't know what the full picture was supposed to be. There were no final drafts, no outlines, no sense of what she was planning with all this work. After sorting through everything, I found only one drafted chapter; everything else was just fragments.

As I sat there among hundreds of pages of articles and clippings with her thoughts coloring the margins in her signature blue ink, I wished so much that she were here to talk to me about it all. Reading and sorting everything was academic but personal, thought-provoking but intimate. I was only nine years old when she died—and it would be a decade at least before I'd come into my own academic interests. She was a leader in the field of human-animal studies, and it saddens me greatly that I never had the opportunity to talk to her as an adult. But reading through her materials felt like a conversation through time and space: me, the vegan animal advocate just embarking on a law career, and her, a long-ago-passed anthropologist fascinated with animal symbolism.

Between us, bridging this gap, were a handful of animal festivals: Groundhog Day, the Jumping Frog Jubilee, the Rattlesnake Roundup, and more. Once I got a handle on the full scope of her materials, I moved to my computer and opened an Excel spreadsheet. I made a column listing the events I found information about in her boxes, a column for each event's date, and a column for notes. I compiled a rough calendar as I searched online and gathered basic information about the festivals she was working on. All but one still existed. My grandmother had visited many of these events throughout the 1990s, and based on my quick searching, it seemed like not much had changed in the intervening decades. My crude calendar in hand, I realized there was a festival in just over a month I could try to attend.

I had no idea how to conduct a research trip. I didn't really know what I was looking for or whether it would be worth it. But I felt pulled to go and find out, to flesh out the scraps of my grandmother's notes with the fullness of what I might see. Excitement—and anxiety—bubbled in my stomach as I confided in my wife over dinner that night that I wanted to make this trip. I sheepishly said, "Maybe I could even finish my grandmother's book."

But when I started to dig into the material and attend some of these events, I realized I couldn't really "finish" my grandmother's work. As an anthropologist, my grandmother was exploring the symbolism humans attach to animals at these festivals. Her notes were academic, focusing on folkloric understandings of animals and the importance of ritual for building community. At first, I studied her notes, trying to see what she saw in these events. I wanted to be faithful to her project; I wanted to finish what she started. But as I attended these events and watched what humans do to animals simply for the sake of *fun*—hunting them, poking them, riding them, and in some cases even killing them—I began to understand there was more at stake than an arm's-length academic assessment might suggest.

The Iditarod exemplifies our complicated treatment of animals. From the inception of dogsledding, as evident in the story about the diphtheria serum relay, dogs have put their bodies on the line in response to human commands. People for the Ethical Treatment of Animals (PETA) has been an outspoken critic of the Iditarod for years. Right near the ceremonial start line, four protesters from PETA handed out flyers and fumed to passersby about the horrors the Iditarod inflicts on dogs. Two of the protesters were dressed in coffins with dog masks on their faces, each labeled with the name of a dog who had died in the race. The flyer they passed out boldly proclaimed, "Suffering and Death for Dogs" and "The Iditarod: A Deadly Race." It reminded attendees that over one hundred and fifty dogs have died in the race's history and that race directors themselves describe dog deaths as "unpreventable."

Dogs do suffer and die on the trail. In the 2024 running of the Iditarod alone, three dogs died during the race.[9] Dogs have died from hypothermia, heart attacks, trauma from vehicle strikes, and asphyxia from inhaling their own vomit while running. Dogs routinely suffer cracked paws, bleeding from stomach ulcers caused by too much ibuprofen, or diarrhea. Many dogs are pulled off the course during the race at checkpoints because of exhaustion, illness, or injury. Even those that complete the course suffer lung damage and other long-term health effects too.[10] In Alaska, to "knowingly inflict severe or ·prolonged physical pain or suffering on an animal" constitutes criminal animal cruelty. But Alaska's animal cruelty laws specifically exempt "generally accepted dog mushing or pulling contests" from their ambit.[11] So the treatment of these dogs is left to their mushers and to the race organizers, who know exactly what mushing entails for the dogs, both good and bad.

The race rules actually assume a drop-off of dog participants throughout the course: mushers must start with somewhere between twelve and sixteen dogs, but they need finish with only five attached to the main towline.[12] The official Iditarod rules also prohibit sheltering the racing dogs at any point during the race other than at veterinary checkpoints.[13] In 2022 two mushers were fined and forced down in the race rankings because of the "competitive advantage" they garnered by seeking shelter for their dogs during an intense and dangerous windstorm.[14] The effect of this rule is clear: choosing safety for the dogs means forsaking the competition. And for born and bred competitors, human and dog alike, that choice is often impossible.

Attention to these welfare concerns has pushed many corporate sponsors to withdraw their sponsorships of the race, including formerly big backers like Alaska Airlines, Coca-Cola, Wells Fargo, and ExxonMobil.[15] Registration to participate in the race has been dropping, partially in response to these changes in public sentiment and partially due to increased costs.[16] And climate change continues to threaten both the race itself and the ability of mushers to train. Snowfall is less certain now than in years past, and ice sheets are not as stable. In 2008 the start line of the Iditarod was moved to Willow, about an hour north of Anchorage, because of uncertain snow coverage in the original starting area of Wasilla. And twice in recent history, in 2015 and 2017, the start line was even moved away from Willow, because of insufficient snowfall there too; in those years, the course started near Fairbanks.[17] Apart from the race itself, the mushers need ample snow and cold to properly train their dogs for the undertaking. Without a sure supply of both, it's becoming harder for mushers to prepare.

But despite these mounting challenges, the Iditarod stubbornly persists. The race still unites the Alaskan community, the larger mushing community, and fans and spectators from all over the world. Local residents seemed to agree. No one I spoke with saw a serious threat to the future of the race. As one resident of Anchorage told me plainly, "It's such an important part of Alaskan culture." Even people outside of Alaska follow the Iditarod every year. National news outlets cover the race, and the cleverly named *Iditapod*, an Alaska Public Media podcast production that releases daily episodes during the race, answers questions from invested callers from all over the country. Even thousands of miles away in Massachusetts, I grew up hearing about the race, watching the animated movie about Balto, and admiring the toughness of the mushers and the dogs. The valiant spirit of the race endures.

The morning after the ceremonial start in Anchorage, we drove to the "restart" in Willow, where the dog teams would officially begin their journey to Nome. The drive was stunning, with snow-covered mountains looming in the distance in every direction. The temperature hovered around seventeen degrees, and the air was dry and crystal clear. We saw a few moose on the side of the highway as we drove.

We stopped at the Iditarod Trail Race Headquarters in Wasilla on the way. A giant sign in front of the small, cabin-like building, indicating it was donated by ExxonMobil, proudly explained the Iditarod race's history. Near the sign were a statue of Joe Redington Sr. and a statue of Balto, dedicated to "the indomitable spirit of the sled dogs." Inside was a one-room gift shop and a back room set up like a gallery, walls covered with artifacts and memorabilia. A video about sled dogs in Alaska, called *Why They Run*, played on a projector. On the left side of that room were two preserved dogs, Togo and Andy, forever alert within their glass displays.

I had read about Togo's exceptional performance in the 1925 serum run, and I felt a little starstruck seeing his body. He had led a team through a blizzard and over the treacherous Norton Sound for three hundred and forty miles, longer than any other team on the lifesaving relay. The run left him permanently injured, so he retired in

Maine. When he died, his body was put on display at Yale University for decades, until it was finally returned to Alaska.[18] While I looked at the compact body of this dog who was, by all accounts, brilliant and hardworking, who had saved countless lives by pushing himself beyond his body's limits, the video playing in the room explained that, despite the controversy around mushing and dog welfare, dogs run only because they want to.

Did Togo want to run so much, in such harsh conditions? Did any of the dogs who were preparing to begin their run today want to do it? The people interviewed in the video said, unequivocally, yes; you can see it in their eyes, they said, the pride and competitiveness the dogs feel in their sport. They are bred for this, the argument goes, so it's what they naturally want to do: to run and to pull. But breeding an animal for a particular purpose does not create an ethically iron-clad defense of that purpose. Breeding monkeys for lab experiments doesn't automatically make any given research method right. Breeding cows to slaughter for food doesn't absolve humans of the ethical pitfalls of factory farming. Just because the dogs were bred to run doesn't mean they don't have limits.

And *want* is different from predilection. I have run marathons, so I can say from personal experience that what you want in a distance event is a fickle thing—from training to the start line, from the middle of the race to nearer and nearer the finish line, the constellation of want and pride and effort morphs as pain and hunger and fatigue join the party. Do sled dogs *want* to run? I have no doubt. What about at mile 793 during a blizzard, when their paws are cracked and their lungs are icy? As someone who cried at mile twenty of my first marathon, I can take a guess: it's complicated.

Human athletes can choose their events. We can listen to our body's needs and act upon them autonomously, stopping for food or injury, and pushing on when we can. The sled dogs don't have the same choices. They are attached to a towline by a harness with other dogs, and a human musher tells them to continue—the same human who has trained them to obey commands, who has earned their trust, and on whom they depend for food, water, and shelter, especially out in the rural Alaskan Interior during the Iditarod. What meaningful choice does any animal have in a situation like that? We don't suggest soldiers can simply fall out of formation and disobey their superiors, even though they could stop walking at any time. The assertion of choice is an illusion meant to justify the command. The fact that these dogs are bred to run may be a prerequisite, but it is no defense. What mushers choose for their dogs on the trail is, ultimately, not up to the dogs.

When we made it to Willow, we followed hundreds of other spectators and trekked through a foot of snow onto the center of Willow Lake. The start chute ran down a short hill, across the lake, and disappeared around the bend into the woods on the far side. While we settled in and waited for the race, people around us drank beer, ate snacks, and gathered around fires. Some set up tents for warmth; one person was ice fishing while we waited. We bought a package of Girl Scout Cookies from an enterprising local father-daughter duo and munched on them. When the dog teams finally started taking off, everyone cheered and took photos, and the mushers high-fived fans as they drove by.

The president of the Iditarod Board of Directors wrote that the Iditarod "celebrates reverence for untamed wilderness."[19] And there is unquestionable romance in seeing a dogsled rush past you before disappearing into the woods on a frozen lake. On the other hand, there's something almost somber about the enormity of the dogs' undertaking, the pain and hardship they inevitably encounter. As most people know from experience, dogs are incredibly smart creatures. In my research, I came across countless tales of lead dogs saving mushers' lives, pulling them out of water when the sled fell through ice, stopping—even when commanded to continue—when they sensed dangers like cliffs or chasms that were invisible to the human eye. Mushing as a sport is full of deep adoration, care, and respect for the dogs and for their skill and athleticism. But it's also undeniable that mushing uses dogs to the point of injury and death for sport. What to do with these two opposing truths is the hard part.

The Iditarod, like every event in this book, raises important questions about how we interact with and use animals to entertain ourselves and to tell our own stories. Mushing is undeniably a huge part of Alaskan culture and history, but with the advancement in arctic flight and machinery like snowmobiles, humans no longer need sled dogs in the way they did a hundred years ago. Mushing is now a sport, having outgrown its use for mail delivery, freight passage, and communication. And the risk-benefit calculation necessarily changes with those developments. Almost everyone would say it was worth the death of a few dogs to save an entire town from a curable disease like diphtheria. But the equation gets much more complicated when the purpose for inflicting the harm is less dire. I'm not sure celebrating Alaskan heritage and history, proving grit and prowess on the trail, and entertaining fans are worth the death of *any* dog. No one is saving lives anymore, so the trade-offs are less clear-cut.

The Iditarod has adapted over the years to address some of the strongest criticisms about dog care. The dogs undergo extensive veterinary checks, before, during, and after the race. The Iditarod website boasts, "No dogs in this world are studied, cared for, or in front of a medical professional more times each year than the dogs that run the Iditarod."[20] In 2023 race organizers for the first time required GPS tracking for dogs who were dropped off at checkpoints. This was in response to a dog who previously went missing for months when he wandered away from a checkpoint. There are three required rests mushers must take during the race—one twenty-four-hour rest and two eight-hour rests—which allow the dogs to recover, eat, and sleep before continuing.

But there are serious and difficult debates about whether these efforts can ever be enough. Pushing dogs to run a thousand miles in a matter of days may never be humane. More precisely, the benefits to humans may simply not outweigh the costs to the dogs, no matter the measures we take to try to minimize harm. Establishing welfare measures is better than ignoring animals' interests altogether, surely. But attending to welfare also serves to push concerns about animals under the rug, assuring attendees that everything is just fine, perpetuating the story that these animals want to be doing whatever it is we are forcing them to do, even to their deaths. It's a way to absolve attendees of our complicity and guilt, to the extent we feel any. It's a Band-Aid on the problem and an imperfect answer to the ethical questions underlying all of these festivals. But doesn't the fact that we need or want this Band-Aid, this assurance, hint at a bigger problem festering like an ulcer deep within us?

We are always struggling to figure out what makes a human, well, *human*. This question undergirds religion, philosophy, morality, biology, chemistry, astrophysics, and more. The simplest way to define something is often by refuting its negative. We may not be able to say with certainty what defines a human being, but we can look around us and see animals and say we are, at least, not that. So we use animals to construct our identity, carving ourselves into the negative space around them.

We have used animals to navigate who we are as humans for millennia. The earliest humans painted images of animals on cave walls and ceilings. These paintings often depicted animals reverentially, looming over human figures. But over time, as humans began to hunt more for subsistence, the images changed. The cave paintings started to show animals as smaller figures, or surrounded by a group of humans, with the humans in more dominant positions.[21] It is a human instinct to compare ourselves to animals, in ways that are both good and bad for the animals. This ancient transition from revering animals to dominating them raises some critical questions: Can our relationship with animals change again in our time? Could we move toward a more respectful relationship with animals? While human supremacy on this planet seems inevitable in the twenty-first century, what would it mean to disentangle dominance over animals from its expression in violence, to separate governance over the natural world from exploitation?

In exploring how humans define our humanity through how we relate to nonhuman animals today, these ageless patterns are still evident. We exert dominance over animals, killing and torturing them, and oftentimes eating them. T-shirts with slogans like "I didn't get to the top of the food chain just to become a vegetarian" (an actual T-shirt I purchased as a child from a barbecue joint in Texas) or "I'll stop eating bacon when pigs fly" (which I spotted in the airport) demonstrate this mentality of human exceptionalism expressed through inevitable—and even self-righteous—violence. We deploy animals for comedy, laughing at how they walk, move, and vocalize. Humor serves to reinforce the solid line between us and them and fosters deep ambivalence. Then there are animal species we revere and idealize, who we put on a pedestal and whose best qualities we celebrate, even as we sometimes forget the real, individual animals that are capable of suffering and joy.

In Anchorage, all of these manifestations of human-animal relationships were present. Mushing dogs involves dominion over animals, but there is deep adoration and respect for sled dogs too. Additionally, there's quite a bit of humor in Anchorage during the Iditarod. The start of the Iditarod coincides with the end of the two-week Fur Rendezvous (more commonly known as the "Fur Rondy"), Alaska's largest and oldest winter festival. The Fur Rondy is older than the state, dating back to 1935 when hunters, miners, and trappers returned from their winter work. The Fur Rondy includes some traditional events, like the world championship sled dog races, a three-day race testing speed rather than endurance, and the blanket toss, a favored Alaskan Native tradition of bouncing attendees into the air with an outstretched walrus skin. But it also includes some quirky modern events, like the outhouse races, where participants build and then push a teammate sitting in an outhouse-style contraption on skis down the street.

We joined the crowds on Fourth Avenue to watch the annual running of the reindeer, part of the Fur Rondy that's advertised as "Alaska's wackiest race."[22] In this interspecies footrace, humans line up in heats and start a jog down the street. After the humans are all released from the start line, a herd of reindeer are released, and they give chase, some weaving among human runners and passing them with ease, others meandering mindlessly. My wife and I burst out laughing when the first reindeer barreled past us. It was hilarious watching reindeer overtake humans and just as funny watching the ones who ambled along next to the humans, not sure what all the fuss was about. Everyone was cheering, laughing, and filming the event with joy. Many people on the sidelines wore foam antlers on their heads while watching the race. There were three or four heats, and the moment the reindeer rushed past the humans never got old, even when we knew it was coming.

Human-animal relationships are not simple. Often, we treat animals with a blend of supremacy and love, making categorization and study difficult. But three categories—dominance, humor, and reverence—offer a starting point, a way to begin to untangle our sometimes complicated relationships with different animals, and a diagnostic tool to understand why we do what we do to different species. This book looks at festivals across the country that exemplify these paradigms, starting with the most obvious examples of dominance, moving to different expressions of humor, and ending with possible versions of reverence.

This book is over thirty years in the making. What materializes from decades of research and festival visits by two different people at two different points in time is one abiding truth: all across the country, in different contexts, for different purposes, we use animals to say something about ourselves. Animals are a source of cultural meaning we reiterate over and over again. My grandmother's work on these same festivals from thirty years ago only reinforces this conclusion. For decades these festivals have remained unchanged. It was remarkable how accurate my grandmother's notes—taken in a time before cell phones and the internet—were to my own experiences at the same events. Some businesses had gone under, key people had passed away, and there was generally more consideration of animal welfare than she described, but the core parts of the event were the same, almost purposefully fixed in time.

Nevertheless, a lot of the circumstances *around* these festivals have changed drastically. The world is a smaller, more interconnected place now. Technology has forever changed how humans engage with enter-tainment. We have the internet, YouTube, TikTok, streaming devices, video games, virtual reality, and more. Our scientific understanding of animal sentience and emotional capacity has grown. The wild-life populations of many of the animals discussed in this book have shrunk or shifted. In this new world—in a time in which we have other options—I'm not sure it still makes sense to rely on these archaic, and sometimes cruel, forms of entertainment.

The animals used in these festivals are living, breathing creatures with their own interests and needs, and with their own capacities for fear and pain. In the process of researching this book, I watched dozens of dogs begin a thousand-mile journey. I stood by as hundreds of snakes got beheaded. I witnessed livestock sold at auction for slaughter. I saw frogs huddled in piles surrounded by stale water and dead cockroaches. I winced as ostriches fell flat on their necks in desperate attempts to escape the humans gripping their backs. And most importantly, I learned that the festivals included in my grand-mother's materials were not unusual or unique; they were only a starting point. Events using live animals happen all over the country and the world during every month of the year. And all of these inter-species festivals have victims: one species decides the contours of the celebration, and another species is subject to our whims.

By skinning rattlesnakes and boiling lobsters, racing camels and jumping frogs, honoring groundhog weathermen and celebrating migrating butterflies, humans undeniably demonstrate our obsession with various aspects of animality. Animal-focused festivals reassert the boundary between humans and animals every year, all over the country, in different ways. These festivals are noteworthy not necessarily for their size or influence but for their prevalence and longevity. They serve as microcosms of how we treat animals more broadly in society:

with scorn, with ambivalence, or with adoration, in turn. Animal festivals offer concrete examples of how we perform our human identities by using—and abusing—animals. We juxtapose ourselves with animals, and animality, in order to claim and assert our humanity, and at festivals, this process becomes literal.

After watching the dogs take off in Willow, we boarded a red-eye flight out of Anchorage. I went to work the next day, just like normal. But this event didn't end when I left—it had only just begun. It felt bizarre to know that for the next week, while I went about my daily routine, the dogs were still running. While I brushed my teeth and drove to work and read the news and slept, the dogs were running.

I followed the race closely. With an endurance race like this, just making it through was its own challenge. And part of the thrill of spectating was watching the number of mushers drop. Within a few days, one musher withdrew because of a broken finger. The defending champion scratched a few days later because of periodontal health issues. While some humans had to take care of their own health needs, the mushers also constantly had to consider whether their dogs could continue the race. I followed along as mushers dropped dogs at checkpoints because of health or safety concerns. That decision is surely a hard one for mushers. But I couldn't stop thinking about the dogs who were left attached to the harness for the entire thousand-mile race, who must have been getting more and more tired with every passing hour, even as their proportion of the weight load grew heavier.

Eight days, twenty-one hours, twelve minutes, and fifty-eight seconds after leaving Willow, Ryan Redington pulled into Nome, winning the Iditarod.[23] This was his sixteenth Iditarod race but his first win.[24] When Redington crossed the finish line, he only had six dogs in harness; the other eight he started with had been dropped off at checkpoints along the way. Redington's grandfather was none other than Joe Redington Sr., who had helped start the race over fifty years ago but had never won it himself. Mushing was in Ryan Redington's blood, and his victory felt a little like a homecoming, or a birthright.

These events and festivals have a natural way of coming full circle like that. The legacy we inherit is one we pass down. When I started researching this book, I wanted to understand the legacy I've received from my family. I hoped to learn more about my grandmother—and myself—by attending these festivals. And I did. Even though I disagreed with much of how the animals were treated, I used the snakes and frogs and butterflies as tools in my own quest too. At every event, as I simultaneously witnessed what befell the animals and enjoyed the celebrations with my fellow humans, I felt my DNA buzz in the knowledge that I was right where I was supposed to be.

PART I

DOMINANCE

RATTLESNAKE ROUNDUP

SWEETWATER, TX

Two things hit me right away: the smell and the sound. The air was saturated with the scent of fried rattlesnake, and throughout the Nolan County Coliseum, no matter where I stood, I could hear incessant rattling. As I shuffled through the doors and down the stairs with a throng of people, I descended from the bright, sunny day onto the dim, dusty floor of the coliseum. I had driven three hours west of Dallas to be here for the sixty-fifth annual Rattlesnake Roundup in Sweetwater, Texas. Four days a year, this celebration turns the little town of Sweetwater into a man-made snake den.

I was prepared for what I would see—I knew snakes would be hunted, killed, skinned, eaten, sold, and more. I had researched the roundup, watched videos on YouTube, and read interviews with the Sweetwater Jaycees, the civic group who organizes the event every year. I talked with people who had attended before and many who hadn't. The problem was that everyone had skin in the game, so to speak. Animal activists, many who have never visited Sweetwater, decry the event from afar as cruel and barbaric. The Jaycees and the town of Sweetwater, on the other hand, seriously benefit from the millions of dollars the event brings in every year to this rural town; they promote it as an important tradition that keeps the local rattlesnake populations balanced. I knew the centerpiece of this festival was killing snakes; I just didn't know what that would be like. Would it be respectful or callous? Would the tone of the event be serious or gleeful? Would the message be based in education or ring of propaganda? Killing animals can mean a lot of different things.

The Rattlesnake Roundup was the event my grandmother had worked on the most before she died. She attended the roundup in 1990, taking copious notes about her time in Sweetwater. She conducted interviews and gathered books and journal articles on snake symbolism. She even had a rough draft of an essay about the roundup. The draft was academic, explaining her experience of the festival from a neutral position. She focused on the long history of snake symbolism in America and made no argument about the future of the roundup.

What worried me the most, though, was a poem I found in my grandmother's files that she wrote after attending the roundup. "Drenched in death," it began, "the arena of nightmare / holds bone and sinew, / skin, blood, and the lidless eyes / of dismembered serpents." One stanza in particular haunted me. As I checked in to my flight and boarded the plane to Dallas, her lines swam in my head:

> None shall escape.
> Those who know earth best
> Wrenched from their dens;
> Now helpless upon cement
> They curl and wait.

My grandmother was empathetic, but she was not overly sentimental. She was a veterinarian who cared deeply for animals, but she ate meat and was not an animal advocate per se. She was an anthropologist who studied the people at the roundup, not the snakes. For her to have been so affected by the roundup that she had to process what she saw in a poem, voicing her more subjective observations, made me anxious. I am an unapologetic empath, so I worried how this festival would affect me, since it had clearly impacted her so deeply. *None shall escape* echoed in my mind as I drove to Sweetwater.

Nevertheless, I wanted to stay objective, or at least open-minded. The world has changed since my grandmother was working as an anthropologist in the 1990s. Today we tend to be more aware of how outsider assumptions can misrepresent a community. As I planned my trip to Sweetwater, I thought critically about what it would mean for me to go to this small town and observe the human-animal interactions there. Could I ever really make a claim about what goes on in a town that is not my own?

As I drove into Sweetwater the Thursday afternoon before the roundup, I felt humbled by how little I knew about this place and these people. It's an odd feeling to step into someone else's community, watch what they do, and still try to enjoy a piece of it yourself. But the roundup, like every event in this book, is designed at least in part for tourists. By attending, I became an audience member to whatever the community wanted to show. One of the benefits of studying festivals is that they are events designed for the public, and they are specifically open to outsiders like me. In my travels I would not be peering into anything private; I am not trying to analyze any particular people in an anthropological or sociological sense. Instead, by paying a fee and watching the activities, I was part of it all. I was not outside the events. I could not observe them safely from afar. Organizers opened their doors to the public, and I paid to witness whatever happened. I contributed to every action I saw by adding to the demand for the festival with my presence and attention.

I parked on the side of the street near the coliseum and stood next to my car. People were stepping out of their houses to watch the opening parade. I had arrived in town just in time. Families with children were passing around plastic grocery bags to collect candy thrown from the parade floats. Directly across from me, a large dog stared out the front window of a home at his whole family, who sat on the curb just below. The parade began with a procession of the ten contestants for the pageant that would be held that night. Each contestant rode in an open-air car, waving to the residents assembled on the side of the street, sashes strung across their bodies. Local businesses organized "floats"—or groups of people in flatbed trucks—and threw candy to the children on the sidewalks. The Jaycees' signature red bus, advertising the "World's Largest Rattlesnake Roundup" on its sides, made an appearance, as did the local high school's marching band. When the last cars passed, kids ran to scoop up candy that had fallen in the road. It was a fairly typical small-town parade.

Later that evening I settled into my seat in the back of the town auditorium. For decades the Rattlesnake Roundup weekend has kicked off on Thursday afternoon with the Miss Snake Charmer Pageant. As one resident put it, "Every festival needs a queen."[25] The competition began with the casual-wear round, in which the contestants are encouraged to wear an outfit that represents who they are. Some wore sneakers and toted sporting equipment, some wore jeans and carried books, and some wore sparkly clothes and waved pompoms. The talent round brought singers, dancers, poetry performers, painters, and more. Lastly, the women donned long gowns for the formal-wear round. As they promenaded around the *Bridgerton*-themed stage to accompanying violin music, you could tell how hard they had trained for this moment. Between each round, the emcee thanked dozens of local sponsors, who had provided meals, transportation, logistical support, and more for this pageant. It was a big event in its own right. Miss Texas was even present, signing autographs at the back of the auditorium during intermission.

The young contestants seemed brave, performing for the entire town, their friends, and strangers like me. You couldn't pay me enough to sing on a stage in front of a few hundred people, but these women took on that challenge with grace. The audience was consistently supportive, even when a note fell flat or a dance step was missed. The point was not perfection; rather, it seemed to be for the contestants to put themselves out there and enjoy a moment in the spotlight as local celebrities.

When the winner was crowned Miss Snake Charmer, the other contestants all cheered and seemed genuinely supportive. The top three contestants were handed enormous trophies, bouquets of flowers, and sashes. As I drove back to my hotel after the nearly three-hour event, I felt heartened. The whole night was pleasant. It was not overly superficial or bombastic; it was not too cheesy or outdated. It was a good-spirited celebration of the ten young women who had decided to be bold and kick off the roundup weekend. The town of Sweetwater, seen through the lens of this pageant, was undeniably charming.

It was hard to square that charm with the gore and violence I witnessed over the next few days.

The drive to the coliseum was different the next morning—cars lined the street in bumper-to-bumper traffic, full of people waiting to park and explore the events. I pulled into a spot, handed the attendant some cash, and followed the crowd to the coliseum. A high school-aged boy stamped the back of my hand with a red-ink coiled snake once I paid my entrance fee.

As soon as I walked into the coliseum, the sunny day gave way to artificial light, and the air was stale. My senses were overloaded. A din echoed around the room, a combination of human murmuring and snake hissing. There were hundreds of people moving in front of me, taking selfies and buying souvenirs. The smell of fried rattlesnake, which looked gray and tough as it passed me in paper bowls, permeated the building. I walked down the steps to the main floor of the coliseum, which had three "pits," or closed-off areas, for spectators to observe different snake activities: a safety/handling demonstration pit, a skinning pit, and a milking pit. When I passed the demonstration pit, I paused to watch the handler interact with the snake and discuss the animal with the crowd. He gripped the snake's head tightly, so it couldn't move, and then held its body out for people to touch. Visitors posed for photographs with the snake, inching only as close as they dared.

Vendors around the pits sold items like preserved snakeskins, T-shirts, and bumper stickers both political and comical: "Live, Laugh, Love. If that doesn't work, Load, Aim & Fire." You could buy almost anything made from rattlesnake skin: bracelets, wallets, belts, key-chains, and more. I wove through families and groups as they point-ed out snakes to each other, posed for photos, and squealed in fear and delight. The Jaycees were clearly identifiable in their bright-red vests holding court all around the coliseum. One Jaycee was "milking" a snake as I passed the milking pit, pressing its open mouth against a glass funnel to force its venom out as people watched, enthralled.

I made my way toward the largest pit in the back. This pit held all of this year's captured snakes—thousands of them. As I got closer to the pit, the sound of the rattling crescendoed into a thick, vibrating chorus. Blood-smeared viewing windows close to the ground allowed me the opportunity to bend down and glimpse a writhing mass of bodies, some defiant and shaking, others subdued and motionless. Within the next two days, every snake in this pit would be slaughtered. My grandmother's lines would ring true: *None shall escape.*

The Sweetwater Rattlesnake Roundup started in 1958 as a way to gather up and remove rattlesnakes from the local community. The Board of City Development called together several rattlesnake hunters who organized a three-day hunt. There was no known market for rattlers at that time. No money was paid for snakes brought in, and no fee was charged for spectators. On the final day, members of the group began discussing how they would dispose of the several thousand snakes that had been captured. They decided to drive a pickup into the armory, cover the pen full of snakes with a tarp, and run exhaust from the truck into the pit. After being subjected to this procedure for an hour, however, the snakes were still alive. The men determined that every snake would have to be killed individually, so they cut each head from the body, piled the parts in steel drums, and hauled them to the town's disposal grounds the next morning. Only the rattles were saved and sold for five or ten cents each.[26]

"Sweetwater ethos" dictates that "if we have to waste our time on them at all, then we might as well enjoy it."[27] So the next year, the event was formalized and moved to the newly constructed Nolan County Coliseum. The Sweetwater Rattlesnake Roundup is not the only event of its kind. Rattlesnake roundups and snake rodeos take place in Alabama, Louisiana, Oklahoma, and elsewhere in Texas. But Sweetwater hosts the world's largest roundup, with up to forty thousand visitors descending on the small town throughout the weekend.[28]

Today a few specialized hunters spend weeks or months traveling around Texas to collect western diamondback rattlesnakes ahead of the roundup. The Jaycees pay them up to fifteen dollars per pound of snake, and the top hunters bring in hundreds of pounds of snakes each.[29] Many hunters use a controversial tactic known as "gassing." Hunters pump gasoline fumes into the back of rattlesnake dens, which forces the snakes to seek fresh air and slither out from their nooks. Often the snakes are still lethargic from their winter hibernation, and when they emerge, the hunters capture the dazed animals. The gasoline has negative impacts on the land and the numerous other animals with whom the rattlesnakes share their dens, and activists have been trying to stop the practice for years. Many neighboring states have made gassing unlawful, but Texas has not yet taken action to curb the practice.[30]

As I stared at the mass of snakes in the pit, I knew many of them had been captive for weeks, if not months, already, and many of them had suffered that gasoline poisoning. It was hard to separate individual bodies with my untrained eyes. The bodies coiled around each other and slid over one another. I wanted to be able to make sense of the sight before me, but the snakes remained inscrutable.

An announcement blared over the loudspeaker and let everyone know the skinning pit was about to open. Dozens of people made their way to the back of the coliseum, excited to see the famed snake skinning. This is one of the main—and most controversial—attractions at the Rattlesnake Roundup. It is both a novelty and a spectacle. Attendees can simply watch the Jaycees do the dirty work, or they can pay a fee to try it themselves.

The skinning pit was fully operational by the time I worked my way to it. There were snakes in every stage of deconstruction: a disassembly line, of sorts, from right to left, from living creature to individual parts, heartbeats gone and blood drained. It was both mechanistic and performative. Jaycees did the work of killing and skinning with practiced hands, but they relished the audience's attention too, often stopping to answer questions, to show off a body part, or to hold a severed snake head out to shock onlookers. Even the newly crowned Miss Snake Charmer got in on the action. In jeans, a sparkly tiara, and a pair of waders, she presided over the pit with a smile on her face as the snakes recoiled and rattled at her feet.

The first stop for the snakes pulled from the pit was the wooden stump where they were killed. The Jaycees worked in a team of two: one grabbed an agitated, furiously rattling snake out of a bucket with a pinching tool and pressed it down on top of the stump; the other beheaded it unceremoniously with a machete. If that description sounds blunt, that's because the reality was blunt—just a quick thwack of the knife, over and over. The Jaycee holding the head dropped it, mouth still agape, into a bucket, while the snake's body was put into a different bucket to await skinning. Every few hours, a Jaycee counted the heads in the bucket and added the number to the ever-growing head tally marked on the wall.

When it was busy, the killing was swift and constant, because it was the first part of the snake-skinning assembly line. But when the stockpile of disassembled snake bodies grew faster than the Jaycees could skin them, the killing duo got creative. One Jaycee demonstrated to the crowd how a snake keeps moving even after it is beheaded. He held up the severed head and put his machete in its mouth, showing the audience how the snake's mouth will still close around it. Even dead, he explained, they can still bite you, so *watch out*.

The skinning process proceeded on a table just to the left of the killing stump. The Jaycees hung decapitated snakes up by their rattle and then sliced a long line up the creature's abdomen, from neck to tail. Once the skin was opened, they pulled out the innards and organs, then the thick, meaty muscle. The skin was then rolled up and set aside to be sold, while the muscle got thrown in large, slimy bags to be carried to the fryer out back.

"Do you want to make a handprint?" a Jaycee asked an adult who signed up to skin a snake. Tourists could skin snakes to the side of the main table, on special rigs strung up over buckets to catch the blood and offal. When this woman agreed, the Jaycee instructed her to hold her hands under the cut-open neck of the strung-up snake. The Jaycee rubbed her hands down the snake's body to force extra blood out of its neck onto the woman's open hands. The wall that lined the skinning pit was white, but workers had begun to leave red, bloody handprints, as was the tradition every year. The woman rubbed her hands together and smiled as she pressed her bloody hands on the wall. She grabbed a Sharpie and proudly signed her name beneath her prints. Renowned animal photojournalist Jo-Anne McArthur nicknamed this the "wall of shame."[31]

"Keep your mouth closed while you're doing it," a mother told her daughter as she stepped into the skinning pit next. The young girl, who couldn't have been more than eight years old, looked a little over-whelmed, but she acted brave. When the Jaycee showed her how to hold the bottom of the snake's neck while he sliced open the skin, the snake's body writhed and recoiled. The girl dropped the neck and took a step back—it was like the snake had come back to life. The Jaycee laughed, grabbed the body, and handed it back to the girl, assuring her it was just a muscle spasm. When the young girl finished pulling out the snake's organs and muscle, she was directed to rinse her hands in two buckets (one with soap, one without) and to pose for a photo.

The audience and the Jaycees alike seemed to relish the macabre nature of this event. Very rarely in our modern society do we see animal slaughter so publicly. But here, people were watching, videotaping, and taking selfies with Jaycees as they held up severed snake heads or other harvested body parts. One Jaycee held out a snake heart in the palm of her hand and people in the crowd stepped up to poke it and take a closer look. The snake's deconstructed body was the central attraction, and onlookers had a morbid curiosity about this creature's inner workings. As fresh blood dripped onto the sawdust shavings scattered throughout the skinning pit, and as the ever-present rattling hummed in the background, attendees remained captivated by the public display of bodily dismemberment.

"Snakes are underdogs that people don't like," Melissa Amarello, a cofounder of Advocates for Snake Preservation, told me. Amarello, a longtime snake lover, attended the Sweetwater roundup in 2015 and is haunted by the experience. She explained to me that snakes rattle only if they are afraid of dying, because in nature they don't want to give away their location to predators. It's a last-ditch effort, made only in times of extraordinary stress. And snakes also musk when they are stressed or upset. "That smell was overwhelming," she recalled when I asked her about her experience at the roundup. "It was like a deafening roar of screams if you understand what snakes are saying."

The problem is that most people do not understand what snakes are saying. Even people who generally like animals often detest or fear snakes. Snakes are cold-blooded and sinuous, and they lack limbs or facial features that we humans can relate to and understand. Everything about them goes against human expectation. Their serpentine form is unlike other patterns in nature. They slither silently. Snakes have no arms or legs, no hair, fur, or feathers. Their scaly skin appears "slimy," even though it is dry, and snakes shed their skin periodically, leaving behind ghost-like forms. Their eyes are lidless, lacking the power to close and open like ours. Their fixed, unblinking stare is disturbing. They are voiceless and they exhibit no facial expressions, so they cannot communicate any of their sensations to humans. These traits set snakes apart, alienating them from the sphere of human understanding and stigmatizing them with a formidable otherness.

Few animals inspire as much disgust or revulsion as snakes. In fact, up to half of adults admit to experiencing anxiety or a generalized fear of snakes.[32] Some researchers believe this fear is innate and biological, shared with primate relatives and part of our evolutionary development.[33] Others argue our fear of snakes is at least partially cultural, passed down through stories, myths, and parental warnings— or through, say, rattlesnake roundups.[34] Hatred of snakes is a kind of cultural currency, and our American society typically relies on imagery and symbolism of snakes to indicate evil.

This association spans millennia. The serpent in Genesis embodied Satan and tempted Adam and Eve, leading to the downfall of humanity. Medusa was an ancient, mythical monster with snakes sprouting from her head instead of hair who could turn a human to stone with a single glance. In a much more modern story, Harry Potter defeats the giant serpent Basilisk, and Slytherin House, whose crest displays a serpent, consistently represents malevolent forces in the series. Draco, the name of Harry's young nemesis, even means "snake" in Latin. Movies—like *Anaconda, Snakes on a Plane*, and the *Indiana Jones* films—capitalize on the fear many people feel for snakes, using that trope for plot devices and cheap thrills.

Rattlesnakes in particular represent a threat in the national mythology of the United States. Settling in America in colonial times necessitated overcoming rattlesnakes, which are native to the continent and presented a new threat to colonists. Rattlesnakes were everywhere in the New World, it seemed, even in New England.[35] As Christopher Irmscher, author of *The Poetics of Natural History*, wrote, "the idea of the New World . . . had come to be intimately connected with the specter of ravenous, rattling reptiles spewing poison as their luminescent bodies disappeared into the dark." Indeed, he continued, the "rattlesnake was the serpent in the American Garden," so that the rattlesnake became "a kind of metaphor for the extraordinary challenge, the danger as well as the promise, of the New World itself."[36] And rattlesnakes took on status as a rallying cry for early Americans too, as they flipped the script on that fear and reclaimed the symbolism of rattlesnakes. The American colonies, threatened by the fist of British imperialism, raised flags emblazoned with a coiled rattlesnake and the motto "Don't Tread on Me."[37] The rattlesnake, native to America, provided the perfect message for the colonies: leave us alone, or we'll strike.

As settlers made their way west, traversing the country and settling on untrammeled land, rattlesnakes of greater number and variety threatened homesteading humans, both literally and symbolically. But unlike other large mammalian predators whose threats were obvious—coyotes, wolves, and bears, for example—rattlesnakes were strange and confounding antagonists who could kill a grown man with a single, potent, bloodless bite. One legend, for example, tells of a cowboy who was bitten on the foot through the leather of his new boots and died a short time thereafter. Months later, a different man put on those same boots and was killed by the fang embedded in the boot.[38] In popular mythology, rattlesnakes lurked everywhere and would strike at children and cattle, posing a fundamental threat to the human way of life. To live in the frontier was to live with rattlesnakes. And to live with rattlesnakes was untenable. Texan folklorist J. Frank Dobie "grew up understanding that a man even halfway decent would always shut any gate he had opened to go through and would always kill any rattlesnake he got a chance at."[39]

From colonial times to the present, the human-snake relationship has seemed zero-sum: either snakes can be present, or humans
can be present, but not both. In colonial times, one writer supposed,
for example, that in the future once settlers established their towns,
rattlesnakes would be "as great a rarity in New England as a wolf is
in Old England."[40] In other words, coexistence was not an option.
The assumption that human presence necessitates rattlesnake eradi-
cation carries forth to modern-day Sweetwater. One rancher told my
grandmother his strategy for keeping rattlesnakes in check: "You just
get him before he gets you." In a similar vein, a Sweetwater resident
interviewed in a 2019 documentary about the Miss Snake Charmer
pageant justified the roundup's wholesale slaughter: "It's either them
or it's me." The woman explained that rattlesnakes do not just live far
away, in the wild, but that they live at people's houses too. The threat
of serpentine encroachment on human habitats evokes an us-or-them
scarcity mindset. We humans need our homes to be safe, and since
rattlesnakes make them unsafe, they have to go. The essential logic is
this: if we don't kill them, they'll kill us, so we have to act proactively.
In his book *Rattler! A Natural History of Rattlesnakes*, Chris Mattison
explained, "Rattlesnakes and people have been killing each other
since the human race first arrived in North America. Yet the battle has
probably always been one-sided—we do more of the attacking than
they do."[41]

The roundup in Sweetwater capitalizes on that ingrained and
socialized fear of snakes and insists on one, supposedly obvious,
solution. The Jaycees reiterate that rattlesnakes are an omnipresent
threat to the community, an assertion they seem to back up by
gathering thousands of rattlesnakes every year without fail. The fear of

snakes overrunning the town is real for some people because they were raised to think the Rattlesnake Roundup is the only thing keeping the snakes away from their own yards, from their own children and dogs. I heard a Jaycee explain to a crowd that before the roundup began, you would see rattlesnakes on sidewalks downtown. He said that they capture thousands of snakes that would otherwise continue to encroach on the town unchecked.

Spreading fear about rattlesnake infestation justifies their slaughter. As Bethany Brookshire writes in *Pests: How Humans Create Animal Villains*, "The instant fear and quickness to label" snakes as pests "is part of how we grant ourselves license to kill." Snakes inspire anger and hate, she writes, that differs from the response humans have to other animal pests and arises from fear, whether innate or inherited. The Jaycees prey on this ingrained fear with their constant refrain that snakes would be everywhere in Sweetwater if they didn't kill them at this roundup. The event provides the town and attendees with an acceptable reason for the slaughter. As Brookshire asserts, "A pest isn't part of nature anymore. It isn't wildlife. A pest becomes an evil influence that must be eliminated, and the ends will now almost always justify the means."[42]

But the threat posed by rattlesnakes in our modern world is almost certainly overstated. While fear of snakes may be natural, and even biological, today rattlesnakes cause far less harm than the Jaycees in Sweetwater would have you believe. In the entire United States, between seven and eight thousand people are bitten by venomous snakes each year, according to the Centers for Disease Control and Prevention.[43] Of those bitten, only about five people die from the bites on average. You are five times more likely to die from being struck by lightning and fourteen times more likely to die from falling out of a tree.[44] Additionally, well over half of all snake bites result from situations where humans seek out interactions with snakes, including handling snakes for religious purposes, keeping them as venomous pets, or finding them in the wild to harass or kill them. Studies have shown that the rate of snake bites is higher for men and that many victims are intoxicated at the time of the bite.[45] So while rattlesnakes and other venomous snakes do present some small threat when humans are hiking or working outside, people seem to be making the problem worse by purposefully interacting with these animals in reckless ways. All snakes want is to be left alone; humans are not their prey. But when attacked, or scared, or messed with, they will defend themselves.

"There are festivals like this for mammals all over the US," Amarello told me, "but they are done in secret. It's only okay here because these are snakes." And she is right—killing contests and festivals happen all across the country. There are crow hunts in New York; coyote-hunting contests in Virginia, Nevada, Wisconsin, Oregon, and elsewhere; and fishing contests all across the country.[46] However, most of the actual killing in those events occurs in the wild, somewhat privately, when the hunter faces the animal for the first time. The Rattlesnake Roundup is decidedly different: live animals are captured, transported, and stored before being ritually killed in full view of the public. To slaughter animals in front of children, families, and spectators makes the roundup more like a spectacle than a contest. The event takes place at a coliseum, after all. Interacting with the violence is not ancillary; it's the point.

The most analogous event I could find was the pigeon shoot that used to occur in Hegins, Pennsylvania, on Labor Day weekend. Gary Francione, an animal activist who spoke to my grandmother at that event thirty years ago, described for me the "carnival atmosphere" that took over the town as spectators drank beer and cheered for the shooters. Organizers would load live pigeons into spring-loaded boxes and then release them, and participants would shoot them as they tried to escape. The pigeons who were hit but survived were either killed by other participants (by being beaten into the ground, for example, or, in one particularly gruesome case that Francione recalled, by having its head bitten off by an attendee) or treated by volunteer veterinarians who waited on the sidelines of the killing fields.

"I've seen a lot of bad stuff in my life," Francione told me. "When you're in the slaughterhouse, you're surrounded by people who believe they are doing something good for people. Same with animal labs—people will passionately tell you how good their work is." Even if that's not true, he acknowledged, "they believe it." But the pigeon shoot at Hegins was "just horrible," he said, because there was not even any nominal reason for it all; instead, the violence was the purpose. "This thing really affected me," he recalled, shaking his head. "It was dreadful." After years of intense pressure from animal advocates, the event was canceled due to a legal victory in state court. The Hegins pigeon shoot was the only event my grandmother attended that has since stopped happening. Even so, a few pigeon shoots still occur throughout Pennsylvania, now held privately and mainly on secluded gun-club land, and legislation to outlaw the shoots entirely has never passed.[47]

Nevertheless, public sentiment has turned away from such killing-based festivals. Animal protection groups have mounted campaigns against wildlife killing contests across the country. Many states have even banned these contests.[48] While these events do still occur, they aren't hugely popular, and for the most part they are no longer central to the hosting town's identity.

But the Rattlesnake Roundup in Sweetwater, and its brazen killing pit, seems to be a massive exception to that general trend.

And while the roundup may be supported by local pride, it is not organized solely for the benefit of the town's participation. Instead, visitors attend the roundup from all over the United States. Sweetwater's population balloons to nearly four times its normal size during the roundup weekend. The Jaycees even visit the state capitol in Austin every year, toting a few rattlesnake ambassadors who they let slither on the ground outside the capitol for theatrical effect.[49] It's a tourist attraction and a major moneymaker for the small town. The Jaycees and the town of Sweetwater are proud of this event, and they advertise it broadly—killing included.

So I was left deciding where on the spectrum of animal violence the roundup falls. Are the Jaycees and the town of Sweetwater engaging in completely senseless violence, like that expressed at the pigeon shoots in Pennsylvania? Or do they really believe there is a justifiable, beneficial reason to kill these snakes? The Jaycees, to their credit, offer a simple answer: they kill these snakes to keep the rattlesnake population in check and to educate people on the dangers they pose.

"It's not that we like to kill the rattlesnakes," one Jaycee explained. "But we do it because it promotes safety. Everything we do is to teach people what to do if they encounter a rattlesnake and just teach people about rattlesnakes in general."[50]

"What I want people to know about the Rattlesnake Roundup is we're not cruel to these animals," Rob McCann, another Jaycee, said.[51] The goal of the festival is to educate the public about rattlesnake encounters, he clarified.

But the education the Jaycees are offering is not exactly unobjectionable. The informational demonstration at the roundup included a lot of casual banter, crude jokes, and moralizing rhetoric. For example, while rattlesnakes do not nurse their young, they typically protect their offspring for a week or two before the baby snakes venture out on their own.[52] In a heavy gloss on the facts, one handler at the roundup explained to the audience that female snakes are "sluts" because "they leave their babies and keep on going." The Jaycees also assure attendees that gassing the snake dens to force the snakes out causes no harm to the environment and that the hunters return to the same dens every year to gather more snakes. But because neither the Jaycees nor Texas Parks & Wildlife regulates snake hunting in any meaningful way, it is impossible to substantiate that claim. Instead, studies have shown that gassing dens more often leads to the unnecessary death of every other animal sharing that den and to the destruction of the den as a possible future resting place.[53] So the facts the Jaycees present about the snakes seem purposive at best and obstructionist at worst.

The reasons offered by the Jaycees to justify killing so many snakes do not necessarily hold up to scrutiny either. Jaycees consistently say the roundup is necessary to moderate the rattlesnake population in Sweetwater, but rattlesnake populations are self-regulated. According to Dr. Emily Taylor, a professor of biology at California Polytechnic State University at San Luis Obispo, "There's predators that eat them. There's droughts and other pressures that limit how much food they can get. And it is not true that rattlesnakes would overrun the town."[54] Moreover, some reports indicate that the hunters who bring rattlesnakes to the Jaycees for the roundup have to travel all over west Texas to procure enough snakes—belying the idea that rattlesnakes are encroaching on Sweetwater.

And even if killing snakes *were* necessary, there are far more humane—and less theatrical—ways of doing it. Even before the snakes are killed, they suffer a lot of unnecessarily poor treatment for the sake of spectacle. They are first captured, often undergoing gasoline poisoning, and transported in boxes that sometimes leave them injured.[55] They are then stockpiled and thrown into a severely overcrowded pit, causing visible external injuries. Many snakes are emaciated by the time the roundup happens. I was startled to see Jaycees kick piles of rattlesnakes around the pit during the roundup. The snakes would slither and recoil and try to right themselves when they landed. And, of course, the snakes are ultimately killed in a callous fashion. The most humane way to kill a snake is to ensure it loses consciousness immediately, by stunning the animal with a firearm or captive bolt in its head, and then "pithing" (or destroying) its brain to ensure the snake does not regain consciousness.[56] Instead, Jaycees behead the snakes and revel in the muscle spasms and biting motions the severed bodies make, showing everything off to gasping attendees.

So maybe none of this passes the sniff test.

"It just does not make sense," Dr. Taylor said, not mincing words. "We can educate people about rattlesnakes, without cutting off their heads and skinning them alive and subjecting them to horrific conditions."[57]

Animal activists agree, and they have undertaken efforts to end these roundups. Dr. Taylor recently worked with Advocates for Snake Preservation to lead a campaign where hundreds of children around the country sent letters to Sweetwater residents, urging them to stop killing snakes.[58] Protestors from PETA were outside the roundup, urging passersby not to support the event. I also spoke with representatives of organizations like the Center for Biological Diversity, who are working on building a coalition with other advocates to organize a campaign against the roundup. The goal for most of these efforts is not to end the roundup but to transition the event to a no-kill festival.

There's a blueprint for this transition. Until recently, Georgia also hosted rattlesnake roundups where snakes were killed en masse. But in 2022, after pressure from advocates and from the State of Georgia, the roundup in Whigham became the last in the state to transition to a no-kill event.[59] Instead of hunting and slaughtering the animals, the organizers of the Whigham roundup displayed captive snakes from a reptile rescue organization, enhanced their educational programming, and teamed up with other conservation groups and the state to make sure their event was still successful. The rest of the event—including vendors, live music, games, and more—remains unchanged. The goals of educating the public, promoting safety, and celebrating local tradition were all still met.

It seemed to me that the same transition could take place in Sweetwater. While killing snakes is certainly at the heart of Sweetwater's roundup, it's important to remember that the weekend includes far more than just celebratory slaughter. The roundup began as a way to gather and eradicate rattlesnakes, but it has expanded dramatically over the years. There are now multiple areas where dozens of vendors set up tents to sell food, souvenirs, and tchotchkes. A gun, coin, and knife show organized by the Sweetwater Rifle and Pistol Club took place right next door to the coliseum. A full-size carnival was set up with rides and other attractions throughout the weekend too. There was a barn dance with live music on Saturday night and a beard-growing contest on Sunday. The pageant kicked off the weekend with a strong showing of community support. The weekend was full even apart from the skinning pit.

And the Jaycees themselves do far more than just manage the Rattlesnake Roundup. They are popular civic leaders, and they raise money and bring meals to people in need in their community. They host other events throughout the year, and the community looks up to them as celebrities of sorts. They also have a "junior" program, where people under eighteen can begin to learn the values of public participation and leadership. The Jaycees I spoke with at the roundup were all more than willing to answer my questions, and they were friendly and welcoming to boot.

The juxtaposition of small-town charm with purposeful violence, of practiced poise and civic duty with what could only be described as bloodthirst, was confounding. I struggled to understand how the same town whose businesses and residents generously supported the pageant contestants, rallying around a common goal, could revel in such unabashed cruelty.

One answer to this confusion might be that I simply cannot understand the importance of the event, because I am an outsider and I don't have a personal connection with Sweetwater's local culture and history. "It's more than a tradition," as one Jaycee explained. "Rattlesnakes are a way of life here."[60] But that's not it, exactly—like anyone, I understand the impulse to value local tradition. I was raised in a small town in rural Massachusetts of about ten thousand residents, comparable to Sweetwater. I attended local Fourth of July parades and festivals, carnivals, and other town events and fundraisers when I was growing up. I know exactly what it feels like to have your town come together around a common purpose. I know what it feels like to have local pride and to look around an otherwise unnoteworthy piece of land and say: this is ours, and this is how we do it here.

But what I saw, more than any recognizable hometown pride, was pure exhibitionism. In Sweetwater, skirting—and maybe mastering—a fear of snakes seemed to be the main commodity the Jaycees were peddling. I watched as a Jaycee pushed a snake head (mouth agape, as always) in a jar toward unsuspecting audience members just to laugh as they recoiled. So many people, mostly young women, screamed and squealed as they posed for photos with live snakes, hating every moment but wanting the proof that they were brave enough to touch that scary animal. Everything was safe because the Jaycees were supervising it. And when the animals were killed, the audience members were able to interact with the body once it was safely in pieces. People could experiment with fear in a controlled way. As the philosopher Jack Weir wrote of Sweetwater, "Nothing unites a community better than a spirited festival and a fight against a common enemy."[61]

Rattlesnake roundups are sometimes called "rodeos" in an invocation of the symbolism, and perceived danger, of the Wild West. Rodeos, too, are places where the boundary between animal and human is tested and reinforced as part of a show for audiences to enjoy. But the traditional American rodeo involves a give-and-take between the wild and the tame. If humans won every time, or won easily, there would be no tension, no excitement, and no reason to perform the events over and over. There must always be more wildness to conquer, or the rodeo loses its purpose. But the Rattlesnake Roundup destroys every creature who enters the coliseum, and not in a fair fight. It's a bloodbath, literally. There's no anxiety, no real threat that the rattlers will win a round against the humans. Rattlesnakes are simply an enemy to be exterminated.

Using snakes in this way—ritually killing them—has a twofold effect. First, it says something about snakes, by reasserting every year that they are bad, scary, and worthy of nothing other than death. It teaches attendees, and especially kids, how to treat snakes. I overheard a parent explaining to her children how dangerous rattlesnakes were as they pressed their noses against the window of the pit. I listened to many Jaycees explain to many different crowds how dangerous rattlers are, what to do if you encounter one, and how important it is to kill them so we stay safe. There are more subliminal elements at play too. Unlike many other animals, snakes are referred to and handled in the aggregate, never as individuals, which further alienates them from us; the roundup reports the "pounds" of snakes captured, instead of the number of individual creatures. Passing down the mythology and symbolism we attach to snakes, instructing the next generation how to handle these creatures as wholesale varmints, is a critical part of this festival. As the Jaycees insist, education is its main goal.

Secondly, the ritual slaughter of snakes says something about us as humans. The fear of snakes the event inculcates is somewhat contrived. Not a single snake in that coliseum presents any meaningful risk to any attendee. They are contained, trapped, powerless, stuck on the bad end of a machete. If someone managed to suffer a bite, antivenom would be available quickly. And even if the fear weren't contrived, the event no longer manages a realistic threat; the community doesn't collect snakes from their own homesteads. Instead, the roundup dramatizes the boundary between human and animal, emphasizing the deadly otherness of rattlesnakes and the absolute right we have to destroy them for our own protection. Specialized hunters help us play out the drama, bringing in thousands of snakes so we can prove ourselves just like we did sixty-five years ago. Humans like being strong, and tough, and dominant. It's natural. Killing the rattlesnakes says we are stronger than they are. We can kill them simply because we want to. Killing them affirms our place in the animal kingdom as the ultimate predator. What greater power is there than that?

Throughout the weekend, I imagined what the snakes' experience of this festival was like. I asked Marc Bekoff, an ethologist who has written numerous books about animal experience and emotion, what he believed. He explained to me that many people think reptiles are unfeeling and insentient, but that assumption is not true. Snakes, like all animals, feel pain and fear, he said, and the snakes must feel "stress from the get-go" at this event, from being hunted to being transported to "being dumped into a cage . . . it must be totally traumatic for them. Their whole lives have changed." Bekoff told me that what a snake feels is not always obvious to human observers, because the animal's stress or fear response looks like anger or a threat to us. When we are cornered, our hearts race, and we scream or cry; snakes rattle and musk. Difference alone does not, and cannot, justify discrimination and abuse. Lack of understanding of another creature is not a sufficient defense for an unabashed exercise of superiority.

Bekoff has proposed a general test for determining whether an action treats animals with respect. Simply ask: Would you do it to a dog? Dogs are known as man's best friend for a reason. They are arguably the best-treated nonhuman animals on our planet. They enjoy some of the strongest legal protections and the most cultural respect in the United States. For the Rattlesnake Roundup, the answer to Bekoff's question is almost absurdly easy. We would never round up stray dogs, keep them without food or water in an overcrowded pit stacked on top of each other, and then behead them one by one. Anyone who tried throwing such a festival would be arrested for animal cruelty.

So we have to ask ourselves, as humans with rational thought: Why is it permissible to do such things to snakes? The answer might well be: it isn't, and we shouldn't. If our only reason is rooted in fear, or in a long-standing notion that snakes are dangerous, then we aren't as rational as we claim we are. We don't have to *like* snakes—I don't, particularly—but not liking snakes is not reason enough to torture and slaughter them.

I asked Melissa Amarello from Advocates for Snake Preservation what she wished for most of all, if she could snap her fingers and change one thing about how people think about snakes. She answered that she would change people's default response to encountering a snake. Instead of treating them as problems to be fixed, she wishes people would marvel at their abilities and appearance, like we do with birds or butterflies. She wants people to think, *What a great day—I got to see a snake!* The roundup teaches the opposite, sanctioning our fear and disgust, imposing the fate of disposability on these mysterious creatures.

When I left the roundup for the day, my clothes and hair smelled like fried rattler. As my grandmother wrote in her notes, "There is never a moment during the three-day roundup that the smell of the deep-frying flesh is not overwhelming." She was right, even thirty years later. I stopped at Walmart to buy some bread and peanut butter to make myself a meager dinner, because I had already eaten the only plant-based offering for miles—Subway—for lunch. Inside the Walmart, a giant display of Coors Light was topped with a preserved rattlesnake, mouth open, body lifted. I sighed and made my way to the checkout. It felt like it was the thousandth preserved and posed rattlesnake I had seen that day.

Even in death we always make them look vicious, arranging their faces mid-bite, fangs prominent. We fear their bites, so we emphasize their ferocity to validate our fear. But then we trade in mythology, proving the threat snakes pose by emphasizing only their attacks, never their repose. It's both self-reinforcing and self-aggrandizing, the worst kind of negative feedback loop, the most senseless chicken-or-egg problem. Which came first, the fear or the symbolism instilling the fear?

We can break out of this cycle, I think. The Rattlesnake Roundup is a weekend-long series of events, only one of which is killing and skinning. It seems possible that the good could happen without the bad, that we could educate the public on rattlesnakes and celebrate the rough-and-tumble frontier history of west Texas without reveling in the snakes' suffering. As I went to sleep after my first day at the roundup, I tried to think of all the good I had seen in Sweetwater. I tried to think of all the civic causes that the money raised, including my entrance fee, would benefit. But I couldn't stop thinking of the snakes still in the pit, awaiting their execution, hissing and rattling into the void.

MAINE LOBSTER FESTIVAL

ROCKLAND, ME
THE LOBSTER CAPITAL OF THE WORLD

First you twist the front arms off the body. You use a metal cracker and a tiny fork to open the knuckles and claws and pull the muscle out from the cavities. Next you crack the tail and remove it from the torso. You pull off two of the back fins, peel back the middle fin, and then use your small fork to push the tail meat up through the big front opening. Be sure to pull off the dark vein running down the center of the muscle—that's poop. Those fins you just popped off? Use your tiny fork to pull out a sliver of meat from each one. You can twist off each smaller leg too, and chew on it to soften the muscle before sucking a small bit of briny tissue out. If you're adventurous, there's even more meat to be found in the abdomen, and the "green stuff" you see there is pancreas and liver (a delicacy). Every bite of meat should be dipped in melted butter, of course, and savored. Don't let any of it go to waste.

Learning how to eat a lobster was a rite of passage for me and many other New Englanders. A lobster dinner was a delicious way to celebrate a special occasion—maybe a birthday or a summer family reunion. Clam chowder and corn on the cob usually rounded out the meal. I have many fond memories surrounding seafood: my mom showing me the best way to extract tail meat at a shack-style restaurant on the North Shore of Massachusetts; my grandfather chewing meat out of the legs with butter dripping down his chin; my dad helping me crack a particularly tough knuckle; my uncle shelling my lobster for me when a kitchen accident sent me to the emergency room for stitches in lieu of dinner.

In New England, seafood and shellfish are staples of both cuisine and culture. But while fishing, broadly speaking, is an important industry throughout the region, lobster fishing carries special significance in Maine. In fact, while you can eat lobster at fancy restaurants all around the country, over 80 percent of all American lobster comes from Maine.[62] The rural state with a rocky coastline is the epicenter of a thriving lobster industry.

The Maine Lobster Festival, located in the port city of Rockland, is an annual five-day party dedicated entirely to the state's most recognizable symbol. Even before I pulled into town, lobster shacks abounded along the side of the narrow, coastal road, marked by giant red claws jutting into the air. The scenery felt familiar to me. I have eaten at lobster shacks like these too many times to count, plastic bib tied around my neck and hands slippery with butter. Though it had been years since I had eaten lobster, I was excited about attending this festival. It would take place along the ocean, in the birthplace of the poet Edna St. Vincent Millay, in the waning warmth of a Maine summer.

I rolled down our windows and inhaled the sea breeze as we entered Rockland, then parked on the town's main street and walked down to the festival grounds. Nearer the harbor, red tents became visible and the smell of brine intensified. Just past the main entrance to the park, where we had stopped to get our bearings, my wife nudged my elbow. A woman walked by us wearing a tan dress splattered in a print of dozens of red lobsters. Around us were thousands of people, a lot of them wearing something lobster-related: T-shirts, hats, or even headbands with red claws sticking up. People here clearly loved lobsters.

This passion for lobster wasn't always the case, even in New England. In the early history of the United States, lobsters were so copious that they were considered cheap, low-class food to be served to imprisoned, impoverished, or enslaved people.[63] Lobster meat was even ground up and used as fertilizer because of its "unbelievable abundance" in the water just off the coast.[64] Lobsters were generally seen as pests and nuisances. The etymology of the word "lobster" emphasizes this connection, as it derives from the Old English word *loppestre*, which in turn came from *loppe*, meaning "spider." As far back as the first century, Pliny the Elder referred to lobsters in Latin as "locusts of the sea." Even today lobstermen still refer to lobsters as "bugs." The symbolic value of the lobster reflected this meager status. Early Americans used the term "lobster" as derogatory slang for British redcoats and deployed the word to call someone a fool or rascal more generally.

By the late 1800s, though, the fate of the American lobster changed. Wealthy people in Boston and New York began to eat lobster, and the bugs' reputation slowly evolved.[65] As prices rose, more and more people began to think differently about lobsters, and the animal came to be considered a delicacy to be enjoyed by the affluent. This shift in perception corresponded with a change in cooking methods. Before the 1880s, most lobsters were killed, cooked, and canned in salt (similar to Spam or tuna). Because lobster carcasses begin developing toxins when they die, a lobster must be killed right before or during cooking in order to avoid making consumers violently sick;

canning lobster was an easy way to transport it without risking illness. In the 1880s, however, Americans rediscovered the ancient practice of cooking lobsters alive, which results in better taste and lower risk of food poisoning.[66] As the technology required to ship live lobsters advanced, fresh lobsters could be served even far away from the coast. Between better taste, easier shipping, and higher costs, lobsters soon became a staple of haute cuisine.

The increased demand for lobster has naturally made catching lobsters more difficult. The shores no longer teem with lobsters so thickly that anyone could wade in and pluck one out of the water with their bare hands. Now, professional fishermen drop specially outfitted traps to the seafloor, with long ropes connecting them to buoys on the surface. The highly individualized buoys are what *The Maine Thing Quarterly* has called "the nautical equivalent of a Medieval knight's coat of arms," as "each lobsterman paints his own design in his own color scheme on his buoys, effectively marking his trap territory."[67] Modern traps are rectangular wire boxes with two compartments: a "kitchen" and a "parlor." Lobsters crawl into the kitchen to eat strung bait, but they have a hard time crawling back out of the funnel that led them in. Instead, they find a different hole leading to the parlor, from which fully grown lobsters can't escape.

James Acheson, sociologist and author of *The Lobster Gangs of Maine*, describes the Gulf of Maine as "one of the world's most prolific fishing grounds."[68] In the late summer, human lobster fishers and lobsters converge on the shallows off the coast of Maine. The fishermen need the warmer temperatures to head to sea, and the lobsters need the warmer temperatures to breed. Lobsters can breed only after molting, and summer is their molting season, when they shed their old shells and grow a bigger one to fit their new size. To do so, they follow the warmth from the deeper water miles off the coast to the sun-warmed shallow ledge nearer the shore. They find a snug hiding place within the rocks and loosen their shells in the safety of their summer nooks. A male lobster deposits sperm into the female's seminal receptacle, where it waits until the female is ready to release her eggs.[69]

Lobstermen drop their traps around and beyond these molting grounds. When the hard work of molting and breeding is over, lobsters are a little bigger, and they head back out to deeper waters. And they're hungry, which makes them especially susceptible to bait.[70] Soon enough, the lobstermen find their buoys and haul up the traps.

This is backbreaking work, from the rough and capricious seas to the overwhelming smell of rotting bait to the heavy lifting (most traps are weighed down to make sure they stay on the seafloor, and some lines connect to more than one trap). And lobstering is temperamental, with catch sizes and market prices varying drastically, so the income from a day's work is never a steady or sure thing. Even more acutely, lobstermen are in constant danger of entanglement in a flying rope, which could snap a bone or even drag them off the boat. The National Institute for Occupational Safety and Health categorizes lobster fishing as a "hazardous occupation" because of the risk of drowning from becoming entangled in traplines heading overboard fast.[71] Lobstermen are sometimes called the "cowboys of the American East," because of how difficult it is to work a lobster boat.[72]

The Maine lobster fishery is also an iconic cultural establishment. People all around the country think of Maine when they hear the word "lobster." The image of a salty, hardy fisherman setting out at dawn into a fog-covered sea comes to mind. As Acheson put it, "In American folklore, the Maine lobster fisherman often appears as the last of the rugged individualists. He is his own boss and his own man," and "he is, along with the farmer and rancher, the quintessential American."[73] And while female lobster fishers make up a small percentage of the industry, in Maine, "lobsterman" is essentially a gender-neutral term; if you have the skills, the equipment, and a license, you are a lobster-man.[74] Lobster is tied to Maine in a strong bond between place and food, between nature and culture, and between folklore and reality. Maine's own tourism website brags, "Few things are as 'quintessen-tially' Maine as the lobster," and celebrates the "rugged, independent, and often admired way of life" of the lobstermen.[75] For a time, lobsters were even on the state license plates, special editions of which can now be purchased to support the fishery.

Though it is a small industry, with about five thousand lobstermen working the Maine coast, the fishery can harvest around one hundred million pounds of lobster each season, worth hundreds of millions of dollars.[76] The lobster fishery contributes over one billion dollars to Maine's economy, including through its ancillary industries, such as tourism, trucking and shipping, boat building, and more.[77] More than thirty million people visit Maine each year, most of them in the summer months, hoping to partake of the state's most famous meal.[78] Unlike many other parts of the food sector, the lobster industry is not made up of faceless corporate conglomerates but of small-scale, in-dependent fishermen who own their own equipment and operate by their own rules. Because of its size and composition, it's an incredibly tight-knit industry.

Today the insular Maine lobster industry feels it is being attacked from the outside, by people who don't see what the lobster-men see on the water. The sustainability of the fishery has long been a source of anxiety for everyone involved. As catch sizes can vary year to year, it is difficult to assess the health of the stock. And everyone has been mindful of the history of the cod fishery in New England, which collapsed due to years of overfishing, a fate no one wishes for lobsters.[79] The problem is that the lobstermen usually have different ideas about what sustainability means than the government officials and scientists who study the species. There is undeniable tension between governmental regulations designed to protect the lobster populations and the conditions the lobstermen themselves see on the water.

A simple regulation like a size minimum and maximum to determine which trapped lobsters can be kept ("keepers") and which must be thrown back to the sea has raised numerous debates between these communities, for example. Since the 1980s, the minimum has stood at three and a quarter inches, and the maximum size is five inches, measured from the eyes to the tail.[80] The minimum restriction ensures lobsters have a chance to grow and breed before they are trapped, and the maximum restriction prevents the older, more prolific breeders from being captured. These restrictions help keep the lobster population stable. Periodically, regulators consider raising the minimum size in order to further protect the lobster numbers.[81] But for lobstermen, even a small change in size limit could be devastating for their livelihoods. Regulators want to do everything they can to protect the long-term health of the fishery, while lobstermen need to ensure they can make a living year to year in a capricious industry with small margins.

Maine lobstermen are not merely myopic and profit-hungry, as critics may suppose. They have always cared for the lobster population, because it is how they make a living; they naturally understand that if they fish all the lobster, there won't be any lobster left to fish. As early as 1917, lobstermen began throwing egg-bearing females back, rather than keep and sell them, as a way to protect future lobster populations. To mark the breeding animal and to protect her from future encounters with fishers (unlike many other animals, female lobsters can breed successfully well later in life), the lobstermen cut a "V-notch" in the middle tail flipper before releasing her back into the water.[82] By the

1950s this practice was a commonplace component of the Maine lobstermen's self-regulation, and in 2002 it became mandatory by law.[83]

Lobstermen do not seem to treat this requirement with frustration; they have always been involved in the conservation of the fishery. A fifth-generation lobsterman posted a video on TikTok, for example, where he "freshened up" the V-notch in a female lobster carrying hundreds of eggs, because her various molts had softened the mark, and he had tenderly removed barnacles from her joints before releasing her back into the water with a fish snack in claw for her troubles.[84] Lobstermen care for the lobsters because they constitute their livelihood, and while the stereotypical ideal of the lobsterman often includes a sea-hardened persona, they are, like everyone else, deeply caring individuals with families to feed and a future to protect.

Today the lobster fishery is designated by the National Oceanic and Atmospheric Administration (NOAA) Fisheries as "not subject to overfishing." The states in New England and NOAA Fisheries manage the American lobster stock cooperatively.[85] Lobster landings (the number of bugs caught, brought to land, and sold) in the Gulf of Maine have generally increased over the past few decades, suggesting the management practices in that area are working well.[86] But while the stock in the Gulf of Maine is strong, the population of lobsters in southern New England has crashed. Some suggest climate change is the culprit for the shifting geographical distribution of lobsters—as the ocean warms, lobsters move to colder water to maintain their preferred habitat. And there is always a generalized fear that this current boom will be followed by a bust. It's impossible to know what the future will bring. But for now, the size limits, the V-notch system, some geographical and temporal restrictions, and limits on the numbers of traps each lobsterman may set seem to be accomplishing the goal of sustainability.

Perhaps the biggest and most controversial threat to the industry comes from another marine species: the North Atlantic right whale. Right whales are critically endangered after being nearly fished to extinction by the commercial whaling industry in the nineteenth century.[87] Today there are fewer than three hundred and fifty individual living right whales. They are protected under multiple federal laws, including the Endangered Species Act and the Marine Mammal Protection Act. Every year right whales die from human-created dangers, most notably vessel strikes and entanglement in lobster fishing ropes. The latter, of course, is where the Maine lobster fishery comes in.

Between 2015 and 2019, an average of 31.4 right whales were killed each year, and 70 percent of those deaths were attributable to entanglement.[88] With the number of remaining right whales so small, every whale death matters tremendously for the future of the species. When whales become entangled in fishing lines, they can suffer severe injuries. Lines can wrap around the whales' fins, interfering with their ability to swim, feed, or even breathe (as whales are mammals, they need to swim to the surface to breathe air).[89] Unfortunately, over 90 percent of the deaths resulting from entanglement cannot be linked to a specific gear type or identity, because the offending gear is not usually found with a dead whale. Even when the gear is found, it is often devoid of any identifying feature like a buoy or license number.[90]

In 2021, to reduce the risk of entanglement, NOAA Fisheries announced new regulations that would be implemented over ten years. The regulations included reducing the legal number of buoy lines and implementing geographical restrictions on lobstering, among other measures.[91] Additionally, the development of ropeless lobster fishing technology has provided new hope for the coexistence of the lobster fishery and the right whales. The new gear is expensive, however, and the industry has expressed serious opposition to transitioning to it.[92]

After the new rules were announced, the Maine Lobstermen's Association filed a lawsuit challenging the plan. The lobster industry maintains there has not been a single right whale death attributed to the Maine lobster industry, and there hasn't even been an entanglement attributed to Maine since 2004.[93] But animal activists say that claim is misleading, because most dead whales have been found with unmarked ropes, making it impossible to know where the entanglement took place.[94] The trial court originally ruled in favor of the federal government and the new rules, but the United States Court of Appeals ruled in favor of the Maine Lobstermen's Association and vacated the plan to protect right whales. The agency will have to begin again.

While that litigation was pending, in the fall of 2022, two industry watchdog organizations took a stance. The Marine Stewardship Council suspended its certificate of sustainability for Maine lobster in large part because of the threats to right whales.[95] Seafood Watch, an organization that works out of the Monterey Bay Aquarium in California to monitor fishing practices, similarly demoted American lobster from Maine to their "red list," naming it a food to "avoid" out of environmental and conservation-based concerns.[96] These moves were not just symbolic—they impacted the marketplace more broadly, the ramifications of which have been felt by the fishermen on the coast of Maine. After those two announcements, Whole Foods announced it would no longer buy and sell Maine lobster because of the concerns about entanglement.[97]

The debate between the Maine lobster industry and a loose coalition of environmentalists, the federal government, and other parties interested in sustainability is a deeply charged one. When outsiders try to tell Maine lobstermen how to do their jobs, they see it as an attack on their way of life, their values, and their ability to manage their own affairs. After all, lobstering is an identity as much as it is a job in Maine.

In the middle of this contentious political and economic climate is the Maine Lobster Festival. This event, which occurs every August, exists to support the lobster industry, which its website complains is "getting assailed on all sides."[98] As I arrived at the festival, reminders of this controversy were everywhere. Patrons wore T-shirts proudly declaring, "I Stand with the Fishermen," and proceeds from the festival went to support the fishery community. The festival program included a panel discussion, called "Save Maine Lobstermen," with Congresswoman Chellie Pingree, the Maine Lobster Community Alliance, and other members of the lobster fishery ready to discuss new plans to support the industry. It also included a whopping five days of activities, ranging from a parade full of lobster-clad floats to the "International Great Crate Race," where people try to run across lobster crates bobbing in a line on the water without falling.

The centerpiece of the Maine Lobster Festival, both in terms of physical layout and thematic significance, is the food tent. When I arrived, a line of hungry patrons was already snaking out of the red-and-white-striped tents and up the small hill. Overwhelmed by the mass of people, I stopped at a board near the entrance, which had a map of the United States on one side, a map of the world on the other, and a container of pins placed underneath. Visitors marked where they were from by sticking a pin into the map. Both maps were full, showing that visitors and attendees apparently came to the small town of Rockland from all over the country and the world. Most of them had come to eat a lobster.

We wove through the crowd to the heritage tent, which displayed grainy black-and-white photos of the festival going back over seventy years. In the marine tent, a few tanks of murky water held some sea critters for kids and families to touch and look at. In one shallow container, a special blue lobster huddled in a corner with its claws banded. There was a crafts tent, where local artists sold souvenirs and artwork to visitors. And, of course, there was an official Maine Lobster Festival souvenir tent. Between these big tents stood a gauntlet of booths and trucks selling typical carnival food and knickknacks.

Eventually we circled back to the food tent to see how it worked. Visitors could buy a single lobster dinner for twenty-nine dollars, a double for fifty-two dollars, or a triple for seventy-seven dollars. Each meal came with corn on the cob, butter, and coleslaw. Workers assembled the plates, pulling a hot lobster out of the bin and dropping it whole on a cardboard tray. Patrons found spots at long tables to crack open their meals. In a different (and only slightly less long) line, customers could buy fresh lobster rolls, with the lobster salad being made by hand right at the stand. A final, and much shorter, line led to other staples, such as steamed clams, mussels, lobster mac and cheese, oysters, corn chowder, clam chowder, and more.

As I watched volunteers stack cooked lobsters onto trays for customers, I saw a few workers in red shirts clamp a lid on a large bin that looked like a cooler on wheels and begin pushing it away from the food tent. We followed them through the crowd to the lobster cooker in the center of the festival grounds. They parked the bin next to one end of a long, rolling conveyor belt. At the far end of the belt was a truck. A small crowd huddled around a brick gazebo–type structure right in front of the rolling belt.

"This is your before picture," a man said to onlookers in a wicked strong Boston accent. He wore a bright-red hat and matching shirt, both of which proudly labeled him a "lobster cooker." The cooking team pushed a large cage full of live lobsters out of the back of the truck onto the belt and then rolled it toward the cookers. One lobster cooker attached a lifting mechanism to the crate and gave a signal to the man holding the control button. The pulley lifted the heavy cage into the air, and the team guided it over the boiling vat. "After, they come out nice and red," the lobster cooker assured us. They lowered the cage into the vat of boiling water, removed the pulley attachment, and covered the vat with a metal lid.

This is the World's Largest Lobster Cooker.[99] Built in 2008, it can cook sixteen hundred pounds of lobster in fifteen minutes. There are eight individual vats housed within the open-air brick edifice. People purchased commemorative bricks to help support the cost of building the cooker in 2008, so the entire unit is covered with sweet memories of loved ones next to engraved lobster emblems. One brick read simply "Lobster for Life!" The entire time I was at the festival, steam constantly emanated from the vats, lifting up and around the bricks and curling out from under the roof. Lobsters were always being cooked.

"Checking number three!"

"Got it," another lobster cooker answered as he moved into place and readied the mechanical pulley system to lift the cage out of the water. When it was lifted out of the vat, the lobster cooker reached in to pluck an antenna off a lobster to test if this batch was sufficiently cooked. The antenna popped off easily.

"Get it outa here," he directed with a sideways wave, confirming the lobsters were ready. He stepped back and helped guide the cage back to the rolling belt behind them. When they had placed the crate down on the belt, he removed the pulley hook from the cage and rolled the container of now bright-red lobsters down the belt toward a waiting bin on wheels. Volunteers helped pull the lobsters out of the cage and place them into the insulated bin one by one, doing what seemed to be a kind of quality control. Every once in a while, a separated claw or arm would appear, and the workers would set it aside or tuck it in their pocket. When the cage was empty, volunteers capped the bin of cooked lobsters, hoisted the wheelbarrow-like contraption, and headed down the path back toward the food tent. The narrow path between the two locations was swamped with visitors lined up for food and perusing tents full of souvenirs, so the volunteers carried big red flags and shouted, "Lobsters, coming through."

It may sound obvious, given the central activity of killing and eating lobsters, but the celebration of lobster in Maine almost entirely focuses on the dead creature as opposed to the live one. Lobsters display their signature bright-red hue only once they have been cooked. Alive, they typically appear brown. But images and souvenirs usually show lobsters in this bright-red state. Christmas ornaments for sale at the festival showed red lobsters stuck in a trap, or red lobster claws repurposed by adding Santa hats and googly eyes (billed as "Santa Claws"). The logo of the Maine Lobster Festival features a bright-red lobster. There was even a large plywood painting of a red lobster right near the cooker, with a cutout for a tourist to poke their head through.

This event, as evidenced by the decor and souvenirs for sale, often celebrates the more macabre parts of the lobsters' journey. Instead of partitioning the fairground with fences, for example, the organizers used piles of lobster traps. Though instruments of death, the traps were not unsightly; instead, they enhanced the coastal scenery. One magnet for sale had a red lobster in a steaming pot with "Eat Me" written around it. A T-shirt in the same store pictured one lobster largely submerged in a steaming pot, with another lobster outside of it asking, "Hey Bob! How's the water? Bob? Bob?! BOB!!" Cooking lobsters clearly does not carry the same taboo or discomfort as other forms of slaughter. For example, I have never seen a T-shirt showing a cow being stunned, hung upside down, and bled while another cow watched. That death doesn't bear quite the same touristic appeal.

Maybe this is because lobster is one of the few foods in American cuisine that consumers often eat whole, with the entire creature on their plate, eyeballs, legs, and all. There is no emotionally protective separation between the live creature and the food, like there is between a cow chewing on cud in a field and a skirt steak doused in marinade. What happens between those two states is an uncomfortable and gritty truth, a deconstruction on which no one much wants to dwell. But there is no hidden processing for lobster. Eating lobster involves picking apart the entire body in a visceral way, with your own hands and teeth. Sucking tissue out of small leg cavities, pushing meat through the tail, cracking and pulling apart knuckle joints—there is simply no way to avoid the fact that this was once, very recently, a living animal, because the dead animal on your plate is so complete.

So instead, the freshness of the kill becomes pointed, a celebrated part of the allure of the meal. There is no fresher meal than a lobster dinner, many say. There's something almost idyllic about plucking your dinner right out of the ocean, minimizing the processing, and feeling connected to your food source.

The redness—and deadness—of lobsters is ubiquitous. When you see a lobster image in pop culture, it is almost always red. Larry the Lobster in the *SpongeBob SquarePants* series, for example, is a buff weight-lifting side character perpetually colored red. The restaurant chain Red Lobster eponymously captures this dynamic. At the Maine Lobster Festival, the parade on Saturday morning heavily featured red lobsters. A red car carrying a local pageant winner had red lobster claws attached to the windows, and the winner wore a dress printed with red lobsters. Lobster balloons, lobster-claw headbands, lobster costumes—all bright red. With so much red messaging it's easy to imagine that their cooked state is actually the most natural, and just as easy to forget that the living, mottled brown creatures were ever really an important part of the equation at all.

Today lobsters are almost always killed by being boiled or steamed alive. Cooks in home kitchens and fancy restaurants simply drop them, legs wriggling, into a pot and close the lid. The lobsters undeniably demonstrate an awareness of the hot water; they thrash about, clanging against the sides of the pot and pushing up on the lid if they can reach. But science has yet to definitively determine whether lobsters feel pain.

Many people argue the bugs cannot, in fact, feel pain, which means killing them by boiling them alive is not inhumane. This school maintains that the lobster's behavior in the pot is simply a "standard escape response," just an instinctual reflex in response to a threatening situation, not evidence the creature actually experiences pain.[100] They argue that lobsters' nervous system is "primitive," most similar to that of an insect. One lobster company says on its website that "for an organism to perceive pain it must have a complex nervous system" and that because "neither insects nor lobsters have brains," they accordingly conclude lobsters "do not process pain."[101] The decentralized nervous system of a lobster, so the argument goes, is too simple to process pain in the same way we would, even when the creature experiences something negative. "Lobsters have stress receptors, but they do not have identifiable pain receptors," Trevor Corson writes in an epilogue to his book *The Secret Life of Lobsters*.[102] The epilogue, titled "How to Cook a Lobster," insists that all of the scientists and fishermen interviewed for his book eat lobster "with enthusiasm," and he encourages readers to do so too. According to this line of thinking, the experience of stress or negative stimuli cannot be equated with the experience of pain, which is more subjective and requires consciousness of suffering.

Animal activists and crustacean advocates, on the other hand, insist the evidence is mounting to prove that lobsters do feel pain. First, many people point to the obvious: the lobsters certainly act like they are in pain when dropped into a pot of boiling water. Demonstrating behavior associated with pain is one of the two key criteria scientists and ethicists consider when studying animals' pain. It is evident, even to dissenters, that lobsters thrash, struggle, and try to escape the pot. In his seminal 2004 essay about the Maine Lobster Festival, "Consider the Lobster," David Foster Wallace writes, "The lobster, in other words, behaves very much as you or I would behave if we were plunged into boiling water."[103] Scientists have also conducted shock experiments on decapods, like lobsters, which prove that they typically try to avoid painful or harmful conditions when possible.[104] What is an escape response—like thrashing against the sides of a pot—if not the manifestation of a preference to avoid harm? And while the legend about lobsters "screaming" when being boiled has been debunked (it is actually the sound of steam escaping from their carapaces), should their biological lack of a vocal mechanism be held against them as evidence they are not in distress? Surely one can be in pain without screaming.

But the second criteria for assessing animals' pain is more complicated. People look to the "neurological hardware" typically required for what we understand to be the experience of pain.[105] "Nociception" is the term scientists use to describe that hardware; it refers to the detection of painful stimuli," or the neurological event that results from encountering something harmful.[106] Nociception relies on nociceptors, or "relatively unspecialized, naked nerve endings that respond to mechanical, thermal, or chemical stimuli."[107] Nociception does not necessarily involve the central nervous system, which is where we typically understand the emotional and subjective experience of pain to occur. In other words, it's entirely possible for an animal's nociceptors to fire in an involuntary reflex without that animal experiencing pain. Wallace admits there is a difference between "pain as a purely neurological event" and "actual suffering, which seems crucially to involve an emotional component, an awareness of pain as unpleasant, as something to fear/dislike/want to avoid."[108] The question is whether lobsters experience the latter.

Even if science is ambiguous on the question of whether lobsters feel pain, the precautionary principle instructs that out of an abundance of caution we should err on the side of compassion until we can definitively resolve the question. Some advocate for other methods of killing lobsters, such as freezing the lobster before boiling it (to loosely stun it) or slicing it in half before cooking.[109] Switzerland, Norway, and New Zealand have made it illegal to boil lobsters alive without stunning them first, following the precautionary principle.[110] These methods try to mirror what the United States requires by law for slaughtering most land animals: stunning a creature to render it insensible before the fatal act. And, of course, some advocates go even further, arguing there is no right way to kill a lobster. Organizations like Crustacean Compassion and PETA have long advocated against eating crustaceans. PETA has conducted "lobster liberation" campaigns, buying live lobsters destined for a meal and releasing them back into the waters of Maine, and they have protested the Maine Lobster Festival many times, urging attendees to "relate to who is on your plate."[111]

For me, these two arguments—that lobsters don't feel pain, so we can kill them in a way that may cause suffering, or that lobsters do feel pain, so we shouldn't—actually reveal the same underlying moral principle: pain matters, and purposefully inflicting it on other creatures goes against our own collective values. Knowingly causing suffering seems to be a line we as a species don't want to cross. It's why our federal government insists on stunning land animals like pigs and cows before killing them in slaughterhouses. We understand there is a difference between different methods of killing. We recognize that inflicting suffering is cruel.

Yet that moral caveat doesn't stop us from killing. To the contrary, it may even facilitate it. If we convince ourselves animals don't feel pain, we absolve ourselves from the guilt of inflicting it. Even when confronted with videos of cows desperately trying to turn around in the chute leading into a slaughterhouse, we are comforted by knowing the animal was rendered unconscious before its throat was cut. Even as we watch lobsters in their death throes, we mutter, "But we aren't sure what that means." We point to science in a way that feels almost willfully ignorant, demanding a definitive finding that a lobster feels pain in the same manner a human does before ever considering a sacrifice as small as not eating one. We think that any potential pain is worth our enjoyment, that the balance of equities is self-evident, as long as our killing stops short of torture. But the more I think about the morality of inflicting pain, I'm not even sure it matters how much pain a lobster actually feels, or whether it compares to ours. As Wallace put it, "Why is a primitive, inarticulate form of suffering less urgent or uncomfortable for the person who's helping to inflict it by paying for the food it results in?"[112]

But some lobster-eating apologists like Corson argue that boiling a lobster, even if it causes pain, is actually an "opportunity" to "acknowledge the philosophical and perhaps even spiritual dimensions of the web of life that sustains us all—all from the safety of our kitchens."[113]

We live in a world where consumers are typically distanced from food production. We buy prepackaged meat cuts and pasteurized dairy products at the grocery store without having to witness or participate in the making of those products. It's almost certainly true that eating a whole lobster puts an average American closer to the source of their food than is possible for any other animal product. As the food journalist Molly O'Neill put it over thirty years ago, "Preparing a lobster is one of the few times that a cook witnesses the transition from 'animal' to 'food,' and confronts the possibility of inflicting pain."[114] While that fact can keep people away from cooking lobsters out of squeamishness, it can also inspire a good feeling. Cracking open a whole lobster always used to make me feel a little more in touch with my carnivore self, rooted into my body's all-too-animal need to eat. Of course, like many, I could not head out to sea and find my own lobster—I have neither the skills nor the brawn—but cracking open a claw makes you feel as if you could, as if you are a self-sustaining pilgrim living close to the land (and sea) around you. It's a relic from a bygone time, this proximity to the animals on our plates.

But if boiling lobsters alive is ethically permissible because of what it forces us to confront about our flesh-eating instincts, I found it hard to know how much of this philosophical consideration actually took place at the Maine Lobster Festival. The sheer number of lobsters being cooked, the quick slam-a-tray-together assembly line, and the slurpy, busy eating in the food tent all belied the notion that there was any time or space for such reflection. Nor was the cooker a huge attraction for visitors; while there were maybe two dozen people watching the cookers at any given time, and while the cooker was in the physical center of the park, attendees were far more densely assembled at the food tent and the music stage. The cooker was there if you wanted to see it, but the festival did not force visitors to engage with the process.

The cooking at times seemed incidental to the main experience of the festival: enjoying a summer Saturday with family and friends while eating a freshly caught lobster. It was a means to an end, not necessarily an end in itself.

Every year at the Maine Lobster Festival, close to twenty thousand pounds of lobster are cooked and served over five days. The briny smell of dying lobsters wafted incessantly out of the World's Biggest Lobster Cooker, and the coastal breeze carried it around the festival grounds. My reaction to the smell was a microcosm of my relationship to the festival more generally: nostalgia at first, followed by a wave of emotional unease. Eating lobster for me was often as much about the meaning and ambiance of the meal as it was about the taste of the meat. Eating lobsters whole was particularly communal, because everyone cracked through their lobster together, and many childhood memories flooded back with the smell of the cooking bugs. But despite those memories, watching a giant crate containing dozens of live, wiggling lobsters get dropped into the unforgiving cooker still made me uncomfortable and deeply sad.

I mulled over where to put the Lobster Festival in this book. This section is called "Dominance," and in my original conception, this section would cover events like the Rattlesnake Roundup, rodeos, or other contests where the point of the event is to kill, master, or best an animal. This festival didn't fit that mold precisely, because the lobsters pose no threat, symbolic or otherwise, to humans. Traps are laid on the seafloor, claws are banded or pegged when the creatures are pulled up, and all that's left to do by the time the festival rolls around is to enjoy your meal. There is no contest, no danger, and no risk for attendees to spectate. Instead, this festival is about eating the lobsters for our pleasure and supporting the local economy, industry, and culture.

But as I thought more about it and separated my own cultural background from what I saw at the harbor, it became clear that the Maine Lobster Festival was not that different from the Rattlesnake Roundup. In each case, wild animals are captured by professionals, hauled in, and transported live to a central facility, where they are killed in front of audiences. Many people think snakes and lobsters do not feel pain, which justifies these practices and assuages the guilt of attendees. While the nature of the death differs, both involve unceremonious killing en masse. Both festivals are deeply important to local identity and culture, and both face steep opposition and doubt from outsiders. Both involve extensive audience engagement with the animal corpses. Both count the killed animals in terms of pounds, not individuals. Both have the freshly killed meat for sale as one of the main attractions. And both sell souvenirs and knickknacks crafted from the leftover body parts. These two festivals were the same, I realized, only with slightly different framing.

The Rattlesnake Roundup dramatizes threats from a predator; the Lobster Festival, however, foregrounds a threat to the lobster fishery: obsolescence. The lobsters themselves are the commodity, not the source of the threat. So instead of emphasizing fear or hatred of the animals, the Lobster Festival celebrates them, even as the over-arching point is to ensure the fishery can continue to kill them for profit. Humans kill snakes at the Rattlesnake Roundup because we fear and hate them, but we kill the lobsters at the Maine Lobster Festival out of some combination of pleasure and sustenance. It's dissonant but logical. This give-and-take with lobsters is what makes this festival—and the fishery more generally—so complicated. It's a dance between needing them, celebrating them, and killing them.

But in the comparison between the Maine Lobster Festival and the Rattlesnake Roundup, differences emerge as well. In Sweetwater, the violence exhibited was, in many ways, gratuitous. No one "needed" to behead snakes, make handprints of blood, and eat the fried meat, even if we accept the goal of reducing the rattlesnake population. The killing that took place in Sweetwater was a spectacle, designed to entertain visitors. The Jaycees were members of a civic organization raising money for local causes, and killing the snakes was a flashy and traditional way to do so. In Maine, on the other hand, lobstermen's livelihoods depend on maximizing a catch. The killing at the festival was not gratuitous—in fact, killing too many lobsters would simply lose fishermen and the festival money, and the cooks often radioed over to the food tent to ask about the supply levels before boiling another batch. And while the cooks did kill thousands of lobsters over the five-day festival, in a potentially excruciating manner for the lobsters, the primary reason seemed to be to raise political awareness and build support for the lobstering industry. The point was not to mess with the live animals but to sell as many as possible as cooked commodities.

While each festival undertook its tasks in vastly different ways, the core of these festivals was the same: public slaughter. As Wallace writes, "If you, the festival attendee, permit yourself to think that lobsters can suffer and would rather not, the [Maine Lobster Festival] begins to take on the aspect of something like a Roman circus or medieval torture-fest."[115] The same could be said of the Rattlesnake Roundup. *None shall escape*, my grandmother wrote, and it was true. These festivals—both carnival atmospheres, both displays of carnivorous indulgence—were eerily similar. Both kill animals to promote local culture and identity and to defend against outsider intrusion. And both justify their actions by the seemingly rudimentary incarnation of the species at the center.

The poster for the Maine Lobster Festival featured a beautiful watercolor painting of two lobsters with their claws intertwined. The piece was titled *Claw Shake*, which the artist explained "highlights the value of empathy and cooperation that [she] believe[s] are lacking in our relationship to others and to nature." The artist finished her statement with a plea: "Let's sit down, shake claws, and listen to each other." That suggestion of teamwork was certainly taken up around the festival, where dozens of volunteers worked on every part of the event. The wider Maine community rallied here, coming out in droves to buy a lobster meal and support the fishery. In the us-versus-them dynamic, the "us" was powerful.

Lobsters do grab each other's claws in real life sometimes, but they do not do so out of empathy. Rather, they enter a better-titled "claw lock," testing each other's strength by squeezing and crushing the other's claw, in what Corson writes is both "a battle of endurance and a game of chicken." Eventually one lobster usually capitulates and retreats, and the winner's dominance is established. If neither steps down after the claw lock, the fight escalates and the combatants often lose limbs in the ensuing battle.[116]

Whether an engagement is a "claw shake" or a "claw lock" is in many ways a question of perspective. Lobstermen need each other's support and camaraderie for their industry to survive (claw shake), but they remain in competition with their neighbors on the water every day to capture the biggest share of a finite resource (claw lock). Lobstermen respect catch limits and size restrictions to safeguard the future of the fishery (claw shake), while still trying to trap as many as they can (claw lock). Fishermen and scientists both want to maintain sustainable lobster populations (claw shake), yet they vilify each other's attempts (claw lock). Animal advocates want to protect a cetaceous species (claw shake) by limiting the success and freedom of another: humans (claw lock). It's like an optical illusion: a collaboration viewed from one angle, a competition from another.

The lobster fishery is a modern tragedy of the commons, where it seems to everyone involved that someone will inevitably lose—whether it be the lobstermen and Maine's coastal communities, the endangered whales, or the lobsters themselves. There are many complicated questions, and the debates are particularly contentious because the solutions appear to be zero-sum. If we overfish the lobsters, the fishermen will suffer in the long term, but if we impose too many restrictions, the fishermen will suffer in the short term. If we protect the right whales, the lobstermen will have to pay an immediate cost, but if we don't, we may well lose a species. If we recognize lobster sentience and admit the moral stain of boiling them alive, the industry and the real people sustaining it will struggle, but if we don't, we risk imposing untold suffering. There are no easy answers.

Eating a lobster was so central to this event that my wife and I weren't sure how to occupy ourselves after a while. We walked laps around the booths multiple times, dodging lines queued for staples like fried dough and "bacon steak on a stick." We listened to live music and meandered through all the tents, twice. But there was only so much killing I could stomach, and the scent of brine was omnipresent. When we left the festival for the last time before driving back to the airport, my wife dug a few dollar bills out of her purse and dropped them in the bucket a volunteer was holding at the entrance.

"Thanks for supporting the lobstermen!" the volunteer called to her. We nodded over our shoulders and smiled back. While most of the festivals in this book bring important and substantial revenue to the hosting communities, the Maine Lobster Festival feels even more directly connected with people's livelihoods. It's political, and pointed, this fundraising. When we were out of earshot of the volunteer, I asked my wife why she donated to their cause.

"Because it felt weird not to," she said. "They've worked so hard." *Claw shake.* Just like the Jaycees in Sweetwater, the organizers and volunteers at the lobster festival poured their hearts and soul into the event, and the results were remarkable. But I hadn't spent a dime in the festival grounds, because I'm sympathetic to the lobsters and their experience of pain, whatever that might be. We left the festival and walked into town for all of our meals throughout the weekend and purchased items only in local stores, not at the festival. *Claw lock.*

"Lobsters are tangible," Linda Greenlaw writes in her memoir about her time lobster fishing in Maine. "Lobsters become the scapegoat, or perhaps it would be more accurate to say that all threats to our ability to catch lobsters become scapegoats." When every problem can be explained in terms of the fishery and its economic success or failure, she writes, it "all boils down to the lobster."[117] The Maine Lobster Festival is in many ways a political rallying cry, using the lobster as a powerful symbol. Celia Knight, the president of the Maine Lobster Festival, explained to me that over the past few years they have specifically worked to make the festival more focused on the meaning of lobsters, rather than it simply being an excuse to hold a carnival. Using lobsters as a symbol here is purposeful, even strategic.

The lobster symbolizes all of the cultural, economic, and personal conflicts at play in this industry and this event. And at the Maine Lobster Festival, the lobsters are the literal embodiment of the celebration of the industry: caught, cooked, and served, these bugs are what it's all about. The human interests involved are played out on the lobsters themselves. We use the lobsters as a symbol, a concrete manifestation of what we think and need and want, a Rorschach test for what values we have. We kill them because they taste good but also because we want to support the human interests involved: the small coastal communities, the hardworking fishermen with lobster in their blood, and the fight against outsider control. But lobsters are their own wild creatures, with their own needs, wants, and interests. I think it's time we add those to the pot instead of using their bodies as living symbols for our own political ends.

PART II
HUMOR

INTERNATIONAL CAMEL & OSTRICH RACES

VIRGINIA CITY, NV
THE RICHEST PLACE ON EARTH

The heat shimmered on the dry desert horizon. Cactuses studded the landscape, which was cracked and brown. Water was scarce. A long pack train of animals and military personnel made its way across the American Southwest, seeking to mark the unforgiving landscape with trails. The year was 1857, and Edward Fitzgerald Beale, a naval officer, frontiersman, and former Superintendent of Indian Affairs, had been ordered to survey and build a road from Fort Defiance, in modern Arizona, to the Colorado River.[118] Journeys like this could be grueling and dangerous. Approaching the raging river, Beale's caravan had no choice but to cross the waters, driving animals through the current. Two horses and ten mules drowned.[119] But in the same attempt, all twenty-five of the American military's newest pack animals surfaced unharmed on the other side, water dripping from their humps. These were the promising, state-of-the-art tools employed in the effort to subdue the western frontier: camels.

By the 1830s, people had begun to move to the West Coast in search of gold, silver, and a new life. Trails connecting California to the Midwest ran through American Indian lands, over and around steep mountain passes, and through arid desert. Until this point, the best technology available to make the journey west was found in animals: horses, mules, and oxen worked hard for American pioneers and settlers. But they required a lot of water, rest, and food on the trail, and many animals died from the difficult conditions, making the trips expensive and even riskier for the human travelers. The American military was in search of something better.

In 1836 a young army officer suggested a novel solution to the challenge of navigating the inhospitable desert: importing camels to use as beasts of burden.[120] No one picked up the idea right away, but in the late 1840s, two things happened: the United States acquired over half a million square miles of arid desert land at the conclusion of the Mexican-American War, and miners discovered gold in California.[121] These two developments combined to intensify the need for safe trails and efficient transportation of goods and people between coasts— trails that would need to traverse newly American desert landscapes.

When Jefferson Davis became President Franklin Pierce's secretary of war, Davis eagerly began promoting the idea of importing camels. In 1855 Congress approved a thirty-thousand-dollar appropriation to purchase and import camels for military and trans- portation purposes, which would be over one million dollars today. The government sent a ship to the Middle East, stopping in Tunis, Turkey, Greece, and Egypt. The officers bought a total of thirty-three camels and began the long trip to Texas with the camels on board. After a few calves died on the journey and a few more were born en route, a total of thirty-four camels arrived safely on the shore of Texas. A second ship left to purchase even more camels upon their return, since the voyage had been so successful and Congress's appropriations not yet fully spent.[122] From these journeys the so-called "Camel Corps" was born.

The Camel Corps proved its mettle on Beale's exploratory trip in the Southwest. Camels were hardworking, gentle, and solid creatures capable of carrying far more for far longer than the horses and mules typically used in the region. The camels required little water and could eat nearly any shrub around, unlike other, pickier pack animals. As Beale wrote in his journal at the time, "My admiration for the camels increases daily with my experience of them."[123] But while it was clear that camels could sustain the grueling work of westward expansion, it was equally clear that the army had no idea what, exactly, to do with camels more generally. Most of the animals stayed stationed at Camp Verde in Texas, but a faction lived in California. The Camel Corps had not yet received a permanent assignment. The future for "Uncle Sam's Camels" was uncertain, and no one knew how they would be incorporated into military strategy and transportation in the region or whether private citizens would begin training the creatures for personal or commercial use too.[124]

The demise of a neglected Camel Corps was perhaps inevitable in a nation on the brink of civil war. There was no room for strategizing and training an entirely new type of cavalry anymore in the midst of such conflict. When war broke out following Abraham Lincoln's election in 1860, it was clear the Camel Corps had to be disbanded. The experiment came to an unceremonious end.

The United States imported camels from the Middle East, but in fact, camels evolved right here in North America over forty million years ago, roaming the continent until about eight thousand years ago.[125] But throughout the relatively young history of the United

States, there have been no known wild camels in North America. What brought them back to the continent in the 1850s was a mixture of military ingenuity and human hubris. We thought we could bend nature to our will by using its own adaptations, mastering the desert by deploying evolution's own solution to cross the arid land.

Camels have adapted to harsh desert environments; they can survive in extreme heat with little water. They have long eyelashes designed to keep sand out of their eyes, special membranes in their noses to retain as much moisture as possible from their breath while exhaling, and tough tongues to allow for chewing sharp desert plants.[126] Advocates of the Camel Corps in the United States admired how foreign nations used camels for freight and transport, and they saw an opportunity in their bodies and labor. Camels were bought and transported to the United States as military tools in the larger nation-building project.

But camels were always outsiders in America, brought here merely to serve human ends. In a 1930 *California Historical Society Quarterly* paper, historian A. A. Gray called them a "queer caravan," composed of "oriental strangers."[127] While camels were seen as useful "ships of the desert" to military strategists and thinkers forging a westward path, they were always decidedly exotic to Americans.[128] That exoticism inspired two general reactions to camels in the general public of the late nineteenth century: frustration and amusement.

Advocates of the Camel Corps highlighted the benefits of camels and their strengths as beasts of burden. But trouble appeared right away once camels were on the ground in Texas. The camels had a distinct, strong odor, which scared horses and mules and was unpleasant to be around. They also had, as historian Odie B. Faulk wrote, a "habit of emitting the most heart-rending and ear-splitting groans." They reportedly spat up half-digested cud when they were perturbed, blowing slimy goo right onto whoever or whatever bothered them, an obstreperousness that irritated handlers used to docile, obedient animals like horses and mules. Also causing frustration was that camels could be mounted only after they were made to kneel, a process that annoyed the animals and produced loud vocalizations and the occasional spit wad, to boot. And during the males' "rutting" season, when they were readying to mate, they were especially cantankerous and prone to biting human handlers.[129]

One of the biggest and most consistent hurdles to the use of camels in the West was that horses and mules were terrified of them. Horses would startle and stampede, and mules would kick and run away at the sight (or sniff) of a camel. In an economy, culture, and lifestyle dominated almost entirely by horse and mule transport and labor, this reaction was untenable, leading many people to decry camels as strange beasts who complicated, rather than simplified, western life.

People were also surprised that camels were so headstrong. In one example, an army private kicked a camel in the belly when the camel moaned at the weight of his load. Such behavior was common at the time, when soldiers wanted—as Faulk recounts—"to get [an animal's] attention" when it was not complying. The camel spat a wad of cud onto the private's face in response. The enraged private then "grabbed a club and swung at the dromedary's head," but the camel "dodged the blow easily, gave forth a shrill scream, and in one quick motion ripped the man's arm to the bone with its sharp incisors."[130] Camels have minds of their own, and they didn't fit neatly into society's paradigms for submissive pack animals.

On the other side of the spectrum, camels' exoticism has long inspired sheer amusement. To westerners, camels are weird-looking, unusual, and unpredictable. In 1787 George Washington hired a camel to visit his homestead at Mount Vernon to entertain guests, a tradition that is replicated to this day every year around the holidays.[131] And in the West of the nineteenth century, when camels would stop near a town while traveling in a caravan, Faulk explains, "many of the people living there went out in a carnival mood to see the strange animals."[132] It was exciting to see camels, breaking up the monotony of their days.

Even at the end of the Camel Corps experiment, entertainment seemed to be a core value to harness from the animals. "The only use for the beasts which came to the minds of the captors," Faulk writes, "was as entertainment for some of the local ladies and children who were given rides." A handful of camels were sold to the Ringling Brothers Circus and to similar exhibitions over the border in Mexico.[133] The novelty of the camel and its humped body was pervasive.

Over a century later, camels are still being imported, bred, transported, and directed to human ends, deployed to entertain and amuse audiences. It was captive camels, after all, that brought me to Virginia City, Nevada, on a hot weekend in early September.

Carved into the hills halfway between Reno and Carson City, this mining boom town cropped up in the 1860s upon the discovery of the Comstock Lode of silver, and today Virginia City is a National Historic Landmark, with dozens of buildings dating from the nineteenth century.[134] Everything in town still evokes the mining days of the Wild West, from building facades to signage. The town sits on a steep hillside, with every horizontal street a full staircase length above or below its neighbor. Because of the town's geography, a broad view opens up past the buildings in one direction, and a mountain rises above you in the other. When my wife and I pulled into the seemingly empty town early on Saturday morning, a voice called down to us.

I looked up, squinting into the sun, to find a shirtless man shouting down from a balcony above us as he leaned on the railing.

"Are you here for the races?" he yelled.

"Yeah," I answered back. I didn't need to yell—the street was quiet, with almost no traffic. Then I hesitated, venturing a guess as to why he was asking: "Do you think it's okay to park here?"

"Oh, yeah," he answered. "The camels will come right through here later." I thanked him, locked my car, and began walking down the street.

The International Camel & Ostrich Races were this weekend. This event dates back to 1959, when the editor of the *Territorial Enterprise* in Virginia City, a man with a penchant for making up news out of whole cloth, invented a story to fill the paper's pages on a slow news day. The story announced the results of a nonexistent camel race in town. The *San Francisco Chronicle,* apparently not realizing the story was fake, republished the results. Humiliated, the *Chronicle* borrowed camels from the San Francisco Zoo and took them to Virginia City to race them the next year, turning the joke into reality.[135] Created out of nothing, the event is now over sixty years old and promises a "weekend of good-old fashioned fun in Virginia City."[136]

But we arrived in Virginia City too early for any fun, new or old, it seemed. We walked up the main street in one direction, peering into closed shops and eyeing the dark-windowed saloons that dotted the town, before crossing the street and walking back on the other side. Much of the sidewalk was made of wooden planks, and the street seemed pulled out of another time. I was surprised to see so few camels decorating the town. Only the town's visitor center boasted a large statue of a camel just outside its doorway. This town was evidently not built around camels in the way that Rockland, Maine, built itself around lobsters. It crossed my mind that this was just a tourist trap designed to draw in people like me, not knowing any better, instead of an event meant to celebrate local heritage and culture.

About an hour before the races were set to begin, we walked down to the Virginia City Fairgrounds—a walk that did not span a long distance but involved a steep decline. Shuttles had just started running for folks who didn't want to make the hike. We scanned our tickets, got our wristbands, and entered the fairgrounds. It was a small arena, essentially an oval-shaped dirt stage with metal bleachers rising on either long side, a VIP tent along one short end, and the starting gate on the other. A couple camels were already saddled up and working. There was a special riser built so people could climb the steps and mount a standing camel, which a handler would lead around the track. Most people in line were children, but some adults were ready for a turn around the racetrack too. The camels seemed exceedingly tame, and kids especially seemed to enjoy the rides, posing for photos, and petting the camels' backs.

I walked past the bleachers to look at the animals in their pens behind the start gates on the far side of the track. Ostriches, camels, zebras, and emus were milling about their metal enclosures. Rather than exhibiting the animals throughout the day for visitors to engage with at their leisure, these races were shows intended to amaze and entertain a captive audience for an hour or two as a cohesive performance. This was unlike the other festivals I attended, where sprawling carnival booths and souvenir tents fanned out around the central animal attraction and where people could come and go as the day went on, interacting with animals as they wished. This was a ticketed, seated performance. Everyone was here to sit and watch the races. The only time we could spend with the animals was now, before the show, as we took photos through the gates.

The animals are owned and managed by Hedrick's Promotions, Inc., an exotic animal exhibition company operating out of Kansas. The company transports the animals out to Virginia City and hosts the camel races, with Joe Hedrick himself emceeing and encouraging contestants throughout the show. When I learned that these exotic animals were transported in from afar for the sole purpose of putting on this show, I realized this festival was essentially a traveling circus. In fact, Hedrick's Promotions offers these races as part of its business, and while Virginia City is a long-standing host, a repeat customer of sorts, it is not the only one.[137] Other locations around the country also hire Hedrick's for special racing events. The Ocean Downs track in Maryland, usually a site for horse racing, for example, offers a special night for Hedrick's show, as has Canterbury Park in Minnesota (there, they call it "Extreme Day").[138] These animals were captive performers, not just captives, sent around the country to entertain.

And unlike the Rattlesnake Roundup or the Maine Lobster Festival, where the animals at the heart of the events are gathered from the local environment, these camels are not from the area, nor does the region have any particular connection with camels beyond the long-ago experiment of the Camel Corps engineering its way through the arid West. All of the other festivals in this book use animals with a link to the host community. Most of these festivals emerged, at least in part, from the tangible relationship humans had with creatures in the wild. The Rattlesnake Roundup was originally a way to deal with dangerous pests, and the Lobster Festival was a way to support the local lobster industry. The Jumping Frog Jubilee, monarch butterfly festivals, and Groundhog Day, discussed later in this book, also revolve around the natural presence and behavior of a certain species.

But the Camel & Ostrich Races do something else. Rather than celebrate a part of the local natural history and humanity's relation to it, this event ships in creatures with little connection to the place. The event has gained status as a tradition because it has taken place for over sixty years, but it is different in kind from the other festivals in this book. It is a literal performance, and it celebrates a history it only recently created. Rather than root down, this festival leans into a form of escapism, where the camels create an exciting, strange, and vaguely foreign atmosphere in this otherwise small, deeply American town.

"It's a lot more like a circus than I realized," I murmured to my wife as we turned away from the animal enclosures and looked back to the visitors lining up for camel rides. We then scanned the fairgrounds, trying to decide how to spend the last half hour before the show would begin. The sky was bright blue and clear, and the mountains rose in the background. There were a few booths with food, drinks, and souvenirs for sale, so we stopped to buy some water. It was still cool out, but the day was forecasted to heat up quickly.

"That's all you want?" the attendant asked. "No beer, cocktail?" I was reminded of an entry I saw on the first page of my grandmother's notes from her visit to these races in the late 1990s: "Have to be drunk to ride a camel."

"No, thank you!" I chirped. It was just past nine in the morning; the show would begin at ten. But when we left the booth and ambled to the bleachers, I could see dozens of other people with drinks in hand. We found seats on the shaded side of the stadium and sat down. As we waited for the show to start, large groups of people filed in around us, laughing and calling out to each other. As the bleachers filled, latecomers had to slot in. Many carried classic carnival food, such as cotton candy, corn dogs, and kettle corn. Everyone was talking loudly and craning to look at the animals kept behind the starting gates.

A man wearing clown makeup and dressed in red, white, and blue with an American flag draped over his shoulder ran onto the track. He began rallying the audience for the performance that was about to start.

While this emcee commanded the track, a memory flooded back to me. My sister and I were sitting with our grandparents in the stands at the Ringling Brothers Circus. I was about six or seven, my sister a few years younger. Our faces were painted with glitter tiger stripes. I cupped a snow cone in one hand and balanced a bucket of popcorn between my knees. My grandfather's eyes lit up when the ringmaster took the stage. My grandfather was a minister, a performer in his own right, and a self-avowed acolyte of P. T. Barnum and other showmen. He relished having a crowd's eyes on him, and he loved the glitz and glamour of the stage. He would eagerly ham it up for my sister and me when we were young, placing a trash can upside down on his head just to make us laugh. That day under the big-top tent, we watched lions, elephants, horses, and acrobats loop around the stage. As a child, I didn't know what any of it meant, what abuses the show must have imposed on the animal performers. But at the time it seemed uncomplicated. I watched my grandfather watch the show, and I believed there was something special in performances like this. It would take me decades to unlearn that or, more precisely, to separate the sweetness of the memory of my grandfather's joy from the complicity in the harm that produced it.

Looking around the stands in Virginia City, I saw so many families. Children were propped up on knees and squeezed beside relatives. Kids were having a day exactly like the one I'd had with my grandparents: a special get-together filled with sugary snacks, revelry, and awe. And all around me, kids watched their parents and grandparents, just as they watched the show. They absorbed their loved ones' laughter and learned, just as I'd learned, that animals make for good entertainment. Events like these are meant to captivate audiences, but they also serve to instruct them. What these festivals normalize is what makes them worth thinking about.

Cheers erupting around me dispelled the ghosts of my grandparents. The first event of the show was the Parade of Animals, where all of the animals were led out of their pens and onto the track for an introductory lap. Camels, ostriches, emus, zebras, and more trotted around with their handlers. As the hoopla intensified, I wondered what my grandparents thought of these races when they attended. My grandmother, a true anthropologist trained to study without personal investment, had jotted down notes that were academic and impersonal, limited to observations and follow-up items. So I had no hints about their subjective experiences here. But the excitement around me was palpable, as wide-eyed kids pointed at the animals and adults cheered and clapped, breathing life into my grandmother's notes. When the camels rounded the track, I inhaled deeply and craned my neck for a better view.

As the clown-faced emcee returned to the microphone, I decided my grandfather probably loved the absurdity and showmanship of these races. "I'm not a real rodeo clown," the patriotic emcee began as the animals were led back into their pens. "They fight bulls. I deal with camels here. But I love camels!" Many of the audience members around me began to chat among themselves, distracted from the show now that the parade lap was over. Someone asked to squeeze by us, climbing over the steps while balancing a plate of what looked like lo mein. "This is the premier camel racing event on the West Coast," the camel clown continued. He then warned us, with a mischievous look, that "there will be a lot of 'what the heck' moments today."

He divided the audience into three sections, one for each side of the arena. This event demanded audience participation. "A combination of human performances and animal performances will determine our winner today," he explained, emphasizing that one of the three audience sections would be declared the "winner" of the races. In addition to the camel races, which have been happening since 1960, the event has grown to include ostrich and zebra races too. The animals would race in groups of three, with each animal released from a numbered pen to correspond to one of the three crowd sections. We were to root for our section's corresponding animal. And there were crowd cheering competitions too. When the camel clown asked for initial cheers in response to his signal to test the audience, all three sections reacted tepidly at first.

"The bar is right over there," he admonished. "You need to work on your motivation, okay?"

The sold-out show began with a camel heat. Joe Hedrick, decked out in a plaid shirt tucked into jeans and a cowboy hat, spoke into a microphone and paced up and down the middle of the track as he narrated it.

"These are very, very healthy camels," Hedrick assured the audience as the animals were led into the starting corrals. The camels wore red saddles with a hole in the middle to accommodate their humps, and a cage-like apparatus around the hump for a human rider to hold on to. As the camels were loaded into the starting chutes, their bridled heads rose over the top of the gates, looking left and right at their surroundings.

The jockeys mounted three camels inside the starting corral, but how they climbed up was hidden from my view. All I could see were the sides of the three flimsy enclosures bumping and shaking as the humans figured out how to situate themselves around the camels' humps. On the cue of some corny horn music, the starting gates slammed open and the camels took off.

Immediately, I realized a core fact about this event that I had, for some reason, not yet considered: these races were quite dangerous. It was nothing like a horse race, a controlled and serious sport where the point is to maximize speed. Instead, this event expected—even rewarded—chaos. As historian and former camel jockey Douglas McDonald put it in his booklet *Camels in Nevada*, the camel's "loose skin, flexible hump, and ability to make rapid turns make staying on a difficult task."[139] Another contemporary writer compared camel riding to "riding a sack of sweet potatoes on a treadmill."[140] The jockeys are not necessarily professionals, they're simply people who are willing to pay or are sponsored by a local company for the $500 riding fee. Even repeat riders admit there is little you can do to train or prepare; camels will simply do what they want, and all you can do is try to balance and hold on.

Barreling out of the gates, the three jockeys all sat behind their mount's hump but leaned deeply forward to hold on to the front part of the saddle. Almost instantly, one rider began to lilt strongly to the right. She slid farther and farther down the side of the camel, but the bar of the saddle kept her knee and lower leg stuck in an unnatural position. I grimaced as audience members around me laughed loudly. The jockey bounced along, precariously stuck in the saddle, until handlers were able to control the camel. The second jockey fell off her camel entirely—a farther distance to the ground than from a horse—landing perilously close to the metal railing lining the track.

"They probably should be wearing helmets," my wife whispered when the second jockey fell.

"I didn't realize it would *still* be so dangerous," I replied. I had read my grandmother's notes before flying to Nevada, so I thought I knew what to expect. She attended the races in 1998 and 1999 and saw a few riders fall each year: one suffered a compressed disc and needed crutches, and another was taken away in an ambulance with an unknown injury. But even so, I naively assumed the intervening decades would have changed the event, somehow, to make it safer. That didn't seem to be the case.

The third camel and jockey in this first heat made it all the way around the track's single curve to the finish line directly opposite from where we sat near the start chute. Although that camel had technically "won," the audience was far more engaged in the experiences of the first two jockeys. The race was short, more like a bull ride than a competitive race. The main goal was to hold on. Crossing the finish line was a bonus.

"What would you tell people about riding a camel?" Joe Hedrick asked the rider who got twisted in her saddle once she dismounted the camel and caught her breath.

"It's very dangerous," she said with a chuckle. Flirting with danger seems to be part of the races' appeal. A homemade documentary called *Dromedary Daze*, which chronicled the 2004 races, showed a heat where a strap on one camel's saddle broke and a rider tumbled off, breaking multiple ribs. Another jockey fell off at high speed in a different heat, breaking his wrist. And in 2011 a rider slid off his ostrich and was run over by another ostrich following behind him, shattering his clavicle.[141] A 2016 rider wrote about her own fall: "I fell . . . about six feet or more off of the camel and landed on my hip. Rocks flew into my mouth like pinballs bouncing up against my teeth."[142]

But the risk of injury doesn't seem to deter the jockeys, who line up every year. Indeed, three more jockeys were already lining up for the second heat of the show: the ostrich races.

Ostriches are notoriously difficult to ride. They are the largest birds in the world and can run over forty miles per hour. But they have not been domesticated and bred to sustain large loads on their backs. Their instinct is simply to shake the weight off. One long-standing jockey stated about ostrich riding: "Sometimes they won't get that far and they'll stop off in a corner and just go into a spin like a washing machine or a clothes dryer, so you just sit there or you just bail out."[143] Ostriches have sometimes been raced with the jockeys sitting in two-wheel carriages attached to the bird, but in Virginia City the humans sit directly atop the birds.

Three adults mounted the ostriches in the rickety start chutes and held on tightly. The birds were jostling the jockeys already, bumping them against the walls in apparent displeasure. My grandmother recorded a similar observation at her first ostrich heat: "terrified, legs quaked and shook. Great fear in chutes." The frantic birds' heads popped up over the gates. To me, riding ostriches seemed even stranger—and more harmful to the animals—than riding camels. What was the point other than pure theater?

When the gates opened, the ostriches immediately started trying to free themselves of their riders. The jockeys didn't make it far. One rider fell off right in front of us, slamming her side into the dirt track. Someone around me audibly winced "Oooooh" as the rider hit the ground. A second ostrich then took a tumble forward too, and that jockey flew forward over the ostrich's head as the bird skidded onto its chest, legs akimbo behind its body. Now free of the jockey, the ostrich righted itself as quickly as it could and sprinted away. People around me were laughing, enjoying the slapstick hilarity of the event.

Slapstick humor is a technique dating back to at least the sixteenth century. It was used by Shakespeare and other theatrical performers to entertain audiences with the "cartoonish reality" created by "purposefully exaggerated" behavior.[144] Slapstick, at its core, involves people getting hurt; the word itself derives from a tool made from two pieces of wood used to make an audible thwack when deployed onstage to mimic a hard slap.[145] Equally critical to the slapstick genre, though, is the buoyancy with which its performers bounce back from encounters with violence. Nothing is meant to be actually harmful, and the humor exists in indulging the absurdity without being chastened by pesky consequences.[146]

But the Camel & Ostrich Races are not carefully choreographed to protect against harm. It isn't a set piece or a rehearsed show. It is a live and unpredictable exhibition, with potential for serious harm, both when a jockey hits the ground and when an animal does. I felt disoriented by my reaction to the ostrich race, which was somewhere between sadness and disbelief. Watching an ostrich fall flat on its chest as it careened out of control in a fear response, watching a human fly into the ground—it all felt cruel, risky, and unnecessary to me. Yet the jockeys and ostriches were all able to walk away on their own, and the laughter around me made my doubts feel almost unreasonable. The handlers on the track hustled to get the ostriches back under control, and the two jockeys who had fallen walked off the track with smiles on their faces.

"We have a lineup change due to Victoria's face-plant there," Joe Hedrick explained bluntly as a new jockey jogged into place for the next camel race. "You sign a waiver, a very strict waiver," Hedrick remarked, joking but not as the new jockey climbed up in the starting chute. I couldn't see where Victoria, the woman who had fallen, went. I hoped she was okay.

The purpose of these races, both originally in 1959 and today, is simple: to entertain. The races are advertised as a family-friendly good time, full of hilarious gaffs, unusual animals, and interactive performances. It is not surprising that camels, zebras, emus, and ostriches are the animals of choice in these races, as they are all exotic creatures not particularly amenable to being ridden and not native to the place where the audience sees them. Everything about this event is meant to be, well, weird. When we were there, a poster for the races in town included this apt teaser: "You'll leave asking yourself *What Did I Just Watch?*"

Flirting with danger is clearly part of the appeal of these races, for participants and spectators alike. Audience members laugh at the lithe human bodies thrown about by the solid animals, shout when someone hits the ground, and clap when they stand up and walk away. In the same vein as the flukes showcased in *America's Funniest Home Videos*, these races are funny in large part because of how dangerous they are. Watching someone flail and fall is an easy way to crack a smile. And in Virginia City, the audience was reactive to this violent form of humor. Spectators around us roared during each heat, taking pictures and videos and lifting children up to see the action better.

But other animal races, like the Kentucky Derby, are not funny. Audience members do not laugh at what happens on the track, and if a fall occurs, it is catastrophic and can even result in the horse being euthanized. And while some countries host camel races that mirror the seriousness of American horse racing—Australia and various Middle Eastern countries, for example—the camel races in Virginia

City are of a different breed. What makes these camel races funny, when other animal races are not?

E. B. White once wrote that "humor can be dissected, as a frog can be, but the thing dies in the process and the innards are discouraging to any but the pure scientific mind."[147] Undoubtedly, overanalyzing a joke or a comedic event can take all the fun out. Doing so might even reveal our worst instincts, suggesting the mechanisms behind our laughter are rooted in something darker or more visceral than the pure joy and effervescence we feel when a giggle rises up our spine. Despite White's admonition, scientists, philosophers, and psychologists have analyzed and debated what makes something "funny" since antiquity, and I'm going to take the same risk here. People race camels and ostriches because it's fun—so to truly unravel the world of exotic animal racing, we have to understand why, in fact, it's a funny thing to do.

At least three traditional theories of humor have tried to explain what makes something funny, but none of them offers a perfect answer. One of the oldest theories of humor is the so-called "superiority theory," championed by thinkers like Plato, Aristotle, Thomas Hobbes, and others. Under this theory, laughter bubbles up when you feel "sudden glory" over the butt of a joke, seeing others' misfortune and feeling your own superiority.[148] But many situations can involve such "superiority" without resulting in comedy. If you learned a friend fell while skiing and broke her leg though you made it down the mountain easily, absent other details, you wouldn't break down laughing. Other thinkers including Sigmund Freud argued for a "release theory" of humor, positing that laughter relieves tension and breaks up social stress by allowing us to engage with socially taboo topics like sex and defecation.[149] But, of course, not all "forbidden" topics are funny in all contexts. Immanuel Kant's "incongruity theory" is one of the best-known theories of humor. Here, humor often contains elements of surprise; something is funny when there is an incongruity between one's expectations and reality, like letting out a fart at a fancy dinner party.[150] But incongruity isn't always funny; an untimely death, for example, is surprising and incongruous but far from hilarious.[151]

Each of these three theories partially covers the humor at the camel and ostrich races, but none of them provides a fully satisfying explanation. There is obviously superiority over the animals and maybe even over the riders who suffer jolting rides and long falls (as the saying goes, better them than me). When those jockeys fall, a communal release of laughter takes place, expressing individual tensions and allowing the audience to engage with the taboo of violence from a place of amusement. And the camel races are definitely incongruous with the expectation of a normal race: from the moment you see the humped creatures and the jostled riders, you know something unusual is going on. But none of these traditional theories perfectly explains why camel and ostrich racing is funny.

A more modern attempt to theorize humor is known as the "benign violation" theory. Caleb Warren, a scholar of humor and one of the theory's main proponents, explained the theory to me as twofold: there needs to be some violation of normal expectations, but that violation also needs to be benign. A violation can be physical, emotional, cultural, linguistic, and more. But a violation alone won't be funny—it will just be weird, or even harmful. To be funny, a violation also needs to be benign, or "okay, safe, or acceptable."[152]

This theory of humor is entirely socially situated, because what people consider a violation in the first place—and what types of violations are then deemed benign—varies drastically among cultures and even subcultures. For example, everyone at the camel races, including me, sensed the violation (riding camels and ostriches instead of horses, say, or people falling off the bucking animals instead of maintaining control). And seemingly, many people considered it benign (because no one, as far as the audience knew, got seriously hurt, maybe, or because it is presumptively permissible to subject the animals to that kind of captivity and treatment).

I, on the other hand, didn't see it as so benign. Cruelty to animals lurked at the edges of the event for me, never overtly, but it was something I worried about throughout the races. Visible behind the pens was the transport truck, the same kind used to drive farmed animals to slaughter—an eerie phantom of how we treat animals more broadly. And the bucking and writhing didn't feel so acceptable to me, because it seemed like at least some of the animals were communicating immense displeasure at being ridden. Because ostrich bodies aren't built to support weight on their backs, forcing the birds to do so causes them stress and fear.[153] When I saw an ostrich fall forward onto its chest and neck, I worried both the bird and the human were hurt, which immediately pushed out any possibility that the race was harmless in my mind. But amid the ubiquitous laughter around me, I couldn't tell if anyone else in the audience was uncomfortable too. I—along with anyone else in the audience who felt like me—kept my buzzkill opinions to myself.

That casual elision of alternative viewpoints plays an important role. There are consequences to laughter, Professor Warren told me. Humor serves a social function. It reminds people about the norms and assessments embedded in the joke in the first place. When the crowd laughed at the ostrich falling on its face and throwing its rider, they reasserted and socially sanctioned the acceptability of the violation. It reiterated what we communally view as okay and, in doing so, renewed the acceptability of the joke. A big group of people laughing at ostriches falling says, yes, this is funny. Doing it all together sanctions the humor. And no one wants to be a buzzkill, so dissenters often stay quiet.

Laughter also reinforces difference between the revelers and who-ever is unfortunate enough to be the butt of the joke. Often what is or isn't considered funny falls along lines of social power, and in this way, humor can be deployed as a tool to maintain status levels among social groups. You have to think no further than schoolyard bullying to understand this concept. While some kinds of jokes that were once considered hilarious, such as those about being gay or overweight, for example, are now harder to stomach because our social norms have changed, targeted humor, even casually deployed, remains capable of being devastating to its subjects.

Animals are often fodder for humor, in part because they are usually assumed to be the lowest strata of society, below all humans. They are safe material, in other words, and we see incongruity in their behavior almost constantly because they don't act like us. The inter-net is full of cat memes, for example, and every year Comedy Wildlife Photography Awards highlight shots where animals are caught doing weird, vaguely human-like things.[154] Television shows like *America's Got Talent* often feature acts with dogs or cats meant to make us laugh. And of course, events like the International Camel & Ostrich Races use animals to play out some classic comedy.

The laughter at these races is more complicated than simple supe-riority over animals, though. The audience members aren't laughing at the camels or ostriches, but instead at the failed attempts of the jockeys to stay atop and control the unruly animals. It is the combination of everything that blends into humor: the speed, the bucking, the falling, the danger, all surrounded by a whiff of exoticism.

To me, it seems that these races are funny, at least in part, be-cause they give animals power they don't usually have in our society.

Usually when riding animals, humans are fully in control, leading the reins with a trained hand and specific cues. We can typically make animals do what we want. But at these races, humans purposefully cede power to the animals. Jockeys aren't in charge of the situation on the track. All they can do is hang on.

"Camels have their own agenda," a losing jockey laughed to Hedrick after his heat, when his camel refused to move forward and instead trotted backward to the starting line. "They have their own personality, just like us," he shrugged.

And that is the crux of why this race is entertaining: it's unpredictable, unserious, and, ultimately, unaffecting. The ridden animals subvert the presumed interspecies power dynamic while on the track, bucking, disobeying, and fleeing instead of acting docile under the weight of human command. We laugh because it's harmless—not to the humans or to the animals involved, who may break bones or fall, but to the stratification of society we have established where humans sit above animals. We can dabble with the alternative, because it's safely contained in an arena. For just a minute, we can experiment with letting animals decide what happens to humans, because when the heat is over we know the wranglers will catch the creatures and lead them back into their pens. No harm, no foul. It's a benign violation of the clearest sort, flipping the script without consequences to how we live our lives.

These human-animal dynamics were continuously on display at the fairgrounds in Virginia City. In the last ostrich heat of the show, for example, one of the jockeys was struggling to mount her bird. The wooden start chutes were shaking side to side, and it was obvious there was a struggle just out of sight. After a few moments, Hedrick announced that jockey was going to scratch, which was "permissible" because the gates had not yet opened. The ostrich ran out of the chute unmounted and trotted alongside the other two competitors. The ostrich may have won the battle, but not the war; despite its temporary independence, handlers got the rebellious ostrich under control and led it back into the same pen where the others waited. The audience didn't laugh quite as hard during that heat as they did upon a spectacular fall. It's not as funny if we're reminded how much the animals don't want to do this. It starts to look a little more like bullying.

The races proceeded surprisingly slowly, and it was getting hotter as they went on. It took time for the organizers to corral the animals between each heat and to reset the saddles and prepare for the next round. During the long breaks, the organizers offered a lot of side entertainments: kids searched for hidden coins in the dirt, raced around to find a performer dressed as Waldo (from *Where's Waldo?*) hidden in the crowd, and chased ducks down the track in a kid-specific race. In another in-between-heats event, adults chased emus, trying to herd them toward the finish line. But the main attraction was the series of "mounted" heats, where adults rode camels and ostriches in wild jaunts around the track. The other events passed time, but audience members around us chatted with each other or went to purchase more food during these filler events.

In addition to showcasing camels and ostriches, the races included a single heat where jockeys rode yet another exotic animal: zebras.

"The only place you'll see zebra racing is right here in Virginia City," Hedrick announced proudly as the riders got situated in the chutes. Zebras can be faster than horses, and they took off from the start chute like rockets. One zebra ran straight forward toward the fence, nearly slamming the jockey's leg against the metal poles before he lost control and fell off.

The presence of these squat, dusty zebras in the high desert of Nevada struck me as particularly anomalous. This is another component of the humor here: the exoticism embodied by the peculiar creatures chosen for these races. These are not "normal" racing animals. They were not animals you see around town, nor do they appear in typical western stories or legends native to the region. These animals hail from far-flung parts of the globe and were there only for our amusement. They obviously did not belong. In standing out, they were somehow funnier—the violation stronger, more poignant, even more benign. Taken out of their own natural contexts, these captive animals were thrown into a human arena where our definitions of acceptability ruled the day. Devoid of a frame of reference for appropriate treatment, we resort to our default paradigms, regarding these foreign animals as curiosities and oddities much like the settlers did in 1850 when camels first lumbered into the region.

Of course, relying on exotic animals to spark excitement and amusement is not unique to Virginia City. Circuses all over the country—like the one I attended with my grandparents decades ago—have used animals in this vein, toting around captive animals and capitalizing on their strangeness and danger. The popular Netflix docuseries *Tiger King* explores roadside zoos exhibiting big cats. SeaWorld and similar companies put confined animals on display, forcing them to perform, mesmerizing audiences with a taste of a distant world. In all of these performances, captive animals are displayed, their differences deployed to spark curiosity and awe.

Animal advocates have long decried many of these captive-animal performances as cruel, barbaric, and unnatural. Keeping wild animals in captivity, transporting them across vast distances in small enclosures, forcing them through intense training to act on command for a human gasp or chuckle—all of it involves deeply interfering with an animal's natural behaviors and desires. Taking an elephant out of the wild and beating it into submission with a bull hook so it stands on its hind legs and lifts its trunk does nothing for the elephant, but it enthralls human audiences. Keeping camels and ostriches in captivity, driving them across the country in a metal truck, forcing them to be mounted and ridden by adults they are so desperate to escape that they thrash and fall—is it really all that different?

I was getting tired. Despite the unpredictability of what would happen in any given heat, the event was growing monotonous for me by the end: another starting horn, another race, another fall. It was already after noon, and I felt oversaturated by the particular brand of slapstick humor embedded in this event. I was hungry, and my body ached from sitting on backless bleachers for over two hours. I was antsy and ready for a change of scenery. My mind was falling away from the animals and the races, and I began thinking about myself and the rest of my day.

Finally, the last heat of the show began, and three camels once again lined up in the starting chutes. The cheesy horn music played one last time before the gates were pulled open and the camels bolted. The first part of the race was uneventful, but a jockey was thrown off near the end of the course and fell hard, nearly six feet down from where he'd sat behind the camel's hump.

"What a dismount!" Hedrick marveled. The handlers rushed to control the camel while the jockey remained on the ground.

"Check on Charlie," he admonished his handlers. "Forget the camel!"

Hedrick's quick direction snapped me back to attention. In this exclamation, I heard a microcosm of the entire event. It may seem counterintuitive, but by foregrounding animals, festivals like the International Camel & Ostrich Races actually demand that we ignore them. In order to accomplish the central goal of the festival—whether killing the animals or deploying them for humor—the animal has to be central but ultimately disposable. The stars of the show cannot matter; if we admitted they did, we couldn't really put on the show.

At these races, the animal performers offer an excuse for families and friends to get together and have a good time. Because of that, humor is at the core of how we relate to the animals at this festival. But humor works to reinforce the animals' insignificance, demanding audience participation in a social hierarchy that excludes animals altogether. Humor instructs audience members which violations are "benign," reminding everyone in the crowd that it's okay to laugh because of the absurdity embedded in the temporary inversion of the typical human-animal relationship. The purposefully slapstick energy of the event minimizes and obfuscates the possibility of serious injury. But if there is any break in the hilarity, human interests necessarily come out on top. And when the last heat wraps up, we leave the fairgrounds and go back to our normal lives, a neat bow tied around the show. Ultimately, we bring animals here to the desert, use them for entertainment, and then forget about them and move on with our day.

It's not a new phenomenon; that's exactly what happened at the end of the Camel Corps experiment, way back in the nineteenth century. When the Camel Corps unceremoniously disbanded, there was never any coordinated strategy to deal with the camels we had shipped over from the Middle East. Instead, as one chronicler describes, "abuse became the common lot of the poor beasts."[155] The camels that were in Texas became property of the Confederacy, which had no interest in training or using them. The Confederate attitude toward the creatures was simple: "They were like a wart on a stick.

We had them and couldn't get rid of them." One confederate soldier pushed a camel over a bluff—the camel broke its neck and died, and the spot became known as "Camel's Leap." Some of the camels were sold to private citizens or to traveling circuses. The camels that were staged in California fared no better.[156]

Because of the camels' size, their obstinance, and their perceived strangeness, most of the camels were eventually released into the surrounding desert to fend for themselves. Citizens and soldiers alike then killed them or shot at them freely when spotted, treating them like pests to be eliminated. The last purported surviving camel from the Camel Corps was Topsy, a Bactrian (two-humped) camel who worked for Ringling Brothers Circus after the Civil War. She changed hands a few times, broke both her humps in a train crash, and eventually died at the Griffith Park Zoo in Los Angeles in 1934.[157] After her death, Topsy was largely forgotten about. She was rumored to have been cremated and buried with her human handler in western Arizona, but the Natural History Museums of Los Angeles County claims to have rediscovered her skeleton.[158]

Topsy is a perfect example of how an animal at the center of human attention can also be obscured and ignored as an individual. The dozens of other camels who were released into the desert and abandoned at the end of the experiment perhaps demonstrate this even more bluntly. These camels were only ever here in the Southwest for our purposes. But when our purposes conclude, we have a bad habit of simply forgetting about the animals and moving on.

We trudged uphill to C Street, where we had parked earlier in the day, and then walked up and down the now-bustling street. People were drinking from cans and cups on the sidewalks, spilling out of the city's many bars. While we had sat watching the races at the fairground, three streets up, Virginia City had apparently turned into one large street party.

We were standing on a wooden-planked sidewalk near the storied Bucket of Blood Saloon when, out of almost nowhere, two dromedary camels ambled past us in the middle of the street, led by a handler. This was the so-called "camel hump," when camels parade down the center of town. I expected the event to be bigger, but it was just these two camels. They seemed unaffected by the crowds and noise of the town. Their eyelashes flitted as they looked ahead, and their long necks swooped slightly as they walked. The camels looked quite out of place, a blip of magical realism in this otherwise stereotypical vision of an old western tourist town.

Before I knew it, the camels were out of sight. We walked up the street to our car, stopping into the now-open souvenir shops. There were very few camel-themed items for sale, a fact my grandmother noted too, and a point of differentiation from all the other festivals in this book. She had jotted down her guesses for the lack of themed merchandise: "Apathy in general? Or general antipathy to camels on the part of spectators?" I can't say for sure, but the party in town continued all afternoon. I don't know if anyone was thinking about camels.

JUMPING FROG JUBILEE

ANGELS CAMP, CA
FROGTOWN, USA

The jockey lifted a frog by its back, dipped it in some fresh, cool water, and then ran his hand down the frog's body, straightening its legs downward. He carried the frog over to the lily pad at the center of the stage and bent down, wiggled the frog a little side to side, and dropped it onto the pad.

"Good set," the announcer's voice echoed over the loudspeaker. The jockey took a half step back before stomping his foot right behind the frog. The frog leapt forward. The announcer prodded, "Now chase him, chase him!" The jockey lunged behind where the frog landed each hop. "One, two," the announcer counted along. "Three!" When the frog completed three jumps, an official placed a cane where the frog had finished its third jump. Another official held one end of a measuring tape in the dead center of the starting pad as the other end was pulled out to where the cane marked the end of the jump. Contestants at the International Jumping Frog Contest, held each spring during the Calaveras County Fair, get three jumps to make a frog go as far as it can. And the jump is measured in a straight line from the starting pad to the landing spot of its final jump, not cumulatively—if a frog jumps in a circle, the jump distance is counted as zero.

"Fourteen feet, two inches," the announcer declared. "Not a bad jump."

The town of Angels Camp, California, has hosted the Jumping Frog Jubilee in one form or another since 1928. But the story of the frog jumping contest goes much further back than that, to California's gold rush days in the mid-1800s. There is more than one story interwoven in this festival. Even in the earliest days of the jubilee, organizers used the frogs to celebrate a particular slice of Americana rooted here in rural Northern California.

Angels Camp sits nestled in lush, rolling hills a few hours inland of Sacramento and San Francisco. This town was an important mining community, because it sat in the mother lode region, and it experienced the characteristic booms and busts that accompanied mining towns all over the West. Prospectors arrived in the 1840s, and by 1849 the small camp had grown to over three hundred people. The town became known as "Angels Camp," because George Angel from Rhode Island was one of the first prospectors in the area to set up shop. In the 1850s, the camp continued to grow as more resources were discovered and more miners arrived, hoping to make a fortune.[159]

One of those hopeful miners was Mark Twain, one of the most famous American writers of the nineteenth century. He arrived in Angels Camp in 1865, when he was still known as Samuel Clemens. Before reaching California, he spent a stint mining in none other than Virginia City, Nevada, and worked for the *Territorial Enterprise* newspaper there—the same publication that invented the story behind the camel races a century later. Deeply in debt, he departed for San Francisco in 1864, where he again worked for a newspaper in the city.

During his time in California, he visited Angels Camp for just a few months to see if he could make a fortune in the mines there. As the county's website puts it, "No, Samuel Clemens didn't find gold, but he did strike it rich in Angels Camp" because it's where he heard and wrote the story that would make him famous.[160] His trip would both change his life and inspire a unique, amphibian legacy.

While Twain was in Angels Camp in 1865, he heard a story about a jumping frog from a local bartender that piqued his interest. He jotted a note in his notebook and soon published a short story titled "Jim Smiley and His Jumping Frog" in the *New York Saturday Press*. It was terrifically popular and would be reprinted numerous times. The story "provided the nation with a nugget from the California Gold Country," which people around the country were hungry for given the lore of the gold rush.[161] Twain eventually renamed the story and used it for the title of his first book, *The Celebrated Jumping Frog of Calaveras County*. A frog graced its cover.[162] By all accounts, this story was an important breakthrough in launching Twain's illustrious career.[163]

In the story, Twain's unnamed narrator seeks out a certain Simon Wheeler to ask about a friend's friend, Reverend Leonidas W. Smiley. Instead of answering the narrator's question, Wheeler responds with an "interminable" story about a man named *Jim* Smiley, who would bet on anything and everything: horse races, dog fights, even which bird would fly away first if there were two birds sitting on a fence. The wildness of Smiley's betting practices escalates with each new tale, culminating in a vignette about Jim Smiley's jumping frog. Jim Smiley captured a frog and taught him how to jump on command, and he would pull him out to hustle people who didn't know his trick.

One day, a stranger inquired about Smiley's frog, and Smiley goaded, "He can out jump any frog in Calaveras County." When the stranger doubted Smiley's claim, Smiley offered a bet of forty dollars to test it. The stranger admitted he didn't have a frog, so Smiley, desperate for the bet, offered to go find a frog for him to jump. While Smiley was gone, the stranger opened Smiley's frog's mouth and poured "quail shot" down his throat to weigh him down. When Smiley returned and the competition began, Smiley's frog wouldn't budge. The stranger took the money he had won and walked away, and only after the fact did Smiley realize his frog had been sabotaged. At this point, the narrative zooms back out to the narrator and Simon Wheeler, who told this whole story-within-a-story about Jim Smiley and his frog. The narrator, seemingly annoyed, leaves Wheeler before he has a chance to tell an even wilder tale about Smiley.[164]

This weird little story has sparked decades of critical inquiry, historical commentary, and literary analysis. Many scholars have studied Twain's use of framing devices, as well as his indebtedness to both Californian and Native American folklore for content and form.[165] Some have delved into Twain's personal experiences in Angels Camp.[166] Literary critics have discussed the story elements, the motifs, and the moral takeaways. As one authority summarized, "The Celebrated Jumping Frog" is "a synthesis of the best American traits: shrewdness, a spirit of enterprise and aspiration . . . [and] the skeptical pragmatism necessary to keep the other characteristics within a useful and realistic framework."[167] Read from this perspective, the story becomes a microcosm of the pioneering spirit of the gold rush years, where speculation was all around and people—including Twain—were willing to bet it all.

It's hard to overstate how central this story feels when one is driving around Calaveras County, as if it were the foundational myth of the town from which all else derived. One journalist visiting town for the fair wrote that the "intertwined historical legacies" of Twain's jumping frog story and the region's gold mining are "impossible to escape," even a hundred and fifty years later.[168] The town of Angels Camp emphasizes this history with both Twain- and frog-themed elements, signs, and landmarks. Spots in town include the Frog Jump Plaza, Froggy's Auto Wash, the Jumping Frog Motel, and the Frogtown RV Park. The high school's mascot is a bullfrog. Street signs are embossed with little jumping frogs. The first building along Main Street features a mural of Twain standing inside a mine cart filled with gold and holding a frog in one hand. A banner over the mural pronounces: "Home of Mark Twain's Famous Jumping Frog of Calaveras County." The original Jackass Hill cabin that Twain stayed in, just outside of town, is gone, but a replica sits atop the hill at the end of a narrow, windy road. Main Street also features the so-called "hop of fame," where bronze plaques adorn the sidewalk to commemorate each winner of the Frog Jumping Jubilee since the 1920s, listing the frog's name, the jump distance, and the jockey. And during the week of the Jumping Frog Jubilee, laundry is strung across Main Street, as a "vestige of an earlier era when residents would wash their clothes and hang them out to dry ahead of festivals in the region."[169]

And, of course, Angels Camp celebrates the legacy of the eighty-eight days Twain spent in the town every year with the Jumping Frog Jubilee, reenacting and embellishing the famous frog jumping competition from his story. The first Calaveras County Fair took place in nearby Copperopolis in 1893, without any jumping frogs.[170] But in 1928, Angels Camp held the first Jumping Frog Contest to celebrate the paving of the town's Main Street by harking back to the town's formative years and Twain's momentous visit. The local booster club wanted to turn "back the hand of time to the days of 1849 and 1865," so they held a jumping frog contest on a table on Main Street. Up to fifteen thousand people attended the first jubilee, many wearing "the clothes of the early-day folk" and visiting replica dance halls, saloons, and gambling establishments.[171] In 1937 the Calaveras County Fair and the frog jump merged to become the four-day event it is today. The combined event occurs every May and now brings up to fifty thousand attendees to the small town of just about four thousand people.[172]

While the county fair today still offers countless other sources of entertainment—rodeo events, livestock shows and auctions, art competitions, and a full carnival with rides and games aplenty—the frog jump is still the heart of the event. The fairground, where the Calaveras County Fair and the frog jump take place, is known as "Frogtown," but the name isn't the only tribute paid to the amphibians there. Giant white wrought iron gates at the entrance of the fairground had the moniker "Frog Town" along with two cartoon frog images welded into them. Images of frogs splayed mid-jump were spray-painted onto the ground outside the main entrance and painted onto parking medians. Above the ticket booth, a large sign proclaimed entrance to Frogtown, USA, and workers admitted attendees by placing a green frog stamp on the back of everyone's hand. The main souvenir booth was marked with green-and-white checkered banners and a sign reading "Frog Mart." T-shirts for sale bore puns like "Frogaritaville" and aphorisms like "Kiss a Frog, Find a Prince." Statues of frogs were situated around the fairgrounds in various themes—one sported lipstick and painted nails, and another had a chef's hat and apron.

The Jumping Frog Contest today has two main components: the smaller fun jump stage, where anyone visiting the fairgrounds can rent a frog and try their hand at it, and the main stage, the professional stage, where teams vie to qualify for the finals by landing one of the top fifty frog jump distances in the first few days of the fair. Jumping takes place on both stages nearly all day, every day. Hundreds, sometimes even thousands, of competitors jump frogs over the course of the weekend. Jubilee organizers collect over four hundred frogs in the weeks leading up to the contest from all over Northern California, and professional teams bring dozens of their own frogs in specially outfitted containers.

I watched the jumping for a couple of hours from under a tree where I had a view of both the main and fun jump stages. It captured my attention far longer than I expected it to as I shifted my attention back and forth between the two stages. Each jump was basically the same: set the frog, chase it, catch it, measure it. Once you see one jump, you see them all, at least mechanically. But you never knew what would happen as you watched. Any given jump could beat the new world record, and that unpredictability was deeply engaging. This particular blend of routine movement and potential excitement was both comforting and captivating, and it kept me entertained for hours. Plus, it was undeniably funny to see adults act so bizarrely, squatting and chasing a frog on a big stage. Watching professionals and amateurs alike struggle to inspire a jump brought a soft smile to my face. Fun jump participants didn't take themselves too seriously. They named their rental frogs when they stepped up onto the Rosie the Ribiter Fun Jump Stage. Puns abounded: The Frogfather, Froginator, Hopscotch, Jerry Springer, Jeremiah Was A, Toadall Terror, Sir Jumps-a-Lot, and Make America Jump Again all jumped while I watched. But despite the silliness of the activity, on the other stage, the announcers narrated the professional jumps with gravity, as if they were commenting on a serious sporting event. This was, after all, the "World Series of competitive frog jumping."[173]

Twain's jumping frog story became so famous, at least in part, because of this exact type of droll and unassuming humor, where the entertainment value is found in the incongruity of serious people behaving eccentrically. The story was steeped in Twain's signature deadpan style, a "new and distinctly American approach to humor" that, according to Twain, prioritized the manner of speaking over the matter.[174] Twain wrote that the "first virtue of a comedian" is "to do funny things with grave decorum and without seeming to know that they are funny."[175] The characters in Twain's story neatly embody this philosophy. The disinterested narrator, portrayed as an elite city slicker, is bewildered by Simon Wheeler's story, not tickled. Wheeler, we are told, relays the story of Jim Smiley with "a vein of impressive earnestness and sincerity, which showed . . . plainly that, so far from his imagining that there was anything ridiculous or funny about his story, he regarded it as a really important matter."[176] The seriousness of Wheeler's narration in contrast with the silliness of the story is what elevates Twain's fiction above mere slapstick or quick, disposable humor. It is subtle, serious, and lasting.

The same dynamic is on full display during the modern Jumping Frog Jubilee. The juxtaposition of humor and sincerity, of ridiculousness and earnestness, is at the heart of this event. It's patently funny to compete by jumping frogs—everyone seems to acknowledge that, from Twain to modern-day attendees and enthusiasts. But on the other hand, the jubilee is, as the *New York Times* aptly reported, "semiserious business, with cash prizes and bragging rights on the line."[177] The professional competitors strive earnestly to find the best frogs and win, even as they employ over-the-top techniques to compel a jump. And the stakes at the "annual Frogolympic"[178] are high. The main stage featured a big sign pronouncing: "WORLD RECORD, 21 FT. 5¾ IN," set by Rosie the Ribiter and jockey Lee Giudici. Rosie's world record jump took place in 1986, and no one has beat her since. And as one documentary narrator rightly commented, "With every year that Rosie's record stands, the frog world grows more and more obsessed."[179] Organizers dramatically increased the purse in 2023:

if anyone set a new distance record, they would win $20,000. With serious winnings and lifetime glory up for grabs, the competition is more than a lark.

It was apparent how seriously people take this event just by watching the professional teams prepare and compete. The professional teams set up camp to the right of the main stage, complete with tents, coolers full of food and drinks, and rows of custom frog-size boxes latched and covered partly with burlap sacks to keep the compartments cool. The teams—including the West Coast Hoppers and the Calaveras Frog Jockeys—wore coordinated uniforms. One young jockey explained to a journalist for *WIRED*, "You wouldn't think something as jumping a frog would be so intense, but it really is . . . it's a serious matter."[180] For a taste of how extensively these teams work to maximize their chances in the competition, I watched a documentary titled *Jump: A Frogumentary*. The film follows some professional jockeys and explains that each team has its own exclusive hunting spots, to which its members consistently return with specially outfitted boats or vehicles to find more frogs. Teams have storage units for the frogs at their homes, and they spend time testing the frogs to see which ones have the capacity to jump far.

But jumping a frog is, well, a funny way to spend time. Coverage of the frog jump almost always capitalizes on the humor of the event. A piece published in 1976 in the *Los Angeles Times* parodied the intense stress frog athletes feel at this event by noting, "Life for a frog isn't always what it's croaked up to be . . . there are those constant jumping competitions. Pressure, pressure, pressure."[181] Another described "thousands of slimy little athletes, primed for the biggest event of their careers." But of course, that journalist quipped, the frogs are "always underpaid."[182] In a riff off Julius Caesar's famous pronouncement, another journalist wrote, "They came. They croaked. They choked."[183]

A 2020 Netflix docuseries titled *We Are the Champions*, which chronicles odd competitions around the world, features an episode on the Jumping Frog Jubilee. Rainn Wilson, who played with Twain-like deadpan the overly serious Dwight Schrute on *The Office*, produced and narrated the series with that same mock solemnity: leading up to the frog jump finale at the end of the episode, he lowers his voice and pronounces, "One jockey, one jump, one chance to go for broke . . . or croak." The episode uses quirky music and clever one-liners to make its point that the jubilee, while odd, is a long-standing, family-focused tradition that brings a lot of meaning to the community and participants. "A group of frogs is an army," Rainn Wilson's voice announces at the end of the episode. "A group of frog jockeys? That's a family."[184]

The jubilee truly is a family affair, no matter where you look. Families dressed in matching T-shirts strategized about which frog athlete to jump on the main stage. Parents cheered on their kids at the fun jump stage. Adults lounged on blankets while young children played games in the grass. Seeing so many families enjoy the event all around me made me reflect on my own family connections to the jubilee. My grandmother's notes indicate she and my grandfather each jumped frogs when they visited the festival in 1993, and I tried to imagine them stepping up and squatting down on the stage. The image was hard to conjure. Would they have been serious or playful? Would they have hammed it up for the audience, or would they have focused on the frog? Judging by what was happening on the fun jump stage in front of me, frustration must have been part of their experience, as it seemed like most attendees who stepped up to try jumping a frog were failing.

I watched people progress through various techniques in their efforts: first stomping behind the frog, then crouching and slapping the ground, and finally poking the frog. (The official rules say you can touch the frog when it is on the starting pad but not once it leaves.) Sometimes a frog would finally hop tepidly, seemingly out of annoyance more than anything else. Occasionally the officials just replaced the frog so the contestant could try again with a more willing athlete.

To get the frogs to jump, professional jockeys have developed their own strategies, which they pass down like proprietary family heirlooms. Some clap, some stomp, some shout. Some kiss their frogs or whisper private encouragement into their ears. Some stay high above the frog, others crouch low, still others charge at the frogs in a sort of horizontal plank position. Some shake their frogs, some blow on them, some keep them in water until the last possible moment.

The strategies don't always work. One professional jockey, for example, got low behind his frog, nearly prostrating his body, and the amphibian athlete took one giant jump forward—a promising start. But then the frog started making short, more frantic jumps to its left. A referee on the side of the stage caught the critter easily with a giant white net. The jockey stopped chasing his frog and looked disappointed as he reached down to grab it out of the net. He shook his head at the official.

The jump was so bad it was not even worth capturing an official distance. "No mark on that jump—the jockey is taking no mark," the announcer confirmed. This particular jockey had been representing the team responsible for Rosie the Ribiter's world record in 1986. But past success is no guarantee for future achievement. The announcer commiserated, "Just goes to show, even for a world champion, sometimes those frogs just don't cooperate."

The kicker about frog jumping is that frogs cannot actually be trained. Jockeys do not spend time teaching the amphibians to jump. Instead, they learn what makes their particular animals tick. As

Wilson explains in the Netflix documentary, "In Calaveras, training is simple. It's a gut check. You either got it, or you don't." Jockeys pay attention to the frog's temperature, the fatigue it develops throughout the day, and the frog's inclination to respond to sounds, or stomps, or ground-level stimuli. They learn how to encourage a jump—but they have little control over whether a frog actually performs.

"The frogs have their own mind," said Lee Giudici, the jockey responsible for Rosie the Ribiter's world record jump in 1986. "And they do not speak English either."[185] The question of whether a frog will respond how the jockey wants it to is a big part of what makes this event so captivating. It's the same as the Camel & Ostrich Races; in both events, the animal's reaction is ultimately an unknown factor that drives the entertainment and humor. Frogs are not inanimate, nor are they trainable in the same way as dogs or horses, whose skills can usually be repeated and performed on command. The will-they-won't-they jump (and if so, how far and in what direction) is part of what makes competing with these frogs worth watching. The frogs with the most promise jumped by world champion jockeys can stumble, and a five-year-old child with a brand-new frog can pull out a win, as happened in 2022.[186]

But even taking the frog's autonomy into account, it remains true that the professionals generally jump frogs much farther than the amateurs do. The fun jump stage is significantly smaller than the main stage, suggesting how much less distance organizers expect the rental frogs to cover. Many people accordingly think the frog jockey is the most important part of the jump. This camp argues the frog knows the "will of the jockey" and will respond accordingly.[187] And there is at least some evidence that the professional jockeys really do know what they're doing.

Scientists who study frog biomechanics have long thought that bullfrogs cannot jump more than about three feet, because in laboratory tests they have never exceeded that distance. But *The Guinness Book of World Records* cites Rosie the Ribiter's record of over twenty-one feet. If Rosie's three jumps were equal, they would be about seven feet each, and if they were not, a single jump would have even exceeded that. Rosie's jump, along with dozens of other jumps reaching distances in the high teens, belies the one-meter ceiling found in laboratory tests. So scientists have "wondered if these claims were little more than a tall tale—rather like the one told in Mark Twain's fictional *The Celebrated Jumping Frog of Calaveras County*."[188]

In 2013 a group of researchers led by H. C. Astley from Brown University decided to go to the jubilee to see this storied jumping for themselves and to study the mechanics and distances of the bullfrogs jumped by the professional jockeys. The scientists recorded all of the jumps that happened over the four-day event and discovered that the "country frogs blew all those lab frogs' jumping records out of the water," with a whopping 58 percent of all jumps recorded throughout the weekend exceeding the previously known maximum jump distance.[189] The scientists cited a large sample size (they were able to record hundreds of jumps) and the jockeys' deep understanding of frog physiology as possible explanations for the improved performance in Frogtown.

"But perhaps the most important reason was motivational," the *Los Angeles Times* recapped. "The jockeys had specific techniques designed to fully trigger the bullfrogs' fight-or-flight mechanism. . . . In other words, they scared the living daylights out of the antsy amphibian."[190] Frogs could apparently distinguish between a harmless scientist in a lab and a jockey trying to resemble "a deadly reptilian-like predator who is going to eat it."[191] The professional frog jockeys know the frogs jump because they are afraid. One jockey divulged in an interview, for example, "I can't give away any secrets, but there's certain kind of environments where they really have to jump to get away."[192] In the Brown University study, frogs jumped by professionals generally launched themselves farther than rental frogs jumped by amateurs. The study concluded, "we believe the most likely explanation for the superior jumping performance of these frogs rests in the techniques employed by the jockeys."[193]

These professional jockeys have worked for nearly a hundred years on maximizing frog jump distances. From the beginning of the jubilee through the 1980s, the winning jump distance increased continuously. But since Rosie the Ribiter set her record in 1986, the winning jump distance has generally plateaued. The 2013 study argued the bullfrogs in Calaveras may have reached their maximal performance and that the steady increase in jump distance since the 1930s was a result of "technique, not of the frog but of the jockey."[194] Jockeys learned what made frogs jump farther over decades of trial and error, pushing these animals to their most extreme performance. But even bullfrog athletes have their limits.

Some people think that forcing these frogs to jump as far as they can by scaring them is cruel. Larisa Bryski, an animal rights advocate interviewed in *Jump: A Frogumentary*, said, "These poor frogs are sort of dragged out of nature and then made to jump on command, more or less, on a stage in front of a big crowd of people in the summer sun."[195] She explained, "it's not like the most violent thing in the world, certainly. But it's not the most peaceful thing in the world to do on a Saturday afternoon."[196] Watching dozens of competitors jump frogs over a few days, I saw what she meant. All of the frogs were captured from their wild habitat in the weeks leading up to the event. At the jubilee, the frogs are kept in tiny containers in order to prevent them from exerting energy until their jump.[197] Some animals, especially the rental ones, seemed reticent to jump at all. Many others seemed frantic in their hops, avoiding everything: the jockey, the giant nets waiting for them on either side of the stage, and the announcer, in turn. By the very act of engaging the frogs' fight or flight instincts, jockeys inevitably stress them.

Apparently answering this objection, there is a "frog spa" behind and underneath the main stage. This is where the rental frogs are kept during the competition weekend, along with any of the professional frogs who need extra care or a place to rest. The frog spa was cool and damp, with frog paraphernalia all over the walls and floor. (My favorite was a sign that read "To Jump or Not to Jump: That Is the Question.") The frog welfare manager and other volunteers were milling about, talking to visitors about the frogs in their care. In the back of the small room were five or six large green metal cylinders, each with an opening on the top covered with wet burlap sacks.

"Do you want to see a frog?" a volunteer asked me. He lifted the sack from a corner of the container and revealed dozens of frogs piled on top of each other, huddled in the corners. Dead cockroaches floated in the murky water—remnants of the frogs' most recent meal. The volunteer reached a hand in, and many of the frogs started moving away, but with a clearly practiced hand he caught one. He gripped the frog by its back and held it up for me to see. "We pamper our frogs, like they're on vacation," the volunteer touted, offering up details on how they feed them and house them and keep them safe from predators while they're here. They even play music for the frogs at night and mandate a rest for the frogs during the long days of jumping. Then, at the end of the jubilee, the frogs are supposedly released in the ponds where they were captured.

After chatting for a few minutes, the volunteer put the frog back in the big metal tube, but before he could cover it with the burlap, a few other volunteers came by with a sack to bring more frogs up to the fun jump stage. One held the sack open while the other picked up frogs and dropped them in. About thirty seconds later, it became clear there was a problem: frogs were escaping. There was a hole in the bottom of the sack. The quick-thinking volunteer holding the sack grabbed one frog and then quickly pinched the hole closed with his other hand, but another frog disappeared behind the metal containers and through an opening in the fence separating the frog spa from the rest of the unfinished basement area. The volunteers looked under the container for a few minutes but couldn't find the escapee. I asked if they would find the frog later, and they assured me they would, because there was nowhere for him to go. In the meantime, they had to bring the other frog athletes up to the stage. There was nothing else to do, so I decided to leave the frog spa and head back up to the stages.

Posted on the wall near the door were "Jumping Frog Facts," including the following: "Our frogs are pampered, they eat crickets each day and listen to relaxing music. We adhere to a strong 'Frog Welfare' policy." That policy was put into place in 1997 to prevent cruelty to frogs at the competition. It covers catching, housing, trans-porting, caring, feeding, handling, and, of course, jumping the frogs. The policy also establishes procedures for when any individual or group endangers a frog or violates the Frog Welfare Policy."[198] There's no doubt the organizers take the welfare of the animals in their care seriously. I even heard about a time a few years ago when the frog welfare manager stopped the jump altogether because the frogs seemed tired and overworked. He mandated they rest for a few hours before resuming the jump.

In addition to voicing concerns about the particular frogs who are captured and brought to Frogtown to compete, people have raised worries about the impact on the environment and frog populations as a whole. In 2003 the California Department of Fish and Game notified the jubilee's organizers that while catching frogs was permissible, releasing them back into the wild violated the law. This was because frogs from different ponds sometimes hundreds of miles away from each other are brought together in close quarters for the weekend, possibly spreading disease among populations. When released back into the wild, the bullfrogs could potentially carry infection back to far-flung parts of the state. Organizers feared the government would make them kill the frogs to prevent this risk, rather than release them, and they knew that would doom the event. No one would want that ending. At the Rattlesnake Roundup in Sweetwater, by comparison, capturing wild snakes and killing them instead of releasing them was the point. Are snakes that different from frogs?

California seems to think so. Facing intense pressure from Calaveras County and the jubilee's organizers, the Fish and Game department did a "policy flip-flop" and found a loophole to let the competition continue as it always has. Fish and Game found a provision in a law from 1957 that exempts frogs to be used in frog jumping contests from general wildlife management rules, so they announced, "it is the department's official position that frogs used in the contest are not subject to prohibitions on release."[199] Luckily for the frogs, they could keep on jumping even after their stints as unwitting but professional athletes. Nevertheless, the original concern—spread of disease—presumably remains.

Lastly, underlying the entire jubilee is a tacit but eerie reminder of humanity's impact on the natural world more generally. The frog Mark Twain wrote about was a red-legged frog, not a bullfrog. Red-legged frogs used to be so numerous in the area that gold rush miners would regularly eat them, which ultimately led to the overharvesting of the species.[200] So to feed the settlers' appetite for frog meat, as *The Washington Post* reported, "entrepreneurs imported even larger, but less delectable, bullfrogs from east of the Rockies to feed the frog leg craze."[201] Of course, that only contributed to the demise of the red-legged frogs, as their native habitats were overwhelmed by the invasive species. The red-legged frog is the official state amphibian, but there has been a 90 percent reduction of its historic population.[202]

Bullfrogs have been the species of choice at the Calaveras County Jumping Frog Jubilee since 1928 (though in the 1990 competition, an exotic animal importer entered some goliath frogs, who failed to jump nearly as far as the bullfrogs despite their mammoth size[203]). This commercial and symbolic reliance on bullfrogs has unfortunately pitted red-legged frogs against bullfrogs in the region. Red-legged frogs are protected under the Endangered Species Act, but organizers of the event explicitly lobbied against designating Calaveras County as part of a protected area for the red-legged frog in the early 2000s, because such protection would, as one journalist put it, "send the bullfrog packing and kill the event."[204] People likely would not be able to hunt for frogs in the same way they are used to doing, and any protection for red-legged frogs might involve inevitable consequences for bullfrogs, who share the same resources and waterways. There are debates about whether reintroducing the red-legged frog into the region is even possible; such a measure would likely involve controlling the bullfrog population or even destroying it entirely, which, for obvious reasons, Calaveras County opposes.

While frogs receive undeniable adoration from spectators, welfare protection from organizers, and glory from everyone at the Jumping Frog Jubilee, they are not the only animals that humans show off and compete at the fair. The fair also includes a rodeo as well as a competition and auction organized by Future Farmers of America (FFA) and 4-H, organizations that use animal agriculture to educate and empower youth. I watched the livestock auction for a while on Sunday morning, the last day of the fair. Rabbits, goats, chickens, and turkeys were auctioned off, one at a time, to be given to the buyer "black" (fully slaughtered and processed into meat cuts), "red" (for resale), or "green" (alive). The auction was packed; families were supporting their young competitors, who had worked for months to raise and care for their animals, and the arenas were full. While there are welfare policies within FFA and 4-H, the underlying principle is to build support for animal agriculture, which, whatever your views on the morality of it, undeniably involves killing animals for human consumption.

I found it a little odd how much support, attention, and protection the frog athletes got, unlike these animals, who by the nature of their species would be killed for our tastes. The whole fair felt like a tangible example of the concept of speciesism—that is, disparate treatment of different species with no genuinely objective or justifiable reason for the distinction. Why should an invasive species like the bullfrog receive more protection and popular support than the threatened red-legged frog? Why do we train our youth to raise and slaughter some animals but not others?

The answer, of course, is human culture. Frogs are (usually, at least in the United States) safe to humans, and they move in a quirky, adorable way. Something about the appearance of frogs—their big,

wet eyes, their large hind legs, or their way of "hopping" around—
lends itself to cultural neoteny, emphasizing cartoonish or infantile
traits. That type of imagery communicates that they are good creatures
and, quite importantly, that they are capable of cuteness.

Frogs are important to American education. Children often learn
about the life cycle of a frog early in school, studying charts of eggs,
tadpoles, and frogs. Many high school biology students are required
to dissect a frog as an entry into more advanced sciences. My grandmother was fascinated by a teenager who refused to dissect a frog
and made national news.[205] Now, animal activists regularly campaign
against the academic rite of passage. But the disposability of frogs—
the fact that we care just enough about them not to condone actively
torturing them, but not so much that we find it morally repugnant to
dissect, use, or kill them—demonstrates that ambivalence can result in
some truly complicated human-animal relationships.

In broader culture, frogs often represent something quirky, harmless but not revered, something humans can relate to but that is also
decidedly different. Frogs feature prominently in western myths, fairy
tales, and American pop culture. In ancient Greece, Aristophanes
wrote a comedy called *The Frogs*, which featured a typical Greek
choral interlude sung—or croaked—by not-so-typical characters:
frogs. Ovid's *Metamorphoses* features a story where humans are turned
into frogs. "The Frog Prince" is one of the Grimm brothers' fairy tales,
where a "nasty frog" morphs into a handsome prince when a curse is
broken. Disney's 2009 movie *The Princess and the Frog* built upon that
basic story, only in this adaptation both the prince and princess turn
into frogs and have to figure out how to become human again. Louisa
May Alcott, who wrote *Little Women*, also wrote her own fairy tale,
titled "The Three Frogs." The *Frog and Toad* children's book series,
a staple in my household and many others, provided lessons about

how friendship can survive differences. And Kermit the Frog is probably the most famous amphibian ambassador, bringing froggy wisdom and jokes to households nationwide.

In Calaveras County in particular, frogs mean even more. By jumping frogs, residents and attendees establish a connection to the area's history and build upon a strong sense of local identity. There's a reason the professional frog jockey teams are usually based around a family. Frogs are an instrumentality of community here, tying generation to generation and family to family. By jumping them, people are able to express who they are. To jump a frog is to join a legacy that began over a hundred years ago. That is a powerful force.

Animal festivals can certainly serve as "rituals of inclusion" in this way, using animals to build camaraderie and companionship among the participants. But on the other side of that same coin, these festivals necessarily operate as "rituals of exclusion" too. Celebrating commonality often involves demarcating and reinforcing boundaries between "us" and "them"—or between "us" humans and "those" animals.[206] While attendees and participants do not exactly laugh at the frogs (or at the jockeys, for that matter), frogs at the jubilee are still considered inferior to humans. Yes, the organizers and teams care deeply about frog welfare, and yes, the frogs are not killed, or tortured, or purposefully hurt—but implicit in the jubilee is the understanding that it is okay, good, or even justifiable to capture wild animals, exploit their fear mechanisms for our entertainment, and then release them. This humorous event that strengthens human bonds simultaneously reestablishes the disposability of frogs.

Demonstrating the relationship between humans and frogs, and delineating the line between us and them, is a big part of this festival. As I watched jockeys jump frogs, it seemed for a few moments that the humans actually became frog-like. They squatted down, jumping right behind the frog, moving on pace with the amphibian athlete in a decidedly unhuman manner. It's one of the reasons this festival is funny: humans don't usually move like that, and they look silly doing so. The border between human and frog has long fascinated humans. Many of the ancient myths and modern stories mentioned above have to do with humans becoming frogs, including Ovid's *Metamorphosis*, "The Frog Prince," and *The Princess and the Frog*. Kermit was originally just a puppet named Kermit, but as his character developed, he took on the look of a frog. Even still, Kermit is the most human-like of the Muppets, as he is "the character through whose eyes the audience is viewing the show."[207] The line between humans and frogs is, in our collective imagination and fears, seemingly a little fluid.

What emerges from the festival is a reassertion of the boundary between human and frog, where we can safely play in the margins between human and animal, making sure we end up on the human side. We can jump with the frogs onstage, but at the end of the round we stand up on our two extended legs and let the frogs go back to the pond. In this way, frog jockeys and attendees use frogs as an idiosyncratic tool to celebrate our humanity and culture by engaging with frogs while also pointing out how different we are. In many folkloric stories, humans want to escape the "curse" of being a frog. In Calaveras, that instinct might be at play in a deeply embodied and subliminal way.

I watched the last of the qualifying rounds as I sat in the shaded grass. Visible behind the stages was a carnival and the Frog Hopper ride, which whooshed kids up and down in the distance. To my right were the rodeo grounds and livestock pens, and behind me were various food booths and stations, along with the "frogeteria," Tom Sawyer Hall, and Mark Twain Hall, where various art shows and other contests were housed. I munched on kettle corn and let myself enjoy the weekend while I took notes and talked with people. As the scientist in charge of the 2013 study at the jubilee had remarked, "How often do you have fieldwork where you eat funnel cake and hot dogs?"[208] The rolling hills formed a peaceful backdrop to the fairgrounds, and I felt grateful to have a chance to spend time at this quirky, cheery festival.

I left the jubilee not quite sure how to feel about it. I'd had a good time, frogs weren't killed, and the community benefited. But this festival has affected the lives of thousands of frogs over the years, not to mention that it has shaped the ecosystem of Northern California as a frog habitat more broadly. And the welfare focus seemed at times performative, crafted in response to the growing consciousness many people around the country have about animals and our treatment of them. Do frogs really care what type of music is played in the frog spa, for example? Or is that just a way to placate human visitors with an aversion to animal suffering? When my grandmother went to the jubilee in the early 1990s, she took notes about the "Tomb of the Unknown Frog" at the festival, which organizers put up to thank the frogs who lost their lives throughout the competition. Today even accidental deaths are not openly tolerated at all. Maybe this is progress. But maybe it simply repackages the reality of animal harm as something more palatable.

I had so many questions running through my head. Should one Mark Twain story and the festival inspired by it have such a broad impact on the natural world? How does the human importance of symbolism and story stack up against the real creatures who are captured and used every year? How do we balance human benefit with animal impact? Aren't both important in the end?

This event was both tied to a specific moment in history and timeless. As it so often goes, life imitates art, and vice versa. Twain's jumping frog story was broadly indebted to California folklore, because numerous stories about jumping frog contests had been published in newspapers prior to Twain's story.[209] Even if Twain had never read them, they may still have factored into the story he heard in Angels Camp, the story that launched his comedic and literary career. In 1894 Twain addressed an allegation that the frog jumping story actually took place "a couple of thousand years earlier," in ancient Greece. Twain insisted "it must be a case of history actually repeating itself, and not a case of a good story floating down the ages and surviving because [it's] too good to be allowed to perish." He seemed to firmly believe the story actually took place in Calaveras County in 1849, adding that the incident "was original when it happened two thousand years ago, and was again original when it happened in California in our own time."[210]

And so it is—every year, individual people and families participate in or watch this event, reenacting and reimagining the formative story of this town with themselves as main characters. When a new champion perches on the bright green throne, they become part of a long, green line of winners that spans a century. But while the event invokes the mythology of frogs and of the West, the jubilee is always, undeniably, a specific event: particular people jumped particular frogs on that exact sunny weekend I visited in May.

In Herman Melville's epic novel *Moby-Dick*, the narrator tells us: "Moby Dick [is not] a monstrous fable, or still worse and more detestable, a hideous and intolerable allegory." Neither are Twain's frogs. Just as Melville wanted to express that Moby Dick was a real whale, and the crew's battle to subdue him was tangible, not just esoteric, so too were the frogs and people in Calaveras County real to Twain. It was their very reality that provided the humor he captured in his droll tale. It is the reality of the frogs and their unpredictable jumping that makes this event exciting even in the twenty-first century, and it is the reality of the strong communal bonds that sustains it.

But it's also their reality that left me feeling uneasy when the jubilee ended. The bullfrogs aren't just symbols, or metaphors, or mascots, any more than the human jockeys are just literary tropes or foils. They are all creatures with heartbeats, with countervailing interests and needs. The jubilee uses real, living frogs. As an ancient philosopher once said, "boys throw stones at frogs for fun, but the frogs do not die for 'fun,' but in sober earnest."[211]

These frogs captured and brought into Frogtown are undeniably pawns for our human ritual. The jubilee treats frogs with a combination of respect and deep ambivalence. On the one hand, strict welfare rules govern the frog experience; on the other hand, there is never really any question that capturing and scaring these frogs so much that they jump to their body's capacity is worthwhile. There is little evidence about the impact of the competition on frogs, and animal advocates rarely raise a flag about this event. Maybe frogs really do experience the jubilee like the organizers insist: as an all-expenses-paid vacation, complete with a cockroach and grasshopper buffet. But maybe they don't.

It's true the jubilee was not nearly as violent as the Rattlesnake Roundup or Maine Lobster Festival; no animals—that I knew of—died during the weekend. Nor was it as exhibitionist and slapstick as the Camel & Ostrich Races were. The jubilee, in some ways, seemed more harmless because it was so silly. But just as at the Camel & Ostrich Races, the humor at the center of the event, the quirky and exotic nature of the animals, and the behaviors they were forced to exhibit combined to sweep away any moral questions about using the animals in this way, to tell these stories. Humor makes it all seem "not so bad."

However, humor distanced attendees from the frogs and dissembled the fact that these animals are captured, held captive, and then pushed to their bodies' limits out of fear. The fun operated as a mask, and lurking beneath it was a growing feeling that humor is actually just dominance in disguise. It's another way of using animals, proving we are better than them, disregarding their interests in favor of our own entertainment. The humans at the jubilee used animals to say something about themselves, just as we had in Texas, Maine, and Nevada. The tone was different, rooted in ambivalence rather than fear. But the end result was the same.

So where does this leave us? So many places around the United States celebrate an animal as part of their culture, history, and traditions. Animals have always been a massive part of humans' symbolic lives, foils to our existence and representations of qualities we hate and admire in turn. After the jubilee, I questioned whether it's possible to celebrate the history of a place using animals without trading in narratives of dominion and ambivalence, or whether using animals for entertainment will always carry the stain of exploitation.

PART III
REVERENCE

GROUNDHOG DAY

PUNXSUTAWNEY, PA
THE WEATHER CAPITAL OF THE WORLD

It was 8:59 p.m., and I was sitting cross-legged on my bed with my laptop in front of me and a credit card in hand. I watched the clock as the seconds ticked by. I had joined "Phil's Phan Club" months before to get early notification of ticket sales, because I'd read online that they were hard to score. As soon as the hour hit, I refreshed the internet page and frantically began adding tickets to my cart. By the time I clicked "check out," I was notified that some events were already sold out. In disbelief I rushed to pay for the tickets I was able to grab, worried that others would beat me to it. When I got the confirmation in my inbox, I was so relieved. I'd be going to Groundhog Day.

I learned about Groundhog Day in elementary school, and I remember waking up early to watch the news with my parents to see if Punxsutawney Phil would see his shadow. Part folkloric tradition, part urban legend, and part modern-day party, this is the festival I thought I knew the most about before attending. I was excited to see how the festival would play out on the ground, instead of waiting for news of the shadow from afar. After a four-hour drive into western Pennsylvania, my wife and I entered the town of Punxsutawney. We passed a handful of groundhog statues, the Groundhog Plaza, and a car wash business with a groundhog logo, before parking at the Punxsutawney Area High School. As we entered the school for the Annual Groundhog Club Banquet, I realized almost immediately that there was a lot I didn't yet understand about this festival.

"Hey there! Happy Groundhog Day Eve!" someone behind us in line said. I turned to see that the greeting had been offered to a passerby in a tuxedo and a top hat.

"Happy Groundhog Day Eve to you too! How've you been?"

The two men chatted for a minute or so before the man in a top hat had to step away for his official duties. He was part of the so-called "Inner Circle," the group of men—only men—responsible for planning the Groundhog Day festivities every year. One past president explained why members of the Inner Circle wear top hats and tuxedoes: "Such an important figure as Punxsutawney Phil should be greeted with a sense of reverence and formality."[212] The Inner Circle also takes care of Phil year-round, along with Phyllis, Phil's groundhog wife. The two of them live in a man-made burrow in downtown Punxsutawney with a completely glass side so tourists and passersby can see them.

Here's one of the first things I learned about Phil: he's immortal. Every summer, Phil takes a sip of the "elixir of life" at the annual Groundhog Picnic, giving him seven more years of life.[213] Happily, this means that Phil has been making weather predictions since at least 1886 and that he never dies; there is only one Phil. Even more luckily, the president of the Inner Circle has a magic cane that gives him the power to understand "Groundhogese," Phil's mother tongue. When

Phil makes his prediction, the president of the Inner Circle translates it to human English. The Inner Circle maintains that Phil has been correct in 100 percent of his weather predictions over the years.

My wife and I walked into the cafeteria, where the banquet was being held. A sign on the wall read "Roll Chucks," and posters with sayings like "Happy Groundhog Day" and "We ♥ Phil" covered the room. A giant, yard-size blow-up groundhog was in the corner. This was a ticketed event, so we made our way to our assigned table, which was covered with a white tablecloth and a centerpiece composed of a plastic black top hat, some fluff meant to represent clouds, sunglasses, and a piece of wood.

We shared our table with three other couples. It was the first time each couple had been in Punxsutawney for Groundhog Day, and everyone was excited. The main Groundhog Day celebration the following morning was free and open to the public, but everything else was ticketed. Buying tickets to these events was not particularly expensive, but it was hard, as tickets were limited and there was extraordinary demand. Tickets to this banquet, the lunch with Phil on the day after Groundhog Day, and the formal Groundhog Ball sold out within minutes of their release.

"It felt like we scored Taylor Swift tickets or something," one woman at our table said. Remembering my experience rushing to secure tickets for this weekend, I agreed. When she said she was able to get tickets to the private, heated pavilion for the morning of Groundhog Day (the so-called "Hogspitality Suite"), I was jealous; those were the tickets that had disappeared while I tried to check out, so we'd be standing in the cold the entire time.

When I shared that I was working on this book, everyone at the table showed interest. One man asked me if I had heard about Buzzard

Day in Hinckley, Ohio. I hadn't, so he explained that it is a celebration of the return of the buzzards, much like the return of the swallows in San Juan Capistrano. I was struck again by how many animal festivals there are around the country and by how many people find meaning in them. This exact type of exchange happened quite a few times while I was telling people about this book. I'd explain the topic, and someone would almost always respond with a variation of "Oh, have you heard of this festival?"

While I hadn't heard of Buzzard Day, I had traveled to San Juan Capistrano, California, for the annual Swallows Day Parade. Every March since the early 1800s, migrating swallows would return to the old Spanish Mission building in San Juan Capistrano to nest in the eaves in early spring. In the 1950s the town started an annual parade to mark the miracle of the swallows' return. Buzzard Day was the same type of event. Both occur in March, and along with lots of other events like these, they mark the beginning of spring. Looking to the habits of wild animals to recognize the changing of the seasons and make sense of the natural world is an age-old phenomenon, and now, events like these honor that tradition, celebrating the returning animals to mark time and look ahead.

Groundhog Day derives from that same idea. February second marks the halfway point through winter, equidistant between the winter solstice and the spring equinox. Ancient Celtic pagan traditions celebrated the holiday known as Imbolc on this day, and Christians call the day Candlemas; both used candles and lamps as a way to mark the return of light in the midst of a season of darkness.[214] During the Middle Ages, a folkloric tradition developed throughout much of Europe about the day itself, connecting the weather on Candlemas to a prediction for weather during the remainder of the winter.[215] As the English saying goes,

> If Candlemas day be fair and bright
> Winter will have another flight
> If on Candlemas day it be showre and rain
> Winter is gone and will not come again.[216]

Right around this time of year, animals begin emerging from hibernation, so people began turning to these reappearances as a similar way to forecast the coming of spring.

Looking to animals for weather predictions was common before modern meteorology. Especially in agrarian societies, weather had an outsized impact on people's lives, so it was important to look ahead and plan accordingly. Much as we check a weather app today for a look at what the week holds, people used to rely on the habits of animals to guess what to expect. Many of these tales have survived: cows supposedly lie down before a storm, the sound of peepers marks the start of spring, geese fly higher in fair weather, and so on.[217]

In Germany the badger became a "weather prophet" connected to the midwinter Candlemas holiday. If the badger awoke from hibernation and saw sunshine on Candlemas, he would return to his hole, thus predicting more winter weather. Groundhog Day began in Pennsylvania in the late 1800s, when German immigrants flooded into the state. These new residents brought their traditions with them, but badgers are not found in Pennsylvania, so groundhogs became the stand-in weathermen. The earliest known mention of groundhog forecasters in Pennsylvania dates to 1840, but the modern iteration of Groundhog Day didn't start until 1886 or 1887.[218] The legend remains much the same: if the groundhog sees his shadow on a sunny day, it predicts six more weeks of winter; but if the groundhog emerges on a cloudy day, his lack of a shadow portends an early spring.

Now, over a century later, that simple tradition has snowballed into a multiday event, which all begins here, at the banquet on Groundhog Day Eve.

The Inner Circle paraded into the room singing, "I need Phil, Phil, Phil." Everyone stood up and clapped along to the music. The emcee introduced the Inner Circle, each of whom has a weather-related honorary name as part of their official roles: Frostbite, Moonshine, Rainmaker, Iceman, and Downpour were among the group. People from twenty-five states and three countries were present at the banquet, and the emcee relished in the diversity represented. He pointed out that this is the "only world-wide holiday with a destination."

Then there was a sort of invocation, or a calling to order—I'm honestly not sure what to call it. One member of the Inner Circle stood and called out, at the top of his lungs, "GrounnnnndddddHAAWW-WWWGGGGGG!" Everyone in the room responded in unison, a bizarre chorus shouting out the familiar name of a rodent in a high school cafeteria. We all giggled and looked around the table at each other. Most of us were filming this, because, really, what were we doing?

The absurdity of the event was omnipresent. Before we broke for dinner, we had to recite "Phil's Pledge: All Hail Groundhog Supremacy." We stood, raised our right hands, and repeated the following oath:

> I hereby pledge my allegiance to the Seer of
> Seers, Prognosticator of all Prognosticators,
> the only true weather forecasting ground-
> hog, and whether (no pun intended) your

motto is eternal warm spring or perpetual
snowy winter, Phil's motto is: May you all
live long like Phil.

After the few hundred people present got their food from the buffet, the program continued. The Inner Circle recognized a local man and woman of the year and then dubbed and named a new Inner Circle member. While open to tourists from all around the country (like us and our tablemates), this event also had a decidedly local focus. The community was celebrating its year of work and progress on community initiatives, and we visitors were merely along for the ride. We received an update from Phil's handler—the Inner Circle member who physically grabs Phil out of the stump for the prediction—about the "state of the groundhog" on the eve of the prognostication.

"There's two kinds of people: true believers and the uninformed," Phil's handler declared. "You look in Phil's eyes, and you *know* it's the real deal." The entire room seemed to chuckle knowingly, both completely earnest in their anticipation of the prediction yet in on the joke. The event closed with some "gifts, prizes, and made-up stuff." The Inner Circle drew table numbers and awarded prizes for random things. I won a prize for being the youngest person at my table: a brown knit hat with a groundhog face on the band and a tail poking straight up from the top. It looked a little like a toilet plunger, but I donned it proudly. Then the event closed with a reminder to arrive at Groundhog Day as early as possible, but no later than 4 a.m.

"What time are you all getting there tomorrow?" I asked our tablemates as we stood up. The grounds would open at 3:00 a.m., even though the prognostication wouldn't happen until sunrise, close to 7:30 a.m.

"I think three o'clock," one woman said. "If we're already here, we might as well do it right!"

"True," I nodded in response, though I doubted we would make the same decision. What were the chances things got going that early?

"Have fun tomorrow," I said as we waved goodbye to our tablemates. It was around 8:30 p.m. There was one more event that night—a dueling pianos event with drinks for some twenty-one-and-over fun—but we weren't going to attend. There are few places to stay in Punxsutawney, and even booking months in advance, I was unable to snag one. So we had a forty-minute drive on dark, winding roads to our hotel in the next town over. We wanted to sleep as much as possible before waking up and making the drive back to town. We weren't the only ones stuck sleeping miles away; when we got to our hotel, a group of women partying in the courtyard wore T-shirts that proudly labeled them "Groundhog Groupies."

We discussed waking up at 2:00 and arriving at the event when the gates opened, but we decided to give ourselves an extra hour of sleep and follow the instruction we heard at the banquet to arrive by 4:00 a.m. Even so, the next morning came far too soon. When the alarm went off at 3:00 a.m., we threw on some warm layers and tried to wake up more fully while we found our car in the parking lot and blasted the heat. We ate a granola bar for breakfast en route to Punxsutawney. The drive was quiet and dark. But as we got closer to town, more and more cars were on the road, and police were at every major intersection directing traffic. In spite of everything I had heard, I was still surprised to see so many people this early in the morning.

The festivities take place at Gobbler's Knob—a rural, hilltop site just outside of town. Don Yoder, a historian of Groundhog Day in Punxsutawney who wrote one of the only books entirely dedicated to the event, called this hill "the sacred gathering place of American

Groundhogism."[219] We arrived at Gobbler's Knob just before 4:00 a.m., and there were already thousands of people there. I was obviously wrong in my assumption that few people would decide to make it to the very start of the day. A small stage sat at the bottom of a cleared hill, forming a natural amphitheater set into the woods. The backsplash of the stage was a huge, green sign with a larger-than-life cartoon image of Phil standing on snowy ground beneath a bright blue sky. The sign read "Gobbler's Knob: Home of Punxsy Phil." A large crowd gathered close to the stage, but people spilled all the way up the hill and around the flat parking lot near the visitor center. Onstage a band was already playing music and energizing the crowd. I rubbed my eyes, partially in disbelief of the raucous gathering, partially from lack of caffeine. I zipped up my jacket; it was cold enough to see my breath. But no one else seemed affected by the time or temperature. To the contrary, everyone around us was shouting, dancing, taking photos, and laughing in groups. It was already a party.

Long lines snaked around the grounds. People waited for a turn at an ideal photo spot. Others waited in line for free hats given out by a major sponsor, Samuel Adams. The hats featured a stuffed ground-hog standing upright holding a Cold Snap beer; they were ridiculously charming. There was a massive line for the visitor center's gift shop, which was housed inside and a little bit warmer. Another line for coffee, hot chocolate, and doughnuts at the Shadow Café ran parallel to the visitor center. Coffee sounded worth the wait, so I hopped in line.

"I saw you on YouTube!" I heard a man exclaim behind me while I waited. "You're the man!" He was talking to a member of the Inner Circle, distinctly recognizable in the classic tuxedo and top hat. So many people watch this event online or on TV every year that these small-town civic leaders become celebrities for the day. The two got a photograph together—the visitor flushed with excitement, the Inner Circle member relishing the attention—before parting ways.

Once we got our cups of coffee and a couple souvenirs, we made our way to the downward slope in front of the stage and picked a place to stand. We still had over two hours until Phil's Prognostication, which would happen at sunrise, around 7:30 a.m. We settled in.

There was a lot of excitement around us to keep us distracted from the cold. People brought signs to wave in the crowd. One sign had "PHIL" in capital letters outlined with LED lights. Another offered two nods to Taylor Swift: "1887, Phil's Version" on one side and "In Our 6 More Weeks of Winter Era" on the other. Another read "Phil's Biggest Phan" and had an arrow pointing downward to its owner. Some people were dressed as groundhogs themselves. Many people, including me, wore brown hats with groundhog faces on them. There was a bonfire on the far side of the grounds, and people were warming themselves in its glow. Multiple bands rotated on the stage, and two indefatigable Inner Circle emcees riled up the crowds in between sets. The excitement mounted with every passing minute.

At one point, Pennsylvania's governor, Josh Shapiro, came on-stage. "Are you ready for Phil?" he shouted into the microphone to audience cheers. "Punxsutawney is the center of the universe right now!" Before leaving the stage, he announced Phil as the new official state meteorologist of Pennsylvania. He concluded simply: "Phil's the man."

"Hey," one of the emcees exclaimed as the governor left the stage, "let's party." This Inner Circle member was temporarily clad in a tie-dyed sweatshirt reading "I am Kenough," in homage to the 2023 movie *Barbie*, along with flag-patterned red, white, and blue pants. "Play something by somebody from Pennsylvania!" he shouted. The

DJ obliged, and the thousands of people gathered at the Knob danced to Taylor Swift's "Shake It Off."

At 6:30 a.m. a fireworks show began behind us, just beyond the nearest patch of woods. The fireworks boomed and fizzled overhead while, for whatever reason, music from *Star Wars* blasted over the speakers. A sign at the Knob touts this as a "once-in-a-lifetime opportunity to experience a fabulous fireworks show during the early morning hours in the middle of winter!" I suppose it was.

"All the *other* groundhogs aren't gonna be happy about this," a man in the audience behind me remarked. I tacitly agreed—fireworks are notoriously dangerous and terrifying for wildlife. I cupped my ears to block out the biggest sounds while the show finished.

Another half hour or so of music, dancing, and waiting passed. My toes were numb, partially from being cold and partially from standing for so long on the sloped, rock-hard ground. During the last song of the preshow festivities, the Philettes—a local high school dance group wearing neon sweatshirts—danced onstage as confetti and fog shot out of cannons into the air above the audience. Kids reached up for pieces of the confetti as it drifted down.

It was finally time. The emcees reappeared, once again dressed in their classic top hat and tuxedo outfits, and asked the crowd to part ways for the Inner Circle.

"Send in the top hats," he announced with gravitas in his voice. "Let's get exceptionally weird."

As classical music blared in the background, the Inner Circle began their trek from the top of the hill near the visitor center, down through the center of the crowd, and onto the stage. The president of the Groundhog Club, who wielded a large cane, held the microphone.

"This cane," he began, "is handed down from president to president. This cane gives me the ability to speak Groundhogese. That's how I communicate with Phil." He explained the ritual of what would happen next: he would rap on the door of Phil's burrow with the cane three times, Phil's handler would "gently" lift the rodent prophet out of the compartment, and they would "have a little talk" about whether Phil saw his shadow. "If it's his shadow he sees, six more weeks of winter there will be," the president exclaimed. The audience booed loudly at the thought. "If there's no shadow, early spring!" Cheers erupted all around us.

"Please place the royal red carpet," the president directed as an Inner Circle member spread a red carpet atop the stump. "Please place the scrolls upon the stump." After the scrolls were put in place, the president exclaimed, "Gentlemen, are you ready?"

As Phil's handler moved toward the stump, the audience chanted, "Phil! Phil! Phil!" The handler lifted Phil out of the small enclosure and raised him overhead as everyone around us cheered and clapped.

"Is he dead?" a small boy next to me asked his dad. Phil was remarkably still and placid, even in the face of this massive, cheering crowd.

"No," the dad answered. "He's probably just tired."

The handler petted Phil's head and smoothed his fur as he placed him atop the stump, next to the two scrolls. The president bent down and looked into Phil's eyes, nodding thoughtfully for a few seconds.

"Okay, we have a decision." A scroll was handed to the announcer, who opened it and began to read.

Hear ye, hear ye.
Another winter's slumber paused so I could
meet the crowd.
Hard to sleep anyway when the party's this loud.

> I envy your energy. I envy the fun. I envy all of
>   you (and your opposable thumbs).
> But it's not what I feel, it's what I see and what
>   you hear. So gather 'round and let me
>   be clear.
> Atmosphere is a wonderful thing. And we can
>   create our own and the weather it brings.
> It brings hope for the future and so much
>   more. Maybe some Punxsutawney Phil
>   write-in votes in 2024.
> But one thing the weather did NOT
>   provide—
> Is a SHADOW and a reason to hide.
> Glad tidings on this Groundhog Day!
> An early spring is on the way!

The crowd erupted. Phil sees his shadow much more commonly than not. Of all recorded predictions, he has seen his shadow over one hundred times but has predicted an early spring only about twenty times.[220] The overcast sky and the dull, gray sunrise made this a special year.

Phil remained calm in his handler's arms, even as he held the groundhog's face close to the scroll, apparently allowing him to read his own prediction. The Inner Circle members and Phil remained on the stage for people to take photos with them. Hundreds of other people started streaming out of the Knob and making the long walk back toward the town.

Just like that, it was over.

Now enlightened by Phil's prognostication, we parked downtown and grabbed bagels at an aptly named coffee shop, Groundhog Grindz, and then made our way down Punxsutawney's main street. A spray-painted outline of a groundhog adorned every crosswalk. We passed many gift shops selling Phil-themed souvenirs, including life-size carvings, stained-glass hangings, stickers, postcards, hats, T-shirts, and more. The shops were packed, and lines to pay led nearly out the door in some cases. At the far end of the town from where we parked, a collection of tents marked the "Groundhog Days in the Park" part of the festival. A band performed music on a temporary stage, and people drank beer and ate snacks from local vendors. Visitors pressed their faces up against the glass to spy Phyllis nestled into her burrow. Phil had to do all the work today, but Phyllis was here on display.

Everything about this event was tongue-in-cheek, and by the Punxsutawney Groundhog Club's own admission, nothing is really meant to be taken seriously.[221] The goal of this event is to have fun and to distract attendees from the seriousness of daily life. The whole celebration indulges in silliness.

So why use Groundhog Day as the start of this section on reverence, instead of as another example of how we relate to animals through humor? Groundhog Day could certainly belong in either part. Just as with camels and frogs, using these rodents for the sake of human humor ignores the experience and interests of the animals themselves. Humor distances us from them, making it harder to bridge the gap between species. And many parts of this event *were* hilarious because of the absurdity. An immortal groundhog weatherman? Men in top hats pretending to speak "Groundhogese"? Four hours of predawn music, dancing, and fireworks to prepare for a mysterious choice of scrolls? This was all a little ridiculous.

But the spectacle is a classic example of how we as humans often open our hearts and love, even revere, one single animal while disregarding other members of the same species. We often find it easier to relate to a narrative story about a single person than to grapple with numbers, statistics, and information presented about the masses. The same principle holds true with animals, and it structures much of how we relate to nonhuman creatures more broadly.

Consider Phil again. Phil is undoubtedly beloved as an individual. He is a celebrity in his own right; you can even purchase a personal greeting from Phil on Cameo, a website where celebrities offer personalized videos for sale. Over the years, Phil has met governors, President Ronald Reagan, and Oprah Winfrey, and he has been on TV and in movies.[222] On Groundhog Day, people wear sweatshirts, hats, scarves, onesies, leggings, and more emblazoned with Phil's name and likeness, much like fans wear specialized merchandise to concerts or conventions. Phil and Phyllis live in a place of honor in the center of town, and Punxsutawney is heavily decorated with groundhog statues and logos. The Inner Circle and tens of thousands of visitors make the annual trek to Gobbler's Knob for the prognostication, with undeniable similarity to how others may undertake a zealous pilgrimage. People cheered for Phil, photographed Phil, and pledged allegiance to Phil. His handler held him up high overhead in one hand to meet the cheering crowd. The attention paid to Phil, as an individual creature, is remarkable.

But people mostly consider groundhogs to be pests. Groundhogs—which are also known as woodchucks—ravage gardens and yards, chowing down on hard-grown produce and digging unfortunate holes throughout the ground below. Many resources online offer ideas for how to discourage groundhogs from moving into your yard or how to eradicate them if they are already present.[223] There have been bounties placed on their heads in the past, rewarding residents for killing as many of the pests as possible.[224] Pennsylvania categorizes groundhogs as "nuisance wildlife," and there is no limit to how many groundhogs hunters can kill in the state.[225] Over two hundred and thirty thousand groundhogs were hunted in the Commonwealth of Pennsylvania alone in 2022.[226] The federal government, through the United States Department of Agriculture's wildlife management program known as Wildlife Services, is also involved in killing groundhogs and removing burrows to prevent conflicts with humans. The Animal Legal Defense Fund reported that in 2022, Wildlife Services killed 2,267 groundhogs.[227]

In light of this landscape, with his species treated as a nuisance pest, Phil's journey to stardom wasn't necessarily a foregone conclusion. When Groundhog Day first started in Pennsylvania, it was in part a day to feast on groundhogs that hunters had killed. German immigrants held an annual groundhog hunt, ending with a large communal barbecue; the Punxsutawney Groundhog Club arose from this hunting tradition in the 1880s and 1890s.[228] In 1899 the people of Punxsutawney, led by Clymer H. Freas (the editor of the town newspaper and a civic leader), adopted the weatherman Phil as an immortal mascot.[229] Phil's growing popularity as a weather prophet began to draw visitors and media attention around the turn of the twentieth century.[230] Because of Phil's rising status, as one journalist put it, "the Groundhog Club stopped hunting his brethren and began catering to him instead."[231] So Phil is one of the lucky ones, having escaped the generalized hatred of groundhogs to become an ambassador of his species, a beloved creature given food, shelter, and veterinary care while other members of his species are trapped and hunted.

There are countless examples of this dynamic—adoring one while oblivious to the many—in human-animal relationships. Perhaps the clearest examples of this dynamic are individual animals who escape slaughter and instead capture the public's attention and sympathy, even while people continue to consume products harvested from the animals' less lucky peers. A Texas longhorn, for example, strolled along New Jersey train tracks in a social media video that went viral; in dozens of other examples, cows and pigs similarly find their way out of the slaughter line into the public eye.[232] And it's not just a social media phenomenon. Two pigs in the United Kingdom in the late '90s escaped a slaughterhouse and were on the loose for a week before being corralled and sent to sanctuary. They would become known as the "Tamworth Two," and a toymaker capitalizing on their fame sold souvenir pigs to celebrate the feat.[233] People cheer for these escapees, admire their tenacity, and hope for their safety. Most importantly, people celebrate their redirection away from slaughter to a happy life at a sanctuary farm. For Ricardo the Texas longhorn from New Jersey—yes, he was even named after his dash to freedom—there was an outpouring of support for his placement to live out his days at a sanctuary when he was recaptured.

But many people who cheer for these fugitives, supporting the underdog journey and sharing endearing videos online, don't make the jump to the fact that all cows could be saved from slaughter if we didn't eat beef or dairy products, and all pigs could be saved if we skipped bacon and pork chops. There is no steak or beef without slaughter, no pork without slaughter, and all dairy ends in slaughter too. Slaughter is not peaceful, and none of the animals are happy to be facing it— there is a reason cows and other animals try to escape their fate. And we humans know this. It comforts us to think that sanctuary exists, that the animals who risk it all can be rewarded with a happily ever after. But cheering on the humane rescue of an individual animal while actively contributing to the suffering and death of others of the same species is willfully blind to this simple fact: every animal who didn't escape also wanted to live. Why celebrate one and ignore the rest?

There are other, more indirect examples of this one-versus-many bias. When Freya the walrus spent too much time around human boats and docks in Oslo, the Norwegian government euthanized her. This decision incited global outrage over the injustice of her unnecessary death, and citizens of Norway even raised money for a statue to commemorate Freya's life.[234] But this outcry over Freya's death has not spurred large-scale efforts to combat climate change or to mitigate harm to wildlife—including walruses—that will inevitably occur as our arctic waters change and warm. Flaco, a Eurasian eagle-owl, escaped from the Central Park Zoo when someone shredded the mesh on his enclosure. Flaco took up residence in the "wild" of Central Park and defied everyone's expectations by adapting and thriving in his new life of freedom. Flaco was a celebrity in the park; one journalist called him "an underdog and feel-good figure in troubled times."[235] And when Flaco died (likely from striking a building, and with rat poison found in his system), thousands of people and celebrities mourned on social media.[236] One mourner highlighted the symbolic power Flaco carried: "I feel like he was showing us how we can break free out of our cages, the mundane, the things that don't serve us, the things that hold us back."[237] But despite our attachment to Flaco as a powerful symbol of freedom, no broader movement to end—or even question—wild animal captivity has ensued. Countless other animals remain in cages, deprived of the chance to experience autonomy and free movement like Flaco. Our collective human focus remains myopic, zoomed in, and specialized, treating particular examples as exceptions, without questioning the underlying rule at all.

The truth is that humans almost always respond more emotionally to individual stories than to large-scale plights. Social movements around the world harness this fact, highlighting narratives about individuals suffering in particularly dire straits or achieving unlikely and powerful success to build support and spark bigger change. Hearing statistics about harm, destruction, or danger almost never packs the same emotional punch as a well-told story about an individual facing or overcoming that harm.[238]

Part of the reason for that discrepancy is found in the concept of "scope of justice," a term psychologists use to describe our "boundary for fairness." If something bad, unfair, or random happens to someone, how much do we care? The answer to that simple question decides so much. Humans ultimately have a limited scope of justice. Our scope of justice is not constant, nor is it uniform among people. I care more about the suffering of my immediate family members than I do about the suffering of people I don't know on the other side of the world, even though I care about all humans in the abstract. It's in our biology to structure our world according to priorities, degrees of separation, and the uncomfortable fact of our limited emotional and physical resources. We can't care about everyone, everywhere, all the time, no matter how much we wish we could, so we structure our care in concentric circles of receding depth and seriousness. Our scope of justice encapsulates those we find morally significant, or more worthy of the same experience of fairness and justice as we ourselves are. It excludes everyone else not out of malice but out of practicality.[239]

Our scope of justice relies primarily on two factors: categorization and proximity. First, we structure our world by categorizing others into broad groups, focusing more on groups that are relatable to us. Most animals live outside most people's scope of justice, and this is often further delineated by species. Living in the innermost circle of many people's lives, pets like dogs and cats enjoy moral significance and protection. We see their joy and pain, and those matter to us. But insects are on the far side of the spectrum. Few people care—in a deep, emotional way—if a fly, mosquito, ant, or wasp gets swatted or killed. But were that same treatment to befall someone's dog, or a human child, we would likely have a different intuitive reaction. Our sense of what justice and fairness require changes according to the moral significance we perceive in a species. On the whole, other humans come first, followed by companion animals and more relatable animals; for example, cows will fare better than snakes in most people's scope of justice, whales better than lobsters.

But our scope of justice also differs based on the proximity of the individual animal to our own lives. Family members matter more to me than people I don't know. My own dog matters more to me than a stray dog in a city I have never been to, even if all dogs pull at my heartstrings more than other animals. We all care more about stories that resonate with our experiences, told by people who look like us, or have backgrounds similar to ours, because it replicates proximity with relatability.

These two dynamics—categorization and proximity—intertwine to build our scope of justice. When humans encounter a compelling story about an individual animal, that particular animal breaks through the din of abstraction and species-level assumptions and elevates itself into our scope of justice. We care what happens to one individual cow because we suddenly see her differently than we see all other cows, and we relate to her. The individual fugitive becomes someone we care about. Slaughter would be unfair, because that individual has overcome the odds and demonstrated human-like ingenuity. Slaughtering such a special, capable individual becomes somehow unjust—even as the rest of the cows and pigs who didn't escape remain outside our scope of justice, where fairness doesn't really play in.

Punxsutawney Phil seems to be inside many people's scope of justice, even as other groundhogs are treated as unimportant pests. Phil's comfort matters, even as we disregard other groundhogs. Phil has broken through the outer boundaries of our scope of justice by being an individual with a story we care about. Caring about Phil as an individual doesn't threaten our categorization of the world around us, because it doesn't demand that we apply our sense of fairness to new entities. Caring about *all* groundhogs, on the other hand, might require radical change: we'd have to drive a lot slower, have rules against interfering with woodchuck encroachment on our gardens, work harder to protect forest landscapes, and more. It's the same with animals escaping slaughter: caring about one intrepid runaway asks nothing of us, but caring about all animals farmed for food would require us to eat differently, multiple times a day. For most people, that's a lot to ask.

But for Phil—and other weather forecasting groundhogs—being the revered "one" instead of the disregarded "many" might not be all it's cracked up to be. These groundhogs are kept in captivity, living in ways that frustrate their natural behaviors. Punxsutawney Phil, for example, lives with Phyllis in tight quarters, even though groundhogs are typically solitary creatures.[240] Phil also lives in a temperature-controlled, artificially lit, glass-sided burrow, which means he doesn't hibernate. Instead of receiving signals from the changing seasons to spur his hibernation, his biological processes are confused by the simulated environment.[241] But if groundhog weathermen are allowed to hibernate, February second comes well before the natural end of their hibernation, and waking groundhogs early can have negative physiological effects.[242] Moreover, accidents can happen whenever humans use animals against their will. Staten Island Chuck, New York's competitor to Punxsutawney Phil, for example, died of "acute internal injuries" after then-Mayor Bill de Blasio famously dropped the squirming creature on Groundhog Day in 2014.[243] Groundhogs sometimes seem agitated in the spotlight, and they have been known to bite their human handlers while squirming out of their tight grasp.[244]

Some groups have advocated against using groundhogs for Groundhog Day in this way. PETA, for example, has asked the Punxsutawney Groundhog Club to reconsider using Phil to celebrate Groundhog Day and urged them to allow Phil to retire to a sanctuary.[245] PETA hasn't called for an end to the festivities around Groundhog Day; instead, they suggest conducting a coin toss to predict the weather, since that would actually be more accurate than Phil. The Groundhog Club responded that they weren't abusing Phil and that they weren't doing anything wrong.[246] Other groups have advocated against the unnatural manner of Phil's captivity and suggested we hit "snooze" on Groundhog Day by pushing it to later in the spring, to allow Phil and other captive groundhogs to naturally hibernate.[247]

But opposition to Groundhog Day still exists mainly on the fringe, likely because the event seems so harmless. How many groundhogs are actually in this position, kept in captivity and toted around to forecast the weather once a year? It's true there are dozens of groundhog weathermen throughout North America. To name a few, Dunkirk Dave, Buckeye Chuck, Chuckles IX, Chattanooga Chuck, Sir Walter

Wally, and Milltown Mel compete with Phil.[248] And many ground-hog personalities have been played by numerous groundhogs over the years; the legend lives on even as the individuals die. For example, Staten Island Chuck was played by Charles G. Hogg when he bit former Mayor de Blasio on the finger in 2009; but a few years later, Staten Island Chuck was played by Charlotte, whom de Blasio dropped, and now a new iteration of the character exists.[249] In Quebec, Fred la Marmotte was played by Big Fred, until he passed the torch to Little Fred when he was old enough to retire; Little Fred died soon after.[250] Even Phyllis, Phil's wife with whom he shares a burrow, is not entitled to immortality; Phil has shared his home with many different versions of "Phyllis" over the years.[251]

Phil's supposed immortality raises questions too. The Inner Circle has to sustain the character of Phil somehow. Inspection and registration records from the United States Department of Agriculture have listed four or five groundhogs in the care of the Punxsutawney Groundhog Club at various points instead of merely confirming the existence of the oft-promoted twosome.[252] In 2024 Phil and Phyllis publicly had babies for the first time (named Shadow and Sunny).[253] Rumors about Phil's death and replacements have also popped up on-line over the years.[254] No matter what you believe about Phil, it's clear that many captive groundhogs are used for this holiday. But it's equally clear that the numbers are not staggering.

So there's an obvious counterargument here: Just how much does this really matter? In the grand scheme of things—with climate change affecting wild animals at an increased rate, with factory farming perpetrating all manner of harm on billions of animals a year, with highly intelligent creatures being kept in inhumane captivity all around the world—even if we care about animals broadly, why should we care about a couple of groundhogs? These groundhogs are handed food and protected from the elements, for the relatively small price of being forced to sit in someone's arms or travel around in a plastic tube a few times a year. These groundhogs are beloved. By numbers, by impact, by seriousness of harm—by nearly any metric, Groundhog Day doesn't do all that much damage to all that many animals.

As I watched the festivities on Groundhog Day, worrying about Phil's feelings and experience of the hoopla instead of enjoying it myself, a basic question swirled deep in my gut: Am I just a massive bummer? While researching this book, I sat through so many events that other people enjoyed, feeling uncomfortable with what was happening around me. I sat silently as people laughed around me at the Camel & Ostrich Races. I worried about the frogs at the Jumping Frog Jubilee. I privately mourned the beautiful animals auctioned off "black" at the livestock auction, along with the thousands of rattlesnakes and lobsters killed while others snapped photos and got in line to buy a piece of their flesh. No one likes the person who rips the curtain open, destroying the fun and reminding people of the reality beneath the pizzazz, but that is the essential work of this book: pointing out flaws in our human-animal relationships, reminding people of the creatures on the animal half of the equation. The words "buzzkill," "killjoy," and "party pooper" all come to mind. So when, like here in Punxsutawney, the "reality" isn't *that* bad, when the harm is just the discomfort of a groundhog or two, is it better to just let the show go on?

For us to begin to wrestle with that question, it's important to remember why we celebrate Groundhog Day and why we use groundhogs in this way in the first place—it's obviously not simply to forecast the weather. Like every festival in this book, Groundhog

Day brings a lot of revenue, attention, and opportunity to the town that hosts it. In Punxsutawney the community has built its identity around Phil and around groundhogs in general. Statues of Phil stand around town, and buildings, plazas, and parks bear his name. Within the Pennsylvania German/Dutch community more broadly, there is a rich tradition of "groundhog lodges," fraternal organizations utilizing the groundhog as a totemic symbol to represent their society.[255] These lodges host gatherings, known as *versammlinge*, that center on groundhogs and involve skits, speeches, and celebrations of heritage.[256] Without Phil, and without groundhogs more broadly, Punxsutawney and Pennsylvania would miss part of their core identity.

On a bigger scale, Phil's prognostications are embedded in time and are often political in some way. During Prohibition, he threatened sixty weeks of winter if he wasn't allowed a drink.[257] In 1958 Phil announced he was preparing to take off in his "Chucknik" spacecraft; the next year, he announced his return from the moon.[258] In 1981, in recognition of the American hostages in Iran, Phil wore a yellow ribbon for his prognostication.[259] In 2000 he "announced the dawn of a 'new Phillennium.'" In 2002, mere months after the terrorist attack on September 11, 2001, the program of the event offered a strong message of patriotism. Phil's prognostication included the stanza

> Thank God I live in the land of the free and
> the brave,
> and I live in a burrow and not a cave.
> I've been sleepin', been noddin', been livin'
> better than bin Ladin.[260]

In 2006 Phil emerged from his burrow with a "Terrible Towel," a symbol of support for the Pittsburgh Steelers' Super Bowl run.[261] We use Phil (and other groundhogs) to say something about our human world. We project a message onto him, using him to tell our stories, placing the burden of human meaning onto him.

Using groundhogs in this way teaches kids—and reminds adults—that it is completely permissible to use animals for our human ends. It proves through example that it's okay, even funny, to use animals however we want, just because we want to. It's okay to take them from the wild; to keep them in captivity; to prevent them from experiencing the world in the way most natural to them; to stick them in a box and hold them up for all to see. The reason for it may be humor, or cultural significance, or something else altogether. We don't even need a reason to justify it. The core message being passed around is one of human exceptionalism. We do this to groundhogs because it brings us value, and that's the only thing that matters.

The next day, the morning of February third, we drove back to Punxsutawney, this time in the daylight. We passed not one but two dead groundhogs on the curvy roads, innards spilling out of their small bodies. It's true that cars are indiscriminate killers—we also saw dead deer, opossums, and birds on the road—but seeing groundhog roadkill was the purest embodiment of the cruel irony, or maybe even hypocrisy, of this event. We spent the weekend worshiping one groundhog, taking photographs of him and seeking his wisdom, while others were squished on the side of the road with little afterthought. There is no rhyme to that reason, no explanation offered for why the worth of one groundhog's life would be different from another's.

We parked and walked around Gobbler's Knob. This time there were no people around, and we had the place to ourselves. Debris littered the ground. Red, white, and blue confetti that had been launched into the air the day before now crunched underfoot. We walked up onstage and peered into Phil's stump. It was just a small compartment filled with straw, barely bigger than Phil's body. I grimaced at the thought of Phil trapped in this tiny stump for hours while music blasted, dancers shook the stage around him, and fireworks boomed overhead. How strange that must have felt.

It was peculiar to see this place empty compared to all the excitement and hoopla of the day before. It was almost sad, like the sticky floors of a club in daylight or the remnants of last night's makeup—a relic of a good time, yes, but something else too. Gobbler's Knob is open year-round, and while tourists visit for other events, nothing rivals Groundhog Day. Now that Phil had done his job, the wooded stage slipped easily back into its rural quiet and peace.

"I can't believe people do this every year," I chortled to my wife as we walked across the eerily empty stage. My eyes were still bloodshot from the lack of sleep the day before.

"It's a pretty big nothingburger," she agreed. A few seconds later, she doubled down. "I mean, really, *nothing* happens."

I was reminded of Bill Murray's cranky line in the 1993 movie *Groundhog Day*: "This is pitiful. A thousand people freezing their butts off, waiting to worship a rat."[262] In some sense, that rang true to me. We barely slept, drove forty minutes in the middle of the night, and then waited for hours in the predawn cold, all to witness a mysterious prediction, supposedly from an animal, which is accurate only about 30 percent of the time—odds worse than chance.[263]

But that perspective misses something critical about this event. Everyone we met expressed so much joy to be there. People took days off work to make the trek to the Knob, driving and flying from all over the region and the nation. Visiting Punxsutawney for Groundhog Day was an item on many people's bucket list. Groups of friends gathered and donned matching outfits. The excitement and delight generated by these early morning festivities with no real purpose were hard to explain, but undeniable. This nothingburger surely means *something*.

We left Gobbler's Knob and headed into town for "Lunch with Phil," a ticketed event held in a two-story fraternal lodge that smelled of stale tobacco smoke. When we walked in, we quickly spotted our tablemates from the banquet a few days before and swapped stories from Groundhog Day. Even with tens of thousands of attendees, Punxsutawney has a way of making this festival feel local and intimate. This dichotomy is part of its lasting charm, I think. It is an event both universal and strikingly particular, boundary-less yet deeply rooted in western Pennsylvania. Every year the Inner Circle broadcasts Phil's prognostication to the nation and the world, but they also celebrate their town of five thousand people and its local leaders. I arrived as an anonymous attendee, but in Punxsutawney I got to feel like I was part of the community.

We found seats on the second floor while we waited for the star of the show to arrive. Because of the crowds yesterday, it was nearly impossible to see Phil up close. This would be my only interaction with the animal at the center of everything. Unlike every other festival in this book, Groundhog Day is about one individual animal only, not a species or a group. Phil is not like the frogs, lobsters, snakes, or camels used for the celebration only because of their membership in a particular species. Phil is decidedly unique. It wasn't *groundhogs* we were there to admire, as evidenced by the roadkill we saw earlier; it was *Phil*.

We waited while pans of food were brought out and a buffet line started forming. After a few minutes, a cheer erupted from behind me. I turned around and saw two members of the Inner Circle flanking Phil, whom they carried in a small, plexiglass tube. Phil stretched up on his haunches and pawed at the side of the tubular enclosure as the Inner Circle members walked him down the center of the room to applause and cheers. Phil circled his small space and continued to look around him as they made their way to the front of the room and placed Phil atop a table for photo opportunities. A line instantly formed as eager attendees jumped up for their chance to meet Phil face-to-face.

"This is going to sound really dumb," my wife turned to me and said, "but I feel like I just saw a celebrity." It wasn't dumb at all. I felt the same way. After all the hype, the fireworks, the hyperbolic orations, the singing and dancing, after anxiously awaiting the news only he could bring, seeing this small groundhog in the flesh right in front of us was affecting. He was real.

We love Phil for what he represents. We use Phil to tell our human stories, over and over again, year after year. Phil is the legend we ascribe to him, a bearer of lore and mystery and fun, a clairvoyant weatherman. And that matters. This story has deep cultural importance, and it creates an entertaining diversion from the darkness of winter. Phil is a symbolic groundhog as much as a real one.

But we also love Phil precisely *because* he is a living, breathing, dynamic creature. Whether meteorological or not—probably not— Phil himself, as a particular groundhog, has some sort of magic power over all of us. Phil is a story made tangible. He entrances us with his particularity, woos us with his cute face and squishy body. And because it is just one, immortal Phil, we can care about him without thinking too hard about the roadkill we passed to drive here. Phil is special.

But Phil's status within our collective scope of justice is not as simple as I have made it sound. It isn't *fairness* we assert for Phil; it's closer to *comfort*. Groundhog Day still operates under the basic assumption that Phil can and should be used for human ends. I think a deep indifference underlies our treatment of Phil as we move him from enclosure to enclosure, gawking and snapping photos, preventing him from hibernating or living his own life. Is any of this what Phil wants? More precisely, is any of this what the particular groundhog forced to play Phil wants? Yes, he receives food and shelter. But imagine the same scenario played out on a human, or another beloved wild species like an orca, kidnapped or born into captivity, given food and shelter but not allowed to live its own life on its own terms. That may be comfortable enough, but it isn't necessarily fair or just. So even Phil, disguised and promoted as a revered individual, may nevertheless lie outside our human scope of justice.

In assessing this one-versus-many dynamic for groundhogs, we have to ask ourselves: Is reverence really worth anything at all for the one? Maybe it is just dominance and apathy packaged in a different, more comfortable form. Maybe it's just another form of disregard, another form of human exceptionalism, to do whatever we want to a creature solely because doing so matters to us. Hunting and killing are the clearest forms of dominance, but there are others too, insidiously wrapped in the language of welfare. Sure, holding a groundhog in captivity to display on Groundhog Day isn't "so bad," compared to a torturous death. But drawing lines between ethical and nonethical treatment is a hard exercise when you get to the margins, especially when we humans don't speak "Groundhogese."

There have been alternative weather-forecasting techniques over the years. In Washington, DC, for example, Potomac Phil is a stuffed groundhog, not a live one,[264] and occasionally, a human child dressed up as a groundhog has played the role.[265] While nothing else has had the staying power of the live groundhog yet, that doesn't mean an alternative ritual couldn't take off. What really mattered about this event was the to-do of it all: the early wake-up; the anticipation; the giant, community-wide party like no other. But it's important to remember that the entire holiday is made up, a ritual full of purposeful nonsense based on a centuries-old legend with little basis in reality. If humans could make this whole weekend-long event up out of nothing, we could certainly create something better to take its place. Continuing to use groundhogs to play Phil isn't inevitable; it's a choice we make.

Phil—or the idea of him—has given tens of thousands of people all across the country a reason to get together and celebrate. He—or the folklore we assign him—offers hope and gives shape to the monotony of winter. Phil is an idea, it's true. But in Phil's reality lies the problem. While more groundhogs are killed each year by magnitudes than are harmed by playing weathermen, the logic underlying the two is the same: groundhogs are disposable, and they are ours to use as we please.

BUTTERFLY DAYS

PACIFIC GROVE, CA
BUTTERFLY TOWN, USA

"It's quite a shtick," my wife commented wryly as we rolled our carry-on suitcases down the hallway of the Monarch Resort. A series of trees grew indoors, fastened to which were a handful of oversized plastic monarch butterflies. It was almost saccharine, glorifying the butterflies with this well-meaning but cartoonish tribute. Then again, that's why we were here too: to celebrate the butterflies. The town's slogan is "Follow the butterflies to Pacific Grove," and we did just that.[266]

Every year, beginning in October, tens of thousands of monarch butterflies migrate to the coast and land in Pacific Grove, California, to spend the winter. "You don't get droves all at once," Stephanie Turcotte Edenholm, an author, educator, and volunteer guide and monarch counter at the Pacific Grove Monarch Butterfly Sanctuary later told me. "Usually, they start arriving in the beginning of October, and you feel a weight of anticipation. You just see one or two at first.

It's a slow build-up." And patterns aren't always easy to spot. "Every year is completely different," she said.

While eastern monarchs overwinter in Mexico, western monarchs travel to various sites up and down the California coast. Monarch butterflies cannot survive freezing temperatures and can't fly when the air is below fifty-five degrees Fahrenheit. To endure the winter, they travel to these so-called "overwintering sites," where they can ride out the winter in protected enclaves. The trees provide favorable "microclimates," where the humidity, temperature, wind, shade, and light are just right for the creatures to hunker down.[267]

Pacific Grove is one such haven for these insects. As John Steinbeck observed in the novel *Sweet Thursday*: "Pacific Grove benefits by one of those happy accidents of nature that gladden the heart, excite the imagination, and instruct the young."[268] Over a century ago, in 1914, author Lucia Shepardson explained, "Each autumn comes a pilgrimage . . . They are not men, they are not beasts, nor are they birds, these travelers of long distances. They are butterflies."[269] The mystery—and miracle—of this natural event arises in part because somehow, every year, the monarchs choose the same exact spot in Pacific Grove to rest: a handful of trees tucked into only about three acres now known as the Monarch Butterfly Sanctuary.[270]

Even more remarkably, the butterflies who "return" to Pacific Grove have never actually been there before. Thousands of butterflies spend the winter here before embarking on their migration, during which the females will lay eggs on milkweed plants before dying. The generation born on those milkweed plants will continue the journey away from the coast before breeding and dying themselves. Multiple generations of monarchs will breed and die before the ultimate "return" to overwinter in California again. This intergenerational migration is a scientific marvel.

But we weren't in Pacific Grove to see the butterflies themselves; it was too early in the season. Instead, we were there for the annual Butterfly Days Festival and Parade, the annual party thrown to welcome the monarchs back to town.

The parade was not scheduled to start until 10:30 a.m., so we stopped for breakfast and coffee. At the coffee shop, families gathered and caffeinated while kids tugged at their costumes. We watched as the main street got busier and families arrived for the parade. I felt more like an outsider than usual. As people greeted each other and began to gather on the street, I could see this was a true community event, put on by the local schools and celebrated by the inhabitants of the town. Tourists were welcome, of course—and everyone we spoke to was happy we were there—but in some ways it felt like we were floating through an event that was not meant for us. It was not really a performance, like Groundhog Day or the Camel & Ostrich Races were. Nor was it a big, formal affair, like the parade at the Maine Lobster Festival was. Instead, this event bubbled up from the heart of the town decades ago, and its current iteration seemed designed not primarily for spectators but for participants. The long-standing requirements that students create their own costumes and that the parade remain unmotorized only highlighted the homegrown feel of the event.

We finished our coffees and walked up Lighthouse Avenue to find a place to stand for the parade. People were casually gathered, and clusters of families and friends found each other along the street. Some brought chairs, but the parade would be short enough that most people remained standing. Bubbles floated in the air as kids shrieked and jumped to catch them. It was a remarkably idyllic small-town scene, and almost everyone dressed for the occasion. Many kids who were too young to march in the parade had nevertheless donned butterfly wings, orange tutus, or themed T-shirts. One mother had two young children in a double stroller, both dressed as monarchs. Adults took part as well. Some simply wore orange and black or a Pacific Grove T-shirt emblazoned with a monarch; others wore full, filmy butterfly wings that draped down their backs. One woman wore a monarch-wing-printed maxi skirt; another wore an orange-and-black poncho that resembled a monarch's wing.

The start of the parade was marked by a vintage police car with two monarchs affixed to its grill and a monarch on either passenger door rounding the corner. Next, a few children carried an orange banner that read "The Children of Pacific Grove Welcome the Butterflies." The first group of schoolchildren followed: preschoolers dressed as caterpillars, with yellow, black, and white striped paper cutouts strung around their necks with a length of yarn. They wore black construction-paper headpieces with yellow dots meant to look like eyes. Their teachers walked with them and encouraged them to wave; many of them did, and their eyes lit up when they spotted their families in the crowd.

Immediately after the caterpillars, naturally, came the main attraction: the monarch butterflies themselves, represented by the kindergarteners. These children, having progressed from the larval caterpillar phase of preschool to the fully formed world of grade school, held a place of honor representing the butterflies The children wore orange or black clothes and wings made from orange and black construction paper and dotted with white paint. In 1994—the year my grandmother visited Pacific Grove for the festival and, coincidentally, the year I was born—a local journalist described the scene: "Monarchs twinkle in the trees. And the children twinkle when they march in honor of the migratory creatures."[271]

This humble parade dates back to 1939, and it seemed to me like not much has fundamentally changed. Images from news clippings in the 1990s when my grandmother visited show children in the same costumes, paper cutouts and all. The idea originated over eighty years ago, when the local parent-teacher association came up with the idea to raise funds by hosting a bazaar and a parade with a butterfly theme. Only about fifty children participated that first year, but by the late 1980s reports noted it had grown to include over two thousand participants.[272]

Over the years, the Butterfly Festival has taken many forms, from the early days of the pageant performance to its current iteration. More recently, the festival has expanded to a full weekend known as "Butterfly Days." The year I attended, there was a welcome event advertised as boasting a "carnivalesque atmosphere," a pancake breakfast, book talks, a ceremonial blessing of the sanctuary, and a ticketed sunset event at the Point Pinos lighthouse. While the parade seems to be the centerpiece of the weekend, I was surprised at how short and simple it was. When the last group walked by us, it was still quite early in the day. The next event—a book talk where the mayor would speak—wasn't for a little while. To pass the time, my wife and I decided to walk up and down the main street, which was lined with banners marking Butterfly Days.

Pacific Grove has built its identity around the monarch butterfly. As one high school student ambassador told me, not at all exaggerating, "Butterflies are everything here in Butterfly Town, USA." Even back in 1954, Steinbeck rightly observed, "The town makes a very nice thing of it."[273] The town logo features a monarch butterfly. Directional signs pointing to landmarks around town include an image of a monarch. Storefront displays when we were there were scattered with butterflies, both two-dimensional stickers and three-dimensional models made of paper or plastic. One jewelry store had a cascading display of faux wisteria flowers with plastic monarchs affixed to the branches. Real estate listings for houses in the area—ubiquitous to any town center—were pinned up with butterfly pins. A map of the town marked "You Are Here" not with a dot, nor with an arrow, but with a small butterfly. Two large statues in town signify the permanent importance of the monarch and the festival more than anything else: one, a statue of a monarch, sits near the coast, and the other, a statue of a young boy and a young girl dressed up for the Butterfly Days Parade, adorns the lawn in front of the post office.

Stores around town capitalized on the monarch motif too, selling a variety of monarch-themed souvenirs and gifts: T-shirts, hats, sweatshirts, mugs, pins, stickers, postcards, notebooks, paintings, magnets, coasters, and bookmarks, to name a few. A "Monarch Butterfly X-Ing" sign hung for sale in one shop, where you could also purchase your own costume wings or children's clothes handmade from black and orange fabric.

One store even offered jewelry made from real monarch butterfly wings, accompanied by a sign claiming that no butterflies were harmed in making the jewelry—an assertion I struggled to believe. The sign explained the butterflies were raised on farms and their wings harvested only after they died natural deaths. I remained incredulous. The very facet of these creatures we marvel at the most is their ability to transform and fly, to stump human scientists and travel hundreds of miles guided by unknown forces. Isn't raising these butterflies in captivity—these creatures born to travel—a kind of harm? How thin the line is, I thought, between adoration and the ever-lurking instinct to own a piece of the thing we adore. Humans always want to capture the qualities of the animals we admire, stretch their skin over our own, co-opt their beauty and adorn ourselves with it instead, using their bodies as totems to invoke their speed, strength, or exoticism. The problem is that we cannot do so without destroying what we admire. Can humans ever respect a creature by letting it be? By protecting the factors that might allow it to thrive, even beyond our eyesight? Even if we get nothing out of it, not even earrings?

I'm not immune. I purchased a small paper monarch butterfly perched atop a wire stand meant to decorate a potted plant, some stickers, and a baseball cap with an embroidered monarch on the front.

Pacific Grove's identification with butterflies didn't seem to stem purely from commercial interests, though. Many privately owned houses we walked or drove past had butterfly decor: we saw decals stuck to windows, metal butterfly sculptures hanging from porches, stained-glass artwork with intricate butterfly wings, and plastic monarchs attached to string lights framing a sunporch. Even some mailboxes were covered with butterfly-themed wrappings. As I said, butterflies were everywhere.

We made our way to the Monarch Pub & Restaurant. It was prominently situated on a corner and hard to miss, so our decision for where to eat was made easy. It was cool outside but warm enough to sit on the patio if we kept our jackets on. The air was humid, and when the sun peeked out from behind the clouds it warmed our faces and hands.

"What can I get you started with?" the waitress asked us. I glanced at the drink menu: cocktail options included a "Flutterby" and a "Monarch Mule." We opted for local beers and veggie burgers and then inhaled the salty air while we waited for our food.

It was easy to see connections between Pacific Grove and the other towns I visited: just like the cartoonish images of jumping frogs decorating Frogtown, USA, groundhogs featuring prominently in local businesses in Punxsutawney, or the lobster-related souvenirs being sold at every shop in Maine, so too are the monarch butterflies the defining symbol of Pacific Grove. But unlike in every other town and festival, here in Pacific Grove, visitors can spot the monarchs in their own natural space. At other events, wild animals are captured or domesticated and transported into the town center for the weekend—think of the frogs caught at families' secret spots, the lobsters trapped off the coast of Maine, or the rattlesnakes gassed and tricked out of their dens. In most cases, we humans bring the animals to us, so we can do something to them in public, killing, harassing, or praising them, in turn.

In Pacific Grove, it's the other way around: the visitors go to the animals. In fact, the commercial interests of the town have long capitalized on the presence of the butterflies themselves, and the town relies on revenue from tourists who come from all over the country to see the butterflies. John Steinbeck observed, "Where there are tourists there is money, and . . . Pacific Grove had a gravy train right in its lap."[274] In 2009, for example, when the butterfly count was fewer than one thousand due to misguided overpruning of the grove, business in the city dropped more than 25 percent.[275] The animals are not just artificially present for the weekend of the festival. Instead, they are naturally present in town for part of the year, separate and apart from the festival. The festival is just the welcome party.

After our lunch, my wife and I drove up the peninsula to see if we might be able to spot any of these butterfly residents. We knew it was too early in the season to see any monarchs in serious numbers, but we hoped we would get lucky nonetheless. How wonderful it would be to see a monarch in its natural habitat, instead of in cartoonish, commercial rendering.

The Monarch Butterfly Sanctuary is tucked behind the Butterfly Grove Inn, a bright pink hotel with a massive mural of monarch butterflies rendered in neon colors on its side. A narrow gravel pathway marked by a white picket fence leads around the hotel to the entrance of the sanctuary. A handful of informational signs and a metal bench cast in the shape of a butterfly greeted us at the entrance. We walked through the single, shaded path in the small grove.

Before 1990 these trees where the monarchs overwintered were on private property. In 1990 the owner sought to subdivide her property in a way that would have destroyed the overwintering habitat. But the city's inhabitants expressed serious resistance to that plan. Ro Vaccaro, who visited in 1988 and became so enamored with the monarchs that she left her job in New York City to move to Pacific Grove, led the opposition. Ro was known as the "Butterfly Lady," and she reportedly had butterfly images on her at all times: on her shoes, on her car, in her apartment. "She always wore a butterfly, every single day, or she felt nude," her sister recounted in an obituary in 2008. Ro's love for the monarchs was infectious, and she used her passion to convince over two-thirds of the residents of Pacific Grove to vote to approve a bond measure to purchase the 2.7-acre plot at nearly market value and to secure a conservation easement over the land. That land is now the Pacific Grove Monarch Sanctuary, protected in perpetuity.[276]

As we quietly walked among the trees, an air of reverence settled around us. It felt like we were in a church, or another sacred space. In 1994, echoing this spiritual feeling, Ro wrote of monarchs as "nature's stained-glass windows, flying high between us and the sun, glowing with the radiance of gems. Standing quietly among thousands of butterflies at the Monarch Grove Sanctuary, we feel our features soften and cares fall away."[277]

Predictably, we didn't see any butterflies. We saw jays and wood-peckers in abundance and watched as they hopped along the ground and around tree trunks. The grove was darkened by the heavy tree cover, and the people we passed were as quiet as we were—all of us hoping for a visitation. In a few minutes, we reached another paved road.

"Is that it?" I whispered.

"I guess so," my wife answered with a shrug. We turned around and headed back up the winding path.

The day we visited the sanctuary was my grandmother's birth-day, and the poignancy of my visit to Pacific Grove for Butterfly Days falling on that exact day was not lost on me. While researching and traveling, I often found myself searching for pieces of my grand-parents. I looked for signs and hints, anything to forge a connection across the gulf of death to the people who, in ways both big and small, formed me. My grandmother's work lay scattered and unfinished, and as I picked up the pieces, I ached for signs that I was on the right track. I sought approval and permission from her that I, of course, would never find. And my grandfather's presence at all of these festivals wove throughout her notes in ways that were frustratingly oblique. A list chronicling the order of the races in Virginia City in 1998, for example, was in my grandfather's recognizable handwriting, not my grandmother's. I could almost picture him sitting next to my grand-mother in the stands, assigned to take notes so she could observe, but the image is hazy and incomplete, composed of gestures and broad strokes without detail. My grandmother's files were only breadcrumbs. I wanted a full story. I wanted a sign.

Butterflies begin their lives as earthbound caterpillars, who eventually wrap themselves in a cocoon and dissolve their bodies before re-forming as butterflies. Their cocoons thin and then crack open, and the butterflies unfurl their new wings and fly up and away into the air. In their lifecycle are obvious and powerful metaphors: that our earthbound bodies do not contain the whole of us; that there is always hope, renewal, and rebirth; that change and transformation can be total, but good.

Humans across cultures have connected butterflies with death, resurrection, and the human soul since antiquity. Boria Sax, writing about symbolic understandings of various species in his book *The Mythical Zoo*, explains that ancient Greeks and Romans pictured the human soul as a butterfly or moth; the words for soul in Greek (*psyche*) and Latin (*anima*) could each be used to refer to a butterfly. Sax notes that in Indonesia people traditionally considered a butterfly to be the spirit of a departed companion.[278] The eastern monarchs who migrate to Mexico are associated with the Day of the Dead celebration, connecting the butterflies' arrival with the souls of loved ones who have passed away.[279] In Pacific Grove too, the American Indians native to the peninsula identified the monarchs with the souls of the dead.[280] Poets including Emily Dickinson, Edna St. Vincent Millay, William Wordsworth, and Homero Aridjis, to name a few, have also written poems about butterflies and used their symbolism in connection with death.

This connection between death and the human soul is also prevalent in Christian imagery and stories. My grandmother's files include an Easter card that reads: "The butterfly has for many centuries been depicted in Christian art as a symbol of the Resurrection. It is a sign of the believer's share in Christ's victory over death. As a very unattractive and earthbound worm, the little creature enters its cocoon for a deathlike sleep . . . then it bursts forth from its 'tomb.'" Wordsworth's ode "To a Butterfly" captures the symbolism of a butterfly's life cycle simply: "Dead times revive in thee."

It's not just death and rebirth that find an example in the monarch but hardship and change too. During the COVID-19 pandemic, people turned to the butterfly as a source of inspiration and hope in a time when the world was pushed into a cocoon, quiet and withdrawn and uncomfortable.[281] At a time when everything had changed—how we worked, who we saw, how we spent our time—and when the concepts of "safety" and "health" seemed evasive to many, the butterfly's radical transformation offered a perfect metaphor for endurance and hope.

Butterflies are consistently one of the most commonly requested designs at tattoo parlors; people like invoking the idea of fragility matched with strength, and of the power of complete transformation in times of change.[282] The jewelry company Alex and Ani sells bracelets with butterfly charms for a less permanent way to wear a symbol of "growth, change and transformation" and "the incredible feats we can achieve when we trust ourselves."[283] Similarly, in the third season of the Netflix series *Bridgerton*, a mass release of monarch butterflies into an indoor ball metaphorically mirrors the emergence of a main character into her true identity. The monarch offers a powerful symbol of what it means to come into one's own.

But butterflies, it's worth remembering, are insects. Insects on the whole tend not to get a lot of human sympathy, and certainly not a lot of human protection. We slap, squish, spray, trap, zap, and swat them regularly. We hire exterminators to rid our houses and yards of bugs and insects. This is generally true even if the bugs are helpful to us. Many people fear spiders, for example, despite the fact that they help keep populations of other harmful insects in check. Even bees, widely recognized as critical pollinators, just like monarchs, are not given as much positive attention as butterflies are. (I, too, cringe when one flies by, instinctually shying away from the threat of a sting.) Even more, monarch butterflies are actually toxic—the milkweed they subsist on produces compounds called cardiac glycosides, which give the butterflies a nasty flavor that protects them from being eaten by predators such as birds.[284] Why we revere and protect these toxic bugs, then, at least on its face presents a conundrum.

But our gut instincts provide easy explanations. Butterflies are beautiful. They don't threaten or hurt us. As a docent at the Natural Bridges State Beach said in 1992, "Butterflies flutter, and beetles creep and crawl. They gross people out. I don't know why that is. People just seem to prefer things that flutter."[285] More to the point, I think, their bodies and lives present a story of renewal and intergenerational perseverance that we can identify with personally. Ants and bees may provide metaphors for social structures and bodies politic, but the story of a butterfly sinks straight to the core of our individual, existential, all-too-human struggles.

When we arrived back to the entrance of the sanctuary, my wife and I decided to sit on a bench for a few minutes to see if stillness would conjure any more animals—maybe even a monarch. Something cavernous, like love or loss, opened in me when I saw the inscription on the bench: "The butterflies' best friend, Ro Vaccaro, for her labor of love." When I started my research, Ro's name was everywhere, because her work was critical to creating and protecting the sanctuary for the visiting monarchs. My grandmother had met Ro on a visit to Pacific Grove and had gone out to dinner with her. After the visit, Ro followed up and sent my grandmother a packet containing dozens of local and national news clippings and articles about her fight to protect the sanctuary (in chronological order, no less, so my grandmother could "get a sense of the drama as it unfolded"). I now have that manila envelope, and all these years later, Ro's meticulous care for the butterflies is still resonating. She closed her note by asking my grandmother to "keep in touch and let me know how your book is coming along." When I read that line, I felt a pang of longing, a message I could never send lodging in an outbox in my chest. Ro cheerfully signed off her note to my grandmother: "Monarchs forever!"

Sitting on Ro's bench, dedicated to her advocacy for the cause she loved most in the world, I was overwhelmed. First, by the feeling of loss. There were so many people my grandmother had spoken with, worked with, received gracious and generous help from, who were now beyond reach. I hated thinking about how many more of these stories I missed by the accident of being born a few years too late. Not to mention my grandmother herself, whose work on this very book slowly, painfully, grudgingly petered out in lockstep with her own energy and breath. But close behind that sadness, and closely related, was gratitude. It was nothing less than a miracle that Ro had fought—and succeeded—in saving the sanctuary, that my grandmother, who lived thousands of miles away on a farm in coastal Massachusetts, had met her, spoken with her, learned from her, and that I, thirty years after that, had discovered pages and pages of cracking, yellowed paper and started to string together a story.

This is the reason humans are drawn to monarchs: just when something seems buried and gone, it can be reborn in an entirely different form. A starving caterpillar eats all it can and turns to goo, but the world keeps turning, and what was once dormant emerges anew. Ro, my grandmother, and countless others are now buried, but their work lives on in new form, having migrated across a continent to alight on me. An informational sign at the sanctuary explains, "This year's over-wintering monarchs are the great-grandchildren of the butterflies that left last spring." And so it is; we, like butterflies, do what we can and push forward, hoping the next generation picks up where we left off, but stronger. The promise of transformation, of a legacy that will outlive us, of progress being made beyond the handful of miles our own feet or wings can take us, is the sweetest hope there is.

As unlikely as it is that a manila envelope from the 1990s would find its way to my desk, so too is it unlikely that a monarch butterfly will survive all that it faces. When I asked Edenholm, who lives in Pacific Grove and published a children's book about the monarch migration, why monarchs have captured her imagination so much, she answered simply, "Their resilience." She continued, "When they come in, some are already tattered from their journey there. We also have storms, with rain and wind, and some of them get knocked down. It's amazing any of them are still alive at the end of the season. Their tenacity and resilience are a miracle."

Their resilience is not endless though. Despite the remarkable universality of the deep meaning humans find in monarchs, the monarch butterfly population has rapidly declined. The Xerces Society for Invertebrate Conservation is a nonprofit focused on invertebrates and pollinators that has been tracking the monarch populations (both eastern and western) since the late 1990s. When my grandmother visited Pacific Grove in the 1990s, the Xerces Society reported that "hundreds of millions of monarchs made the epic flight each fall" and "more than a million monarchs overwintered in forested groves on the California coast."[286] Today scientists estimate a decline of more than 95 percent of the monarch butterfly population has occurred in California.[287] An exhibit at the Natural History Museum in Pacific Grove demonstrates this loss poignantly: one thousand white paper butterflies hang in an arch over a doorway, and tucked among the white cutouts is a single orange one. The exhibit's sign reads: "In 2020, the overwintering Western Monarch population fell to a record low, a loss of 99.9%. This means that for every thousand butterflies that came to California in 1997, by 2020 there was only one."

The natural world my grandmother knew when she conceptualized this book, in other words, was entirely different from the one I face now. Butterflies are still beloved, the festival in Pacific Grove has continued on and even expanded, but in the last thirty years something drastic has shifted underfoot. The butterflies themselves can no longer be taken for granted.

Threats to the monarchs started long ago, when people used to throw objects at them to make them fly. When monarchs overwinter in Pacific Grove, they often cling motionless to tree branches because they are incredibly sensitive to temperature. A 1959 booklet called *Mystery of the Monarchs* explains, "When seen in this manner, clinging together with folded wings almost hiding the foliage, they are a great disappointment to visitors who cannot discriminate between leaves, bark and butterflies." The fact that butterflies did not demonstrate their much-lauded beauty on demand for human visitors, tourists, or onlookers frustrated some. In the early 1900s, *Mystery of the Monarchs* continues, "humans, dissatisfied with observing them inactive during periods of inclement weather, their beautiful color folded into their wings, used to pelt them with sticks and stones to make them fly."[288]

In 1938—the year before the first Butterfly Parade took place—the citizens of Pacific Grove enacted a municipal ordinance to protect the creatures from such abuse. Pacific Grove was beginning to understand the value the butterflies brought to the community, so local lawmakers codified protections to reflect as much. That city ordinance, once described as "one of the country's most unusual pieces of legislation,"[289] stated: "It shall be unlawful and is hereby declared unlawful for any person to molest or interfere with in any way the peaceful occupancy of the Monarch Butterflies on their annual visit to Pacific Grove." The ordinance further prescribed a penalty of a five-hundred-dollar fine or imprisonment of six months in jail. There was only one exception if butterflies "choose to spend the winter clustering about some private home." In that case, the homeowner could work with the chief of police to relocate the unwelcome visitors.[290]

The earliest iteration of Butterfly Days used monarchs in the same way we have seen animals used elsewhere: captured from the wild for our entertainment. Organizers put on a pageant, where the local schoolchildren performed a butterfly dance, sang songs, and retold a legend about monarchs in an Indian village on Point Pinos.[291] As part of that pageant, author Lucy Neely McLane wrote, "hundreds of captive butterflies were released at the climax of the play to fly over the audience—an impressive and highly dramatic scene."[292] But by 1947, after the pageant was paused for the second World War and then revived, many residents of Pacific Grove found the use of live butterflies to be problematic: "Too many butterflies were blinded by the light and battered to death"[293] or "scorched in the stage lights."[294] Citing the unique ordinance prohibiting harm to monarchs, animal advocates charged the organizers with "butterfly murder" and eventually won the debate.[295] While the use of live butterflies ended, the parade continued on.

Beyond naive rascals with sticks and ignorant performers, monarchs face serious and omnipresent threats to their safety wherever they cluster in huge numbers, relatively defenseless, for the winter. When a storm arrives, or when weather patterns include more frosts than usual, these can have outsized impacts on an entire population of monarchs, killing thousands at a time. In 2002, for example, a storm in Mexico killed most of the butterflies in two of the largest overwintering colonies in the largest known mass die-off ever.[296] As climate change intensifies storms and changes weather patterns, the impact on butterflies may become harsher.

On a smaller scale, changes to the fragile composition of the overwintering sites can also have dramatic effects. In 2004 an eighty-five-year-old woman named Ann Thomas was killed in the Pacific Grove Monarch Sanctuary when a branch fell and hit her. In 2009, mindful of that history and trying to ensure the sanctuary's safety for human visitors, the city made what the mayor later admitted was a "horrible mistake" by cutting down old limbs and pruning the trees throughout the sanctuary. The cost of ensuring human safety in the sanctuary was, unfortunately, sacrificing the safety of the sanctuary for the monarchs; the pruning removed critical branches that filtered the sun, offered protection from wind, and created space for clusters to gather. The butterfly census that year counted only 793 monarchs, when the census at the same time the year before had counted more than 17,800.[297]

And it's not just the overwintering sites where monarchs face threats. On their migration, these butterflies rely on a supply of milk-weed plants to breed and nectar-producing plants to eat throughout their journeys. Pesticide use across the country has led to drastically reduced supplies of both. Particularly where corn and soybean crops span acres and acres of the country, spraying carcinogenic herbicides over those crops has destructive consequences for the other plant life that sustains the monarchs. Small-scale pesticide use affects monarchs too, even in homegrown gardens. Edenholm, who participates in the annual monarch counting efforts in the Pacific Grove Sanctuary, told me about an encounter she had with a monarch suffering from pesti-cide poisoning. "It probably went out to get nectar from someone's garden." She recounted seeing the butterfly "shaking on the ground," with "the wings flipped right side up, the wrong way, and the abdomen distended and curled up." She continued, "I knew it wasn't typical monarch behavior. It was pretty disturbing."

In light of these numerous and serious threats, the Center for Biological Diversity, together with partners including the Xerces Society, filed a petition in 2014 urging the Fish and Wildlife Service to officially list the monarch butterfly as "endangered."[298] Under the Endangered Species Act, a variety of conservation and protection mechanisms kick in when a species is officially listed as either "endangered" or "threatened." The Fish and Wildlife Service must create a recovery plan for the species and designate a critical habitat where additional protections are put into place. Listing is like an on-off switch. When a species is listed as endangered, it becomes illegal for anyone to "take" an individual member of that species. "Take" is a term of art that is defined in the statute to mean "harass, harm, pursue, hunt, shoot, wound, kill, trap, capture, or collect, or to attempt to engage in any such conduct."[299] Unlisted species, no matter how at risk they are, receive none of these protections.

The Endangered Species Act is one of the most powerful laws we have for protecting animals. In 1978, the Supreme Court famously decided that the presence of the snail darter, a tiny fish listed as endangered, rendered finishing construction on the multimillion-dollar Tellico Dam project in Tennessee illegal under the Endangered Species Act.[300] That listing on-off switch really does matter, it turns out: when it's flipped on, a tiny species can block massive infrastructure projects, but when it's flipped off, even our most beloved species continue to struggle and disappear without protection. While the monarchs were listed as endangered by the

International Union for Conservation of Nature in 2022, the move was largely symbolic; the American legal system does not make such international gestures actionable.[301]

In 2020 the Service finally issued a decision finding the listing of the monarchs was "warranted but precluded," meaning they found the plight of the species was grave, and they agreed that listing monarch butterflies was "warranted." However, they simultaneously decided that listing the monarchs was nevertheless "precluded by higher priority actions."[302] In late 2024, the Service at last took a step toward protecting monarchs. They proposed listing the species as threatened and sought public comment on the proposal.[303] But for now, the switch is still turned off for the monarchs, which means there are no federal legal protections for the species, so everyday harms—like heavy use of pesticides and insecticides, carbon emissions contributing to climate change, and land development—can continue unabated.

Even if monarchs are someday listed, protecting them from harm will still present a tricky challenge, both practically and legally. Unfortunately for the monarchs, the cause-and-effect chain of events is hard to pin down, in part because of the intergenerational migration that makes the species so special. What affects the population at one point in the journey may not become visible until later. For example, a drought affecting the availability of milkweed one year might not reveal itself in that year's butterfly counts, but the next year, the population at a certain overwintering site might hit record lows. Historically, the Endangered Species Act works best with respect to concrete and readily attributable harms, like blocking an action that would hurt a species in the immediate vicinity. The law is strong, but it is an imperfect vehicle to protect from harm that is not easily matched to an individual wrongdoer and may take generations to appear.

Even so, people care about monarch butterflies more than ever. You can see it in the proliferation of websites, festivals, proposed laws, and conservation efforts. Monarchs are a uniquely accessible species— they are not hidden in a forest, or atop a mountain, or at the bottom of a lake. They are in your backyard, eating your milkweed, or flying through your town once a year like clockwork. They are bright and flashy, and they move unlike anything else, sure to catch your eye and make you look. Their greatest weakness as a species—the very, very many places something can go wrong, from egg to caterpillar to butterfly, from inland to coast, from Canada to Mexico—is also their greatest asset: their range is almost everywhere, so we all have a chance to see them and to learn to care.

Without federal protections under the Endangered Species Act, local protections and conservation efforts take center stage. One major contribution Pacific Grove offers is in conducting annual butterfly counts to gather data about the species. The Pacific Grove Museum of Natural History and the Monarch Sanctuary work with volunteers to conduct weekly counts. It's a technical process that involves heading out at dawn (before it warms up enough for the butterflies to fly), learning how to spot clusters of butterflies, checking your counts against those of your neighbors, and ultimately coming up with a reasonably accurate number. It's harder than it sounds. As Natalie Johnston, the Natural History Museum's volunteer and community science coordinator, told me, the butterflies can look like "triangular pine cones," and learning to count by cluster instead of how we all learned as children takes some adjustment. But these annual counts provide critical data for the city and the scientific community at large. As I sat in the same sanctuary where they make these counts, I tried to imagine thousands of butterflies, wings tucked together, clinging to the trees. The effort to count them seemed tremendous.

After failing to see a butterfly in the sanctuary, and after learning more about the plight of monarchs and the numerous risks they face as a species and as individuals, a nagging and painful question surfaced: What will happen to Butterfly Days, or to the town's identity more generally, if the butterflies no longer visit Pacific Grove?

I had a vague idea. I had visited San Juan Capistrano, California, to attend the annual Swallows Day Parade, which similarly celebrates the return of migrating swallows to the old Spanish Mission building in the town, a phenomenon that used to happen every year around Saint Joseph's Day. In the 1940s Leon René wrote a song called "When the Swallows Come Back to Capistrano," first recorded by the Ink Spots and later by artists including Elvis Presley, solidifying the birds' relevance in popular culture.[304] Just as butterflies decorate Pacific Grove, swallow motifs and souvenirs with their pictures proliferated in downtown San Juan Capistrano. I planned on writing a chapter about this event, so I attended the parade and visited the Mission, hoping for the same kind of engagement with animals I had seen elsewhere.

But there were few swallows to be seen, either literally or symbolically. In the late 1990s the Mission underwent a restoration project that removed the swallows' nests. The swallows stopped returning in nearly the same numbers as in prior years, despite additional interventions like building man-made nests and laying tasty bait to try to draw the birds back to town.[305] In the absence of living swallows, I tried to focus on the symbolic ones. But the parade did not feature swallows or the story of their annual return. Only one or two floats even referenced the birds.

In some ways, the Swallows Day Parade might be a *post-animal* animal festival. The event still engaged the community, even without the animals. Attendees—including me—had a great time, and the local equestrian history was evident in the entirely horse-drawn parade. But the Swallows Day Parade felt a little shallow, divorced as it was from its original source of meaning. There was no attention paid to swallows at all. Revelers instead donned their best cowboy-inspired outfits and grabbed a beer to watch the festivities. It's true that a festival can do a world of good for a local community, regardless of the animal at its center. It's also true that the Swallows Day Parade was incredibly fun. But when an animal is an absent referent, a phantom limb, a dying species being pushed out of its habitat, throwing a festival in its name without acknowledging the change and loss seems myopic at best. I felt almost guilty about celebrating a phenomenon that no longer happens reliably because of us.

Pacific Grove isn't there yet. But the specter of the post-animal animal festival loomed large as I sat at the entrance of the empty butterfly sanctuary.

It is indisputable that animals everywhere are under serious threat: climate change, habitat loss, overuse, human ignorance and cruelty, and more wreak havoc on the lives of billions of creatures every day. Humans are not good at handling diffuse sources of harm. We like to point our finger, lay blame, and assign consequences. For every harm, there is a remedy; for every action, a stream of foreseeable effects. These concepts are built into the social structures we have designed. We assign liability through concepts like causation. But when there are multiple causes—perhaps infinite causes—of a given harm, what can we really do? When there are nearly eight billion individual polluters, humans who eat and drive and consume and dispose and dump and fly and burn, it may be ineffectual, even inequitable, to hold any one person accountable. Even as corporations profit off destruction, we consumers pump their gas, buy their meat, and air-condition our homes, diffusing and democratizing the blame among us all.

But the interconnectedness of our world is not solely a cause for distress; it's also a reason to hope. Just as the causes of harm are dispersed, so too are solutions available to each of us, wherever we are. Monarchs democratize science and conservation by taking them out of the ivory tower labs and courts and putting them into our own backyards. People can get involved easily, begin to compare what happens this year to what happened last year, and experiment with small efforts that make a big difference. Restoring native plants, for example, or not using harmful pesticides can have a positive effect that reverberates well beyond our yards.

"Monarchs utilize the entire ecosystem," Natalie Johnson, from the Pacific Grove Natural History Museum, explained to me when I asked her about conservation efforts underway in Pacific Grove. "They rest in the trees, they feed from the flowering plants, they even use the underbrush. So when someone tries to protect the monarchs, they're helping the entire ecosystem." The accessibility and visibility of the butterflies are a boon not just for monarchs but for the natural world as a whole. Johnson continued, "Monarchs are important conservation ambassadors because the things one does to help monarchs have good impacts for so many other species."

Small actions matter. Protecting one species may help more. It's not too late or too big to solve; we can all get involved. Every one of us, every day, makes decisions about how we will engage with the animals around us. We can choose to engage with them from a place of compassion and care, understanding our individual decisions reverberate.

A few weeks after we had left Pacific Grove, at the end of October, I woke up to an email from Edenholm, the author who volunteers as a butterfly counter in Pacific Grove: "I thought you'd enjoy hearing our first official count of the monarch season in Pacific Grove was 3,823 this morning!" That was over thirteen hundred more butterflies than were counted at the same time last year, and obviously well over the record-low of zero in 2020. I smiled as I tapped out a response on my phone, recalling the earnestness with which people had asked, as they entered the sanctuary and we made our way out, "Did you see any?" Today, people would.

Butterflies don't offer a simple metaphor—they are a living symbol, embodied proof of what we know to be true. Threats are everywhere, but so, too, are causes for hope. Earthbound caterpillars dissolve before reforming as a creature with flight. Butterflies adapt and find new havens, and humans watch, baffled, trying to figure out how they work. The unlikelihood of these processes is enough to make even skeptics feel something numinous at play.

These unlikely harbingers of philosophy give us a way to grapple with the inevitability of mortality. So we celebrate them for it. But the celebration should not be divorced from the animals themselves. Festivals that celebrate animals can encourage visitors to engage with the risks animals face, educate the public on harm reduction, and use funds to advocate for better protections. Pacific Grove offers an example of how we can use butterflies to tell our stories without harming them in the process. And even more importantly, Pacific Grove demonstrates how we can learn from our mistakes: from the first iteration of the parade and pageant, where humans accidentally killed dozens of butterflies, to the time less than a decade ago when humans wanting to watch the monarch miracle pruned away the very branches that sustained it, the community in Pacific Grove has adapted and corrected its relationship with the butterflies who share their home. And the work isn't done.

The truth is, we still don't understand what the monarchs know; we probably never will. But we humans gain so much from living on a planet with these small, orange insects who inspire us and teach us fundamental truths about being embodied on this earth: the struggle of life, the impermanence of death, the value of resilience, and the drive to move forward not just for ourselves but for our descendants. We should protect them, both for their sake and for ours. Our fates are intertwined.

A few hours before our flight out of town, my wife and I sat on a bench that overlooked the Pacific Ocean. We watched seagulls, pelicans, and sea otters loll in the surf. The coastline was forbidding, foamy sea crashing against the rocks. But the sun had burned away the fog, turning the water from indigo to cobalt, and now it was warm and bright on our faces. Every once in a while, massive groups of pelicans would fly up and away.

Our time in Pacific Grove had been cheerful and sweet. The community was warm and welcoming, and the parade was adorable and suffused with small-town charm. But I felt melancholic. My grandparents' absence was so acute here. At other festivals, I was curious about them. I thought about what they would have done on their trip, and I was almost objectively interested in what my grandmother would have written down or thought. But here, I missed them. This endearing town, with its humble parade and quaint events, made me reflect on everything an animal festival could be: a way to explore interspecies relationships based in reverence and hope.

Before long, an erratic shadow caught my eye. A single monarch butterfly, bright orange against the blue sky, flitted and swooped above our heads. I pointed it out to my wife, and we sat and watched it fly. *How?* I thought, incredulous. How does a creature like that travel so far? The mystery of the butterfly migration compounds when you watch the hapless and seemingly inefficient way they fly. These are not osprey, gliding and diving with a precision that stumps even the best human eyes. These are dainty, paper-like waifs, whose bodies plunge to a different part of the sky with every wing flap or gust of wind, what the poet William Butler Yeats described as a "zig-zag wantonness."[306] This lone ambassador of its species fought the ocean breeze valiantly as it made its way down the coast. More would follow soon.

As we watched it swoop and rise in the air, it moved away from us until it was only a dark pinprick in the sky, and then nothing. I inhaled deeply and grabbed my wife's hand. Whether it was a sign, a message from my departed grandmother, or just a serendipitous nature sighting, I can't say. I was just happy to see one of the first monarchs of the season. I wished it well on its journey as we stood up to make our own flight home.

SCOPES TRIAL PLAY AND FESTIVAL

DAYTON, TN

I arrived at the courthouse early on Friday evening and settled into my seat in the back row. According to the woman checking tickets, the show was nearly sold out. Dozens of people filed in as a slideshow of photographs from the original trial of John T. Scopes in 1925 rolled on a screen behind the judge's desk. The historic courtroom had been completely transformed into a theater: blackout shades blocked the waning daylight, air-conditioning mercifully protected us from the sweltering summer heat, and stage lights sat atop risers of seats in the gallery. Judging by the pleasant, drawling accents around me, I suspected I may have traveled the farthest to be there.

"All rise!" the bailiff instructed. We did, as the cast—the judge, lawyers, and defendant—entered and took their places around the courtroom. The twelve audience members who were chosen to stand in for jurors sat in the jury box on stage left, looking eager and proud to participate. And when the proceedings began with a prayer, just like they did in 1925, nearly everyone in the audience bowed their head unprompted. This play was not one an attendee could passively witness. To the contrary, the projection screen hanging above the judge's desk cued our reactions, adding depth to the play: "Hubbub" meant we needed to murmur; "Humor" meant we needed to laugh out loud; and calls for "Applause" and "Cheering" were self-explanatory.

This play was meant to be experienced, felt, and imagined, and the normal line between audience and performers was purposefully blurred. As such, it was supposed to feel real, like something was at stake for us too, even all these years later. The fact that the play took place in the historical courtroom only emphasized this blending of reality and performance: the actor performing the role of the judge sat at the same bench the real judge had, the men acting as prosecution and defense sat at the original counsel tables. The actors fanned themselves to portray the oppressive Tennessee heat of July, even as the air-conditioning thrummed along and kept us cool. Without that anachronism, it would have been easy to lose myself in the re-enactment.

In the summer of 1925, this very courtroom in Dayton, Tennessee, became the epicenter of an American media sensation for hosting the so-called "Monkey Trial," in which the state of Tennessee prosecuted the schoolteacher John T. Scopes for teaching evolution in schools. The Tennessee legislature had recently passed the Butler Act, named for the representative who introduced the bill, John Washington Butler. The act prohibited teachers in public schools from promoting "any theory that denies the story of the Divine Creation of man as taught in the Bible, and to teach instead that man has descended from a lower order of animals."[307] The ideological debates between creationism and evolution were intense at this time. One anti-evolution book published in 1922, for example, referred to the theory of evolution as the "ape-man hoax now scattering its corruptions throughout the world and impressing its deceptions upon the world's 'best minds.'"[308] Equally fervent were calls on the other side in defense of individual liberty and academic freedom to learn and teach evolution, free from the imposition of the state.[309] In this contentious climate, the Butler Act wouldn't stay on the books without a fight.

Following the passage of the Act, a then-nascent civil rights organization—the American Civil Liberties Union (ACLU)—placed an advertisement in the *Chattanooga Daily Times* seeking "a Tennessee teacher who is willing to accept our services in testing this law in the courts." The ad continued, "Our lawyers think a friendly test case can be arranged without costing a teacher his or her job. Distinguished counsel have volunteered their services. All we need now is a willing client."[310]

Enter John T. Scopes. In the story that has become legend, a group of townies in Dayton saw the advertisement and gathered at the local watering hole—a drugstore run by Frank Robinson, known as a "hustling druggist"[311]—to discuss the idea of Dayton hosting the test case. As serious as the national debates between fundamentalism and modernism were, the proposed trial would obviously be contrived. Neither Chattanooga nor Knoxville showed interest in the case, but Dayton—situated midway between the two and nestled in a beautiful, lush valley on the Trail of Tears—was facing a serious economic downturn and saw an opportunity for traffic and revenue in what would undoubtedly be a sensationalized trial.[312] From the beginning, everyone seemed to understand the trial as an unabashed publicity stunt, not merely a legal proceeding. Professor Ed Caudill, an expert on the Scopes Trial, described the trial to me in one simple word: "hucksterism."[313]

In his memoir, Scopes wrote about the conception of the trial in a chapter titled, naturally, "Getting Down to Monkey Business." The leader of that drugstore meeting, Dr. George Rappleyea, asked Scopes if he had taught evolution while substituting as a biology teacher. Scopes admitted to doing so, because, as he said, "you can't teach biology without teaching evolution."[314] The group of men asked if he would be willing to be arrested for violating the anti-evolution law to start the test case. Scopes, a twenty-four-year-old football coach and substitute teacher, agreed, but he was a reluctant hero who later described the trial as "just a drugstore discussion that got past control."[315]

Nevertheless, once Scopes agreed, Rappleyea sent word to the ACLU, which, in turn, agreed to finance the case. Scopes was arrested, and as the machinery of the court system began to churn, residents of the town of Dayton picked sides and prepared for the onslaught of the trial. For the defense, Clarence Darrow volunteered to lead the team. He was one of the best-known criminal trial lawyers in the country at the time, having defended accused killers Nathan Leopold and Richard Loeb in an infamous murder trial the year before.[316] Darrow felt personally invested in the fundamentalism-versus-modernism debate and was so eager to participate in the Scopes Trial that he offered free legal representation.[317] On the other side, William Jennings Bryan—a three-time Democratic presidential candidate and renowned orator—led the prosecution, in large part to further promote his personal support of populism.[318] This trial was, by all accounts, set to be a clash of titans.

On July 10, 1925, the "trial of the century" began. As the trial progressed and the procedural debates wore on, a carnival atmosphere swallowed the town of Dayton. Scopes himself described the "Monkey Trial" as a circus: "From the beginning to the end of the test case Ringling Brothers or Barnum and Bailey would have been pressed hard to produce more acts and sideshows and freaks than Dayton had."[319] Vendors sold souvenirs and knickknacks, hot dogs and sodas. Musicians played along the streets outside the courthouse. This was also the first trial to be broadcast live over the radio, expanding the reach of media attention around the country.[320]

On the afternoon of the seventh day of trial, the judge moved the proceedings to the lawn outside the courthouse, likely because of the heat, the overcrowded courtroom, and the excitement surrounding the closing arguments he knew everyone would be jockeying to see. Instead of progressing right to closing arguments, the defense surprised everyone and called William Jennings Bryan—the prosecutor himself—to the stand. Bryan agreed despite his cocounsels' objections and took the witness stand as the crowd swelled from hundreds to thousands in expectation of his testimony.[321]

This encounter between Darrow and Bryan was a microcosm of the entire trial. Religious freedom, local control, and fundamentalism were on the stand, with modernism and academic freedom firing question after question in an attempt to break down the logic of dogmatism. The trial was all about this moment: idea pitted against idea, both sides represented by celebrities, the whole country watching. Scopes himself was just the vehicle, his prosecution a technicality. The core of this trial was here, in the verbal sparring between Darrow and Bryan. As Bryan announced to applause from the spectators, "These gentlemen . . . did not come here to try this case. They came here to try revealed religion. I am here to defend it, and they can ask me any question they please."[322]

The ninety-minute examination began with Darrow asking Bryan, "You have given considerable study to the Bible, haven't you, Mr. Bryan?" to which Bryan responded, "Yes, sir, I have tried to." Darrow set some groundwork by asking, "Do you claim that everything in the Bible should be literally interpreted?" Bryan answered carefully: "I believe everything in the Bible should be accepted as it is given there; some of the Bible is given illustratively." Then Darrow proceeded to ask Bryan about particular beliefs and lessons from the Bible, starting with the story of the whale swallowing Jonah.

"You believe that the big fish was made to swallow Jonah?" Darrow asked.

"I am not prepared to say that. The Bible merely says it was done," Bryan demurred. "A miracle is a thing performed beyond what man can perform," he continued. "When you get beyond what man can do, you get within the realm of miracles; and it is just as easy to believe the miracle of Jonah as any other miracle in the Bible."

Darrow sought to clarify: "Perfectly easy to believe that [a whale] swallowed [Jonah]?"

"If the Bible said so," Bryan answered, before quipping, "the Bible doesn't make as extreme statements as evolutionists do."[323]

Darrow went on to question Bryan about Noah and the flood: "You believe that all the living things that were not contained in the ark were destroyed?" Bryan cleverly answered, "I think the fish may have lived."[324] They argued about the evidence for the age of the earth, the biblical account of the seven days of creation, and where Cain got his wife. Bryan defended the beliefs in these accounts vigorously, often garnering applause from the crowd. He concluded, "the only purpose Mr. Darrow has is to slur at the Bible, but I will answer his question. I will answer it all at once, and I have no objection in the world, I want the world to know that this man, who does not believe in a God, is trying to use a court in Tennessee to slur at it, and while it will require time, I am willing to take it."[325] The court adjourned for the day soon after, the questioning left unresolved.

The next morning, before the examination could continue, the judge struck Bryan's entire testimony from the record. He announced that "the testimony of Mr. Bryan can shed no light upon any issues that will be pending before the higher courts." Rather, he said, the simple and sole question at issue "is whether or not Mr. Scopes taught that man descended from a lower order of animals."[326] Given that ruling, Darrow capitulated. Darrow reiterated that Scopes had indeed taught evolution—which was never really in dispute—and asked the judge to instruct the jury to find him guilty of violating the statute.[327] The end of the trial was a letdown in light of the media hype and dramatized warnings about the clash between religion and science. The jury deliberated for nine minutes, returning a "guilty" verdict without even sitting down.[328]

It was not immediately clear who the "winner" of the trial was, though. As historian Edward Larson put it in his Pulitzer Prize–winning book about the trial, "the prosecution claimed a legal victory; the defense a moral one."[329] Popular reactions outside of the courtroom and around the country mattered almost more—to the debates, and to the legacy of the trial—than what happened to Scopes in particular. Perhaps because of the unsatisfying and uncertain legal outcome in 1925, the trial's meaning and legacy were left open to interpretation immediately after the verdict. Journalists and activists on both sides immediately began recasting the events in the media to fit their preferred agendas.[330]

Most famously, *Inherit the Wind*, a 1955 play and 1960 film adaptation, brought the trial back into public consciousness and sensationalized its story. In this telling, the fictionalized Dayton is filled with bumbling fundamentalists and townspeople with pitchforks pitted against the bastions of reason and modernity from the North. While the play and movie take pains to distinguish fact from fiction, changing people's names and locating the trial in a fictional town, the connection to the real-life trial was lost on no one. The huge popularity of the fictional retelling soon blurred into a mainstream narrative of the historical trial itself. Everyone I spoke with from Dayton—and many of the people my grandmother spoke with thirty years ago—took issue with how the film depicted the events, the town, and the outcome of the trial. The events were much more civil, and the sides much more balanced, than the movie depicts, they argue; Darrow and Bryan were friendly out of the courtroom, and the residents of Dayton welcomed Darrow and his colleagues warmly.[331] Nevertheless, *Inherit the Wind* continues to dominate the national mythology of the Scopes Trial.

The Scopes Trial Play and Festival that I traveled to Dayton for materialized from this battleground to claim the cultural legacy of the trial. In 1988 a producer arrived in Dayton intending to put on a production of *Inherit the Wind* in the Rhea County Courthouse. Instead, the producer met with Dr. Richard Cornelius, a professor at Bryan College, and realized that the legacy of the trial was more complex—and more interesting—than the Hollywood interpretation suggested. Rather than stage *Inherit the Wind*, the producer decided to write his own play to be more faithful to the transcripts of the actual trial. Two years later, the Scopes Trial Play and Festival was born, and the town of Dayton tried to revive the circus atmosphere of the 1925 trial. Musicians and vendors lined the streets outside the courthouse. There have been a series of plays put on over the years, all written by local writers and all telling the story of the Scopes Trial from different angles.[332] The play I traveled to Dayton to see was called *Monkey in the Middle*.

The audience around me laughed and nodded along as a modern cast reenacted that famous interrogation once again. As during the trial in 1925, the present-day audience seemed to understand that while the consequences of the debate were important, the combination of topic and medium—whether a trial then or a play now—invited extravagances and dramatics that made it fun. The transcript of the 1925 trial reveals the original proceedings were full of humor, despite the fact that this criminal trial took place in a setting that invited, even demanded, seriousness and professionalism. And as the lights came up for intermission and people stepped past me to buy a soda or popcorn from vendors in the hallway, the entertainment value of this whole monkey debate was hard to ignore. After all, there's something undeniably funny about thinking of your grandparents as chimps, even as that question cuts to the core of who we are as humans.

The Scopes Trial Play and Festival is remarkably resilient and adaptable. It has survived changes in leadership, new scripts, budgetary restrictions, and a global pandemic in turn. Bryan College put on the play for many years, and in 2014 the Rhea Heritage Preservation Foundation was created to protect and promote the history of the trial and the courthouse. Rick Dye, the president of the Rhea Heritage Preservation Foundation, explained to me that the foundation aims to expand the festival to generate interest in the history of the town. As part of that effort, the basement of the courthouse has been turned into a small museum, containing a handful of artifacts, including a copy of the biology textbook Scopes was convicted of teaching from.

The people who put on this festival, and who safeguard this history, care deeply about the facts of the trial and the legacy of everyone involved—both creationist and evolutionists alike. The town as a whole seems to identify with the trial. The hotel I stayed in, for example, named its conference room the Bryan Room. A stained-glass window at the Best Western down the street, where my grandmother had stayed on her visits to Dayton, depicted monkeys. I got coffee one morning at Jennings Coffee and Tea. The museum in town sells *A Field Guide to the Scopes Trial*, which offers a detailed map of the town along with "then" and "now" photograph comparisons of various spots. Commemorative plaques decorate the town too, indicating landmarks like the spot where Robinson's drugstore once stood. The lawn in front of the courthouse features two prominent statues: William Jennings Bryan on one side and Clarence Darrow on the other, forever representing opposing sides of an eternal debate.

The Scopes Trial captures too many tensions to name: local versus national control, majority rule versus tyranny of the few, fundamentalism versus progressivism, religion versus science. The arguments presented at the Monkey Trial continue to reverberate today. Our country is still caught between fundamentalism and liberalism, between minority and majority rule, and between religious dogmatism and academic freedom. There was no easy winner of the Scopes Trial, and there will not be today either. As the Bryan College librarian, Kevin Woodruff, summarized to me, "Americans are still asking these questions that were first asked in that courtroom in Dayton."

But to me, the Scopes Trial also explores another critical question: What makes a human different from an animal? When we review the history of the trial and of the play and festival, this issue emerges as a powerful, if underexamined, driver of the events.

The principal problem that the Butler Act, and Bryan, sought to prevent was the challenge that evolution posed to human exceptionalism. The Butler Act criminalized the teaching of "any theory that denies the story of the Divine Creation of man as taught in the Bible" in favor of "teach[ing] instead that man has descended from a lower order of animals." It follows, then, that teaching evolution as applied to plants or animals would not have violated the law. Bryan himself acquiesced that evolution as applied to plants and even "up to the highest form of animal" could be accepted "without raising a presumption that would compel us to give a brute origin to man."[333] No one cared if a dog evolved from a wolf, in other words; what angered people was the suggestion that humans were part of that schema. As a reporter noted at the time, "Hands off one thing and one thing alone: the divine creation of man, the human being with a soul."[334]

Since medieval times, Western culture has situated humanity squarely, and categorically, above nonhuman animals in the Great Chain of Being. Traditional Christian teaching maintains a teleological view of humanity, with humans as the ultimate capstone of seven days of creation, created in God's own image, separate and apart from the rest of the world. But the theory of evolution questioned anew, as Thomas Huxley put it, "man's place in nature" and fundamentally challenged this long-accepted hierarchy by blurring seemingly clear-cut lines.[335] Within evolutionary theory, when, exactly, did humans become *humans* and consequently separate themselves from the "lower order of animals"?

Considering humans to be just another type of animal was a demotion in this worldview, where the hierarchical relationship between animals and humans was foundational. As Bryan argued at the Scopes Trial, "the Christian believes man came from above, but the evolutionist believes he must have come from below," that is, "from a lower order of animals."[336] Evolution threatened the hierarchy altogether, which, in turn, threatened humanity's comfortable seat atop it.

American society more broadly still generally engages with animals from a place of superiority and treats efforts to change that paradigm as nonsensical at best, misanthropic at worst. For example, my grandmother's notes summarize a conversation she overheard when she was in town for the festival in 2000. A man recounted a night when his friend swerved the car they were driving to avoid hitting a squirrel; he wrecked the car and nearly killed them both. The man described being disgusted with his friend for caring about a squirrel, so much so that he got out of the car in a rage, intending to find and kill it himself.

My grandmother didn't write what she thought about this anecdote, but I identify with the driver in this story. I've experienced similar frustration in others when I've made decisions for the benefit of animals. While I was in law school, my peers often asked me, skepticism tinging their questions, why I cared about animals when so many humans suffer from injustice. At the end of law school, my classmates assigned each other "superlatives." Mine was "most likely to kill a human to save an animal." Though meant in jest, the superlative reveals the same stark reality my grandmother's story relays: caring about animals is often seen as a direct threat to human wellbeing. Animals and humans have long been placed on opposite sides of a neat species-based divide. Challenging that boundary by protecting animals seems to threaten the place of humans in the hierarchy, as if the world is zero-sum.

Bryan articulated this same thought over a hundred years ago. The theory of evolution questioned human superiority over animals, and, even more worrisome, it threatened to drag us down to the lowly level of beasts. He wrote,

> The Darwinian theory represents man as reaching his present perfection by the operation of the law of hate—the merciless law by which the strong crowd out and kill off the weak. If this is the law of our development then, if there is any logic that can bind the human mind, we shall

turn backward towards the beast in proportion
as we substitute the law of love.[337]

Evolution was not a neutral theory that described the state of the world; it was a dangerous theory that threatened to change it. Bryan believed that "if a man links himself in generations with the monkey, it then becomes an important question whether he is going towards him or coming from him."[338] Acknowledging evolution might mean destabilizing the parts of us that make us special: love, generosity, kindness, rationality, forgiveness. If we admit we are just predators, competing with each other for space at the watering hole, what reason would there be to promote goodness? On the other hand, if we do embrace our humanity and operate under Bryan's "law of love," might the animals, according to the logic of the survival of the fittest, overtake us in our weakness? Think of the residents in Sweetwater, justifying the slaughter of snakes with this exact "us-or-them" mentality; the fear of losing our place in this world to animals is, for some, all too real.

The question of what separates humans from animals was the crux of the controversies about evolutionary theory in the first place. It was also the beating heart of the Scopes Trial, which capitalized on the anxiety about the relationship between humans and animals—and between humans and primates, our closest relatives, in particular—by making monkeys the symbol for the trial. Dayton became known as "Monkey Town," or "Evolution Arena."[339] Newspapers frequently published cartoons about the trial featuring monkeys. Merchants decorated their shops with monkeys and apes. Robinson's drugstore sold drinks like "Simian Sodas."[340] Children purchased and played with monkey dolls.[341] On the fourth day of the trial, Bryan reportedly gave Darrow a monkey figurine as a souvenir of the case.[342] Even today, monkey symbolism continues to be a fundamental part of Dayton's identity. One night in town, I got a beer called "Survival of the Fittest" at Monkey Town Brewing Company (also on the menu: an IPA called "Evolutionary Theory"). Every time I drove downtown, I passed a mural of a monkey. The festival's marketing materials, T-shirts, and signage all featured cartoon monkeys.

Two actual apes were also brought to town in 1925. "Mindy the Monkey," a chimpanzee, was toted around the courthouse, and tourists and spectators could take photos with him or watch him play music on a tiny piano.[343] "Big Joe" was kept in a cage through which visitors could shake his hand.[344] The presence of these apes, and the attendees' reactions to them, demonstrates the obsession with differentiating humans from these creatures who look and act a lot like us, and the threat posed by blurring the lines between them and us. When one juror saw Big Joe, for example, he apparently exclaimed, "Well, I'll be dogged!" The ape's keeper responded, parroting Bryan's fears that the theory of evolution might send mankind spiraling backward: "That's just what it is, gentleman. That chimp is just man long ago gone to the dogs."[345]

This anecdote shows the core fear underlying the evolution debate: animality, a part of us we like to think we've tamed and domesticated, might still threaten to encroach on our own comfortably human lives if we're not diligent.

Animal festivals are one aspect of that diligence. At every event, the line between human and animal is tested and reinforced as humans flirt with animality, leaning into our animal selves, acting like the animals around us for a small period of time. At the Iditarod, mushers are on the trail with the dogs, enduring the elements together, lashed to the same sled. At the Rattlesnake Roundup and Maine Lobster Festival, attendees explore our carnivorous instincts and the thrill we get from being at the top of the food chain. We become one with the camels, ostriches, and frogs we're ambivalent about, mounting them or chasing them while adopting their gait. In Punxsutawney and Pacific Grove, we identify ourselves closely with aspects of animals we admire. At many of these festivals, people even dress up as the animals, donning costumes in the shape of worms, lobsters, groundhogs, or butterflies in turn. At all of them, we align ourselves, however briefly, with the animals in the center.

But when each festival wraps up, the human organizers and attendees go back to their fully human lives. After eating a snake or a lobster, the consumer tosses the refuse and goes about her day. After jumping a frog or racing an ostrich, the jockey stands up or dismounts on his own two feet again. After a weekend dedicated to a certain species, we find it difficult to change our behavior to benefit a species other than our own, despite our admiration. To affirm our humanity, we dip our toe into animality—but we always resurface. By testing the limits, we ultimately reaffirm the boundary between our human selves and our animal selves.

Despite the controversies I've pointed out, most of the animal festivals I visited while researching this book were, at the end of the day, fun, with parades, live music, themed food and drink, and creative souvenirs. I traveled to unique corners of the country I never imagined I'd visit. I met people who expressed infectious love for their homes and for their local history, who believe strongly in protecting and passing down the stories and traditions they have learned themselves. The festivals bring important revenue to small towns and often raise money for local schools, charities, or civic fundraisers. Participants and organizers alike look forward to them all year. These events carry immense importance.

But, of course, these festivals involve—and harm—real animals. In just the handful of festivals I visited during my research, thousands of snakes were hunted and slaughtered, and innumerable other creatures sharing their dens were likely killed too; six hundred dogs began a thousand-mile run to Nome through record warm temperatures; tens of thousands of lobsters were trapped and boiled alive; dozens of camels, ostriches, emus, and zebras were transported over a thousand miles before being mounted and kicked around a dusty track in the desert sun; hundreds of frogs were captured and terrified onstage; and groundhogs were kept in tiny enclosures for human merriment. And this list doesn't even begin to cover all of the other animals I saw during my research. In Pacific Grove, when we landed late at night for Butterfly Days, a half dozen deer skirted the windy road to our hotel. On my drive from Nashville to Dayton, I passed a massive poultry processing plant. In Sweetwater, a vendor offered photographs with a captive monkey held on a leash, and in Virginia City, a booth sold hands-on experiences with live owls. Animals are everywhere if you stop to notice them.

While the festivals in this book are prime examples of how we literally use animals to celebrate our own history and build community all across the country, they are by no means the only examples. This is not an isolated phenomenon or one found only in random pockets of the country but a widespread and common part of our daily lives. We use animals in ceremonial ways as we gather for important events. Pig roasts, clambakes, and barbecues, for example, are all types of human gatherings centered on the consumption of animal flesh. Many people scoff at the idea of Thanksgiving without eating a turkey, or Christmas or Easter without a ham. During the Super Bowl—where a "pigskin" is thrown around—people consume millions of chickens' wings. Many people go fishing or hunting as a beloved family event. Families go to zoos or aquariums for educational day trips.

Every one of us interacts with animals, sometimes multiple times a day, in ways both overt and hidden. We eat them as food; we wear their skin and feathers; we spoil them as our companions; we watch them on TV in quirky advertisements and on animated shows; we manage and kill them as pests in our houses and apartments; we hit them on highways; we use products and medicines tested on laboratory animals; we train them both as guides and as scouts. These animals include pigs, cows, chickens, fish, dogs, cats, horses, sheep, snakes, rats, mice, cockroaches, ants, mosquitos, rabbits, foxes, coyotes, deer, opossums, squirrels, chipmunks, birds, and more.

Even the most urban city dweller is not insulated. Consider waking up to eat breakfast and watch the morning news. Breakfast might include eggs and bacon, buttered toast, or cereal with milk, all of which come from animals. The apartment may have been treated for pests, but even so, there may be a mouse or a cockroach in the walls, and pigeons roam outside the door. On the local news might be a segment about a family who lost their dog and is offering a reward. When a commercial comes on, an emu or gecko might greet the viewer. When we get dressed, maybe we pull on leather shoes, a leather belt, or a wool sweater. Maybe our shampoo was tested on laboratory animals, or maybe our makeup has animal-derived ingredients. We don't have to go far afield to study human-animal relationships; even before we leave the house, animals are embedded into the quotidian fabric of our lives.

———————

Animal festivals are examples of living history, rituals played out every year to commemorate the past and project it into the future. In Dayton, nearly a hundred years after the monkey trial took place, felt this surreal time warp. Pulling into the historic downtown, I imagined this town in 1925: the heat and religious fervor are oppressive, and a circus barker totes a chimpanzee in a suit around town while vendors sell monkey-themed souvenirs. I pictured the same town in 2000, my grandfather driving down this exact stretch of road in a white button-down and loafers while my grandmother takes notes in a small yellow notebook, noticing the horse-drawn carriage pulling tourists down the street. And here I was, in the twenty-first century, sipping my iced coffee as I made my way in my rented Hyundai to the old courthouse, where actors performed lines pulled from the original trial itself. The past is purposefully present at these festivals.

And at each of these events, humans use animals to tell stories about who we are as humans. We want to teach our children what we know about the world, to remember and honor our heritage, and to have fun while doing it. These festivals do all of that. In Texas parents teach kids how to master a fear of snakes, invoking a pioneer past when rattlesnakes threatened homesteads. In California families compete and trade secrets about frog jumping techniques. In Alaska parents teach kids about dog mushing and its role in the state's history as they lift them onto their shoulders for a better view of the sleds. These festivals are opportunities to instruct, reiterate, and pass down cultural mythology and assumptions about animals. The past is renewed in the present when we re-create it every year.

But tradition is not an everlasting defense. Humans have rebuilt our world many times, giving up traditions we once thought integral to our society in light of ever-expanding views of equality and justice. Maybe it's time we think about extending some of these principles to animals, instead of doubling down on traditions that seem to have overripened into something slightly rotten. Just because an event made sense fifty or a hundred years ago doesn't mean we have to continue it now, in the same form, to the detriment of animals. We can honor the past while moving forward.

To many, both in 1925 and today, the idea that humans might not be fundamentally different from animals is anathema. Humans think of ourselves as superior to animals. We use animals for endless purposes: food, clothing, companionship, humor, entertainment, scapegoats, religious objects, and more. We would never treat another human the way we treat most animals, because we view humans as morally superior. The differentiation between humans and animals is part of what allows us to use animals without guilt. But if we admit that humans *are* animals, if we understand that our experiences of pain and joy and sadness and love are not fundamentally different from animals' experiences of those same feelings, the justifications for treating animals differently (and poorly) crumble. It would mean we aren't as superior as we think we are.

So we continuously fight against thinking of ourselves as animals, asserting instead that being a human is supposed to mean something special. We insist we are *more* than our animal instincts, *more* than our emotional connection to the past, *more* than our mere desires. Bryan captured this sentiment in his speech, simply titled "Man," when he wrote: "Man must be more than a perfect animal; he does not rise above the level of the beast if he permits his thoughts to rest entirely upon blood, and bone and muscle."[346] Maybe Bryan was right. But if we are going to claim to rise above our animal selves, I think we need to lead with the best of our human selves. Rather than worrying about animality sucking us down in a dark undertow, I wonder what it would mean instead to extend core aspects of humanity—like dignity and intrinsic moral worth—to animals. If animality is a threat, I think humanity might be the answer.

This book proceeds from dominance to humor to reverence, from the most obvious examples of harm and mastery over animals to a possible model for future human-animal relationships based on respect, protection, and individual dignity. This is a journey we can all make. Every one of us can reconsider our relationships with animals, shifting our mindset from one of commodification, dominance, or ambivalence to one of respect. We don't have to lose who we are, and we don't have to give up our traditions. We just have to remember who pays the price and decide to honor our past in a different, more humane way. We can renegotiate our relationship with that past; we don't have to be beholden to it. If we truly are more than our animal selves, I believe that means we can overcome our impulses to cling to our history and find a better way to celebrate it. This is the project of life: moving forward, getting better, learning and growing. It's not a loss or an admission of defeat, and it doesn't have to be a condemnation of those who came before. It's just change. It's growth. It's progress, rooted equally in humility and hope.

I spent so much time thinking I could not write this book because I wouldn't write it the way my grandmother would have. I am not an objective anthropologist, like she was. I have a strong interest in protecting animals, changing how the world treats them, and persuading people to think of them as fellow creatures rather than as objects. My grandparents ate meat; my grandfather loved seeing circus animals; they both deeply enjoyed some of the events in this book I found hard to watch. I thought that honoring my grandmother's work meant I couldn't write this book the way I wanted to, because I knew I would say something different from what she had in mind.

But I was wrong. Through writing this book, I've connected to my family's past, learned how my grandmother thought about animals, and explored the legacy of compassion and curiosity I have been lucky enough to receive. But I've also felt emboldened, as a thinker in this particular moment, buoyed by all that came before me to emit this message of compassion to the world. Someday I hope my grandchildren move beyond what I have done, pick up the baton, and run forward. I don't want them trapped in the limits of where I exist today. I don't think our grandparents would have wanted that either. There is love in this process, and forgiveness. There is grace, and courage. Just because things have been done a certain way for a long time does not doom us to repetition. Change is not always a rebuke of the past; it can be a revived commitment to a better future.

MORE ANIMAL FESTIVALS

Below is an inexhaustive list of animal festivals that occur every year throughout the US.

JANUARY
- National Western Stock Show (Denver, CO)
- Montana Winter Fair Skijoring (Bozeman, MT)

FEBRUARY
- Groundhog Day (Punxsutawney, PA)
- Hashknife Pony Express (Scottsdale, AZ)
- Chicken Roping (Moorcroft, WY)
- Goldens in Golden (Golden, CO)
- Whale Festival (Mendocino, CA)
- Hatteras Village Waterfowl Festival (Hatteras, NC)

MARCH
- Iditarod Trail Sled Dog Race and Fur Rendezvous (Anchorage, AK)

- Rattlesnake Roundup (Sweetwater, TX)
- Swallows Day Parade and Festival (San Juan Capistrano, CA)
- Buzzard Day (Hinckley, OH)
- Dana Point Festival of Whales (Dana Point, CA)
- Wild Chicken Festival (Fitzgerald, GA)
- Mule Day (Columbia, TN)
- Ostrich Festival (Chandler, AZ)
- Ocelot Conservation Day (Brownsville, TX)
- Whigham Rattlesnake Roundup (Whigham, GA)
- Rattlesnake & Wildlife Festival (Claxton, GA)
- Opp Rattlesnake Rodeo (Opp, AL)
- World Championship Rattlesnake Races (San Patricio, TX)

APRIL

- Prairie Chicken Festivals (KS, WI)
- Blessing of the Fleet (Darien, GA)
- Apache Rattlesnake Festival (Apache, OK)

MAY

- Jumping Frog Jubilee (Angels Camp, CA)
- Kachemak Bay Shorebird Festival (Homer, AK)
- Duckling Day (Boston, MA)
- Southern Ute Bear Dance (Ignacio, CO)
- Mule Days (Bishop, CA)
- Horned Toad Derby (Coalinga, CA)
- Willows Lamb Derby (Willows, CA)
- Indiana Dunes Birding Festival (Porter, IN)
- Blue Crab Festival (Little River, SC)
- Kentucky Derby (Louisville, KY)
- Soldier Hollow Classic (Midway, UT)

JUNE

- World's Oldest Rodeo (Prescott, AZ)
- Noxen Rattlesnake Roundup (Noxen, PA)
- Meridian Dairy Days (Meridian, ID)
- Acadia Birding Festival (Mount Desert Island, ME)

JULY

- Slug Fest (Tacoma, WA)
- Sedona Hummingbird Festival (Sedona, AZ)
- SharkCon (Tampa, FL)
- Frontier Days (Cheyenne, WY)
- World's Largest Salmon BBQ (Fort Bragg, CA)
- Alabama Deep Sea Fishing Rodeo (Dauphin Island, AL)
- Chincoteague Pony Swim (Chincoteague, VA)

AUGUST

- Maine Lobster Festival (Rockland, ME)
- Omak Stampede and Suicide Race (Omak, WA)
- Wausau Possum Festival (Wausau, FL)
- Yurok Salmon Festival (Klamath, CA)
- Fisherman's Feast (Boston, MA)

SEPTEMBER

- International Camel & Ostrich Races (Virginia City, NV)
- Llama Show at The Big E (West Springfield, MA)
- American Royal World Series of Barbecue (Kansas City, MO)
- Butterflies in the Pass Monarch Festival (Pass Christian, MS)
- Original Lobster Festival (Fountain Valley, CA)
- Woollybear Festival (Vermilion, OH)

OCTOBER

- Butterfly Days Festival and Parade (Pacific Grove, CA)
- Monarch Butterfly & Pollinator Festival (San Antonio, TX)
- Woolly Worm Festival (Banner Elk, NC)
- Trailing of the Sheep Festival (Hailey, ID)
- U.S. National Oyster Festival (Saint Mary's County, MD)
- New York State Sheep & Wool Festival (Rhinebeck, NY)

NOVEMBER

- Alaska Bald Eagle Festival (Haines, AK)
- Turkey Pardon (Washington, DC)
- Waterfowl Festival (Easton, MD)

DECEMBER

- Issaquah Reindeer Festival (Issaquah, WA)

ADDITIONAL EVENTS

- 4H/FFA Fairs
- State Fairs
- Rodeos and Livestock Shows
- Fishing Contests
- Hunting Contests
- Live Nativities

SELECT INTERNATIONAL EVENTS

- Palio Horse Race (Italy)
- Grindadrap Whale Hunt (Faroe Islands)
- Ieper Cat Festival (Belgium)
- Cat Slaughter (New Zealand)
- Puck Faire (Ireland)

- Running of the Bulls (Spain)
- Woofstock (Canada)
- Appleby Horse Fair (England)
- 'Obby 'Oss Festival (England)
- Monkey Buffet (Thailand)
- Jaipur Elephant Festival (India)
- Tihar Festival (Nepal)
- Rabbit Hopping (Denmark)
- Gadhimai Festival (Nepal)
- Snail Races (England)

ANCIENT FESTIVALS

- Medieval Feast of the Ass (Beauvais, France)
- Lupercalia (Rome, Italy)
- Ritual Slaughter and Sacrifice Practices (Worldwide)

NOTES

PREFACE

1   Nancy Meyer, *Festivals of the West* (Ward Ritchie Press, 1975), 7.

IDITAROD TRAIL SLED DOG RACE

2   "Iditarod Trail History," U.S. Bureau of Land Management, https://www.blm.gov/programs/national-conservation-lands/national-scenic-and-historic-trails/iditarod/history.

3   *See generally* Gay Salisbury and Laney Salisbury, *The Cruelest Miles: The Heroic Story of Dogs and Men in a Race Against an Epidemic* (W. W. Norton, 2005).

4   Christopher Klein, "The Sled Dog Relay That Inspired the Iditarod," History.com (website), March 10, 2014, https://www.history.com/news/the-sled-dog-relay-that-inspired-the-iditarod.

5   Ibid.

6   "Balto," Centralpark.com, https://www.centralpark.com/things-to-do/attractions/balto/.

7   Don Bowers, "Iditarod Race History," Iditarod: The Last Great Race, Iditarod Trail Committee, 2020, https://iditarod.com/race-history/.

8   Ibid.

9   "Third Dog Dies in the 2024 Iditarod," *Anchorage Daily News*, March 12, 2024, https://www.adn.com/outdoors-adventure/iditarod/2024/03/12/third-dog-dies-in-the-2024-iditarod/.

10   Shad Clark, "The Iditarod: How Long Is It and How Many Dogs Die in the Race?" *Sentient*, July 29, 2022, https://sentientmedia.org/iditarod/.

11   Alaska Stat. § 11.61.140(a)(1), (e).

12   "Official Rules 2025, Rule 17," Iditarod Trail International Sled Dog Race, https://cloud.iditarod.com/wp-content/uploads/2024/06/2025-Iditarod-Race-Rules.pdf?eeb77a0b.

13   "Official Rules 2025, Rule 37," Iditarod Trail International Sled Dog Race, https://cloud.iditarod.com/wp-content/uploads/2024/06/2025-Iditarod-Race-Rules.pdf?eeb77a0b.

14   Zachariah Hughes, "3 Iditarod finishers receive penalties for sheltering dogs indoors during fierce windstorms," *Anchorage Daily News*, March 26, 2022, https://www.adn.com/outdoors-adventure/iditarod/2022/03/25/3-iditarod-finishers-receive-penalties-for-sheltering-dogs-indoors-during-fierce-windstorms/.

15   Alicia DelGallo, "Iconic Sled Dog Race at Risk. Iditarod's Economic and Environmental Challenges Stack Up," *USA Today*, March 2, 2023, https://www.usatoday.com/story/sports/2023/03/02/iditarod-2023-worlds-most-famous-sled-dog-race-faces-challenges/11381992002/.

16   Mark Thiessen, "'A Little Scary': Iditarod begins with smallest field ever," *Boston Globe*, March 1, 2023, https://www.bostonglobe.com/2023/03/01/nation/little-scary-iditarod-begins-with-smallest-field-ever/?event=event12.

17   Allison Chinchar, "Iditarod route changed due to lack of snow," CNN.com, March 5, 2017, https://www.cnn.com/2017/03/05/us/weather-iditarod-race-moved-north/index.html.

18   Salisbury, *The Cruelest Miles*, 252–253.

19   2023 Official Race Guide of the Iditarod Trail Committee, 8.

20   "Leaders in Dog Care," Iditarod (website), Iditarod Trail Committee, https://iditarod.com/leaders-in-dog-care/.

21   Melanie Challenger, "How 'Being Animal' Could Help Us Be Better Humans," interview by Ezra Klein, *New York Times: The Ezra Klein Show*, June 27, 2023, https://www.nytimes.com/2023/06/27/opinion/ezra-klein-podcast-melanie-challenger.html.

22   "Running of the Reindeer," Fur Rondy (website), Greater Anchorage, Inc., https://www.furrondy.net/events/running-of-the-reindeer/.

23   Final Race Standings, Iditarod (website), Iditarod Trail Committee, https://iditarod.com/race/2023/standings/.

24   Mark Thiessen, "Grandson of Iditarod co-founder wins Alaska sled dog race," Associated Press, March 14, 2023, https://apnews.com/article/iditarod-2023-ryan-redington-wins-a9b7d7a789bf032e3d1538058901b249.

RATTLESNAKE ROUNDUP

25   Emalee Arroyo and Rachael Connelly, dir., *Miss Snake Charmer.* A Misspent Day, 2018. At 12:03, https://www.misssnakecharmermovie.com.

26   Jack Kilmon and Hooper Shelton, *Rattlesnakes in America and A History of the Sweetwater Jaycees Rattlesnake Roundup* (Shelton Press, 1981), 106–107.

27   Ibid., 186.

28   Ted Williams, "Despite Criticism, the Last of the Rattlesnake Roundups

Hang On," *Yale Environmental 360*, June 4, 2024, https://e360.yale.edu/features/rattlesnake-roundups.

29   "Snake Hunters," Sweetwater Jaycees, http://www.rattlesnakeroundup.net/snake-hunters.html.

30   Eleanor Cummins, "Rattlesnake roundups are a southern tradition. They're also an ecological disaster," *Popular Science*, March 8, 2019, https://www.popsci.com/rattlesnake-roundup-ecology-gassing/.

31   Jo-Anne McArthur, *The Wall of Shame*, 2019, photograph, Natural History Museum, https://www.nhm.ac.uk/wpy/gallery/2019-the-wall-of-shame.

32   Jakub Polák et al., "Fear the Serpent: A Psychometric Study of Snake Phobia," *Psychiatry Research* vol. 242 (August 1, 2016), 163–168, https://www.sciencedirect.com/science/article/abs/pii/S0165178115306211?via%3Dihub; Taylor Orth, "Three in 10 Americans fear snakes—and most who do fear them a great deal," YouGov, June 16, 2022, https://today.yougov.com/society/articles/42863-americans-fear-snakes-heights-spiders-poll; Brittany Brookshire, *Pests: How Humans Create Animal Villains* (Ecco, 2022), 34.

33   *See, e.g.,* Vanessa LoBue, "Why So Many People Fear Spiders and Snakes," *Psychology Today*, October 11, 2021, https://www.psychologytoday.com/us/blog/the-baby-scientist/202110/why-so-many-people-fear-spiders-and-snakes; Carl Zimmer, "Afraid of Snakes? Your Pulvinar May Be to Blame," *New York Times*, October 31, 2013, https://www.nytimes.com/2013/10/31/science/afraid-of-snakes-your-pulvinar-may-be-to-blame.html.

34   LoBue, "Why So Many People Fear Spiders and Snakes," https://www.psychologytoday.com/us/blog/the-baby-scientist/202110/why-so-many-people-fear-spiders-and-snakes.

35   "Rattlesnake Conservation in Massachusetts," Mass. Division of Fisheries and Wildlife, https://www.mass.gov/info-details/rattlesnake-conservation-in-massachusetts.

36   Christopher Irmscher, *The Poetics of Natural History* (Rutgers University Press, 2019), 159, 162, 166.

37   Ibid., 165.

38   J. Frank Dobie, *Rattlesnakes* (Little, Brown, 1965), 19–20.

39   Ibid., 60.

40   Irmscher, *The Poetics of Natural History*, 169.

41   Chris Mattison, *Rattler! A Natural History of Rattlesnakes* (Blandford, 1998), 85.

42   Brookshire, *Pests*, 52.

43   "Venomous Snakes at Work," The National Institute for Safety and Health, Centers for Disease Control and Prevention, August 28, 2024, https://www.cdc.gov/niosh/outdoor-workers/about/venomous-snakes.html?CDC_AAref_Val=https://www.cdc.gov/niosh/topics/snakes//.

44   Greg Pauly "Misplaced Fears: Rattlesnakes Are Not as Dangerous as Ladders, Trees, Dogs, or Large TVs," Natural History Museum of Los Angeles County, https://nhm.org/stories/misplaced-fears-rattlesnakes-are-not-dangerous-ladders-trees-dogs-or-large-tvs.

45   Ibid.; see also Willis Wingert and Linda Chan, "Rattlesnake Bites in Southern California and Rationale for Recommended Treatment," *The Western Journal of Medicine* (January 1988), https://www.ncbi.nlm.nih.gov/pmc/articles/PMC1026007/pdf/westjmed00137-0039.pdf; Wes Siler, "Let's Talk about Snakebites," *Outside*, May 9, 2018, https://www.outsideonline.com/outdoor-adventure/exploration-survival/lets-talk-about-snakebites/.

46   "Wisconsin's Largest Coyote Killing Contest Exposed by Undercover Activists," Wolf Patrol, March 13, 2021, https://wolfpatrol.org/2021/03/13/wisconsins-largest-coyote-killing-contest-exposed-by-undercover-activists/; "Facts about Wildlife Killing Contests," The Humane Society of the United States, https://www.humanesociety.org/wildlifekillingcontests; "Killing Contests," Animal Legal Defense Fund, https://aldf.org/issue/killing-contests-and-the-law/.

47   John Kopp, "Pennsylvania Clings to Pigeon Shoots That Have Nearly Vanished Nationwide," *Philly Voice*, June 5, 2017, https://www.phillyvoice.com/pennsylvania-clings-to-pigeon-shoots-that-have-nearly-vanished-nationwide/.

48   "New York Ends Wildlife Killing Contests," Animal Legal Defense Fund, January 5, 2024, https://aldf.org/article/new-york-ends-wildlife-killing-contests/.

49   Abigail Jones, "State Capitol sees slithery visitors this week. Here's why," KXAN, February 14, 2023, https://www.kxan.com/news/texas/state-capitol-sees-slithery-visitors-this-week-heres-why/.

50   Brandi Addison, "Sweetwater's Rattlesnake Roundup is this week. Snake advocates are pushing for change," *Lubbock Avalanche-Journal*, March 9, 2023, https://www.lubbockonline.com/story/news/environment/2023/03/09/sweetwater-rattlesnake-roundup-this-week-snake-advocates-push-change/69984675007/.

51   Arroyo and Connelly, *Miss Snake Charmer*, at 2:01.

52   Ellis Garvin, "Do Baby Rattlesnakes Stay with Their Mom? (For How Long?)," Rattlesnake HQ, https://rattlesnakehq.com/do-baby-rattlesnakes-stay-with-mom/.

53   "Petition to Ban Use of Gasoline and Other Toxic Substances to Hunt Snakes," Center for Biological Diversity, et al., March 8, 2016, https://www.biologicaldiversity.org/campaigns/outlawing_rattlesnake_roundups/pdfs/Texas_gassing_petition_3_8_2016.pdf.

54   Julia Sewing, "Researchers question the ethics of Sweetwater's Rattlesnake Roundup," KTTZ, March 17, 2023, https://radio.kttz.org/2023-03-17/researchers-question-the-ethics-of-sweetwaters-rattlesnake-roundup. See also "Rattlesnake Roundups Fact Sheet," Advocates for Snake Preservation, https://www.rattlesnakeroundups.com/wp-content/uploads/2018/01/RattlesnakeRoundups.pdf.

55   *See* Manny Rubio, *Rattlesnake: Portrait of a Predator* (Smithsonian Institution Press, 1998), 153–154.

56   *See, e.g.,* "Humane Killing Methods for Nonnative Reptiles," Florida Fish and Wildlife Conservation Commission, https://myfwc.com/wildlifehabitats/nonnatives/python/humane-killing-methods/.

57   Sewing, "Researchers question the ethics . . ." https://radio.kttz.org/2023-03-17/researchers-question-the-ethics-of-sweetwaters-rattlesnake-roundup.

58   "Rattlesnake Love Letters," Rattlesnake Roundups, Advocates for Snake Preservation, https://www.rattlesnakeroundups.com/love-letters/.

59   Press Release: "Last Rattlesnake Roundup in Georgia Replaced by Humane Wildlife Festival," Center for Biological Diversity, February 28, 2022, https://biologicaldiversity.org/w/news/press-releases/last-rattlesnake-round-up-in-georgia-replaced-by-humane-wildlife-festival-2022-02-28/.

60   Lizzie Chen, "Rattlesnake Roundup: A Texas Community Tradition," NPR, April 3, 2020, https://www.npr.org/sections/picture-show/2020/04/03/821397097/rattlesnake-roundup-a-texas-community-tradition.

61   Jack Weir, "The Sweetwater Roundup: A Case Study in Environmental Ethics," *Conservation Biology*, vol. 6, no. 1 (March 1992): 123–125.

MAINE LOBSTER FESTIVAL

62   Christopher White, *The Last Lobster: Boom or Bust for Maine's Greatest Fishery?* (St. Martin's, 2018), 2.

63   History.com Staff, "7 Things You May Not Know About Lobsters and Their History," History.com, September 29, 2023, https://www.history.com/news/a-taste-of-lobster-history.

64   David Foster Wallace, *Consider the Lobster* (Back Bay Books, 2006), 238.

65   "7 Things You May Not Know About Lobsters and Their History," https://www.history.com/news/a-taste-of-lobster-history.

66   Nathaniel Lee and Abby Tang, "Here's why we boil lobsters alive," *Business Insider*, April 11, 2018, https://www.businessinsider.com/why-we-boil-lobsters-alive-2018-4.

67   "A Lobstering Life: Meet the Coombs," *The Maine Thing Quarterly: Lobster Issue*, Maine Office of Tourism, https://visitmaine.com/quarterly/lobster/lobstering-life.

68   James Acheson, *The Lobster Gangs of Maine* (University Press of New England, 1988), 9.

69   Trevor Corson, *The Secret Life of Lobsters* (Harper Perennial, 2004), 34–35, 48.

70   Ibid., 38.

71   Ann Backus et al., "Dangers of Entanglement during Lobstering," National Institute for Occupational Safety and Health, *Workplace Solutions* (August 2005), https://www.cdc.gov/niosh/docs/wp-solutions/2005-137/pdfs/2005-137.pdf.

72   Corson, *The Secret Life of Lobsters*, 4.

73   Acheson, *The Lobster Gangs of Maine*, 1–2.

74   Ibid., 3; "Women Are Lobster Fishing and We're Excited About It," *Maine Lobster Now*, March 2, 2021, https://www.mainelobsternow.com/blog/women-in-lobster-fishing; Lobster Institute, University of Maine, https://umaine.edu/lobsterinstitute/educational-resources/job-descriptions/.

75   "Lobster," *The Maine Thing Quarterly: Lobster Issue*, https://visitmaine.com/quarterly/lobster.

76   "Maine Lobster Fact Sheet," Maine Lobster (website), https://lobsterfrommaine.com/article/maine-lobster-fact-sheet/; "American Lobster," NOAA Fisheries (website), https://www.fisheries.noaa.gov/species/american-lobster.

77   Melissa Waterman, "Lobster's claw-hold on Maine is strong," Island Institute (website), July 6, 2022, https://www.islandinstitute.org/working-waterfront/lobsters-claw-hold-on-maine-is-strong/.

78   Thomas Gibbons-Neff, "For Maine Lobstermen, a Perfect Storm Threatens the Summer Season," *New York Times*, July 3, 2020, https://www.nytimes.com/2020/07/03/us/maine-lobster-summer-virus.html.

79   Corson, *The Secret Life of Lobsters*, 212.

80   Maine Rev. Stat. Title 12, Part 9, Subpart 2, Chapter 619, § 6431.

81   Corson, *The Secret Life of Lobsters*, 134–135; Patrick Whittle, "Legal sizes for lobsters could change to protect population," *News Center Maine*, February 6, 2023, https://www.newscentermaine.com/article/news/local/lobster-regulations-maine-legal-sizes-for-lobsters-could-change-to-protect-population-new-england/97-9ee0768b-8e1c-40cd-982a-ffc5f7d783f6.

82   Frankie Adkins, "Not for the pot: how 'V-notching' lobsters may help save them," *The Guardian*, April 6, 2023, https://www.theguardian.com/environment/2023/apr/06/not-for-the-pot-how-vnotch-lobsters-tails-may-save-way-of-life/.

83   Corson, *The Secret Life of Lobsters*, 101; Jessica Hall, "V-notched lobster decline is a threatening sign in Maine," *Portland Press Herald*, May 8, 2014, https://www.pressherald.com/2014/05/08/v-notch_decline_is_a_threatening_sign_/.

84   Jacob Knowles (@jacob_knowles), "Another day at the claw spa," TikTok, September 2, 2023, https://www.tiktok.com/@jacob__knowles/video/7274310525163523370.

85   "American Lobster," NOAA Fisheries (website), https://www.fisheries.noaa.gov/species/american-lobster.

86   "American Lobster," Atlantic States Marine Fisheries Commission, http://www.asmfc.org/species/american-lobster#contacts.

87   Michael Levenson, "Whole Foods to Stop Buying Maine Lobster Amid Risk to Endangered Whales," *New York Times*, November 28, 2022, https://www.nytimes.com/2022/11/28/us/whole-foods-lobster-maine-whales.html.

88   Francine Kershaw, "Experts Advise Administration on Right Whale Entanglement," NRDC, May 19, 2022, https://www.nrdc.org/bio/francine-kershaw/experts-advise-administration-right-whale-entanglement.

89   "Women Who Help Entangled Whales," NOAA Fisheries (website), July 10, 2023, https://www.fisheries.noaa.gov/feature-story/women-who-help-entangled-whales.

90   "North Atlantic Right Whale Updates," NOAA Fisheries, https://www.fisheries.noaa.gov/national/endangered-species-conservation/north-atlantic-right-whale-updates.

91   "NOAA Fisheries Announces New Lobster and Jonah Crab Fisheries Regulations to Help Save Endangered North Atlantic Right Whales," NOAA Fisheries, August 31, 2021, https://www.fisheries.noaa.gov/media-release/noaa-fisheries-announces-new-lobster-and-jonah-crab-fisheries-regulations-help-save.

92   *Financial Impact of Transitioning Two Sectors of the Northeast Lobster Fishery to On-Demand (Ropeless) Fishing*, Conservation Law Foundation (March 2023), https://www.clf.org/wp-content/uploads/2023/03/CLF-Economic-Analysis-On-Demand-Fishing_FINAL-03_2023.pdf.

93   Angus King, "What Sustainable Seafood Activists Get Wrong about Maine's Lobsters," *Time* magazine, September 21, 2022, https://time.com/6215218/sustainable-seafood-activists-get-wrong-maines-lobsters/.

94   Levenson, "Whole Foods to Stop Buying Maine Lobster," https://www.nytimes.com/2022/11/28/us/whole-foods-lobster-maine-whales.html.

95   Marine Stewardship Council, "MSC Certificate suspended for Gulf of Maine lobster fishery," press release, November 16, 2022, https://www.msc.org/en-us/media-center/news-media/news/msc-certificate-suspended-for-gulf-of-maine-lobster-fishery.

96   Annie Roth, "To Save Whales, Don't Eat Lobster, Watchdog Group Says," *New York Times*, September 13, 2022, https://www.nytimes.com/2022/09/13/science/lobsters-right-whales-maine.html.

97   Levenson, "Whole Foods to Stop Buying Maine Lobster," https://www.nytimes.com/2022/11/28/us/whole-foods-lobster-maine-whales.html.

98   "What Can You Do to Support Maine Lobstermen?" Maine Lobster Festival (blog), https://mainelobsterfestival.com/blog/2022/10/28/what-can-you-do-to-support-maine-lobstermen/.

99   "The World's Largest Lobster Cooker Returns to the Maine Lobster Festival," *Maine Lobster Festival* (blog), June 1, 2018, https://mainelobsterfestival.com/blog/2018/06/01/worlds-greatest-lobster-cooker-returns-maine-lobster-festival/.

100   Corson, *The Secret Life of Lobsters*, 275.

101   The Lobster Institute, "Do Lobsters Feel Pain?" Cape Porpoise Lobster (website), https://www.capeporpoiselobster.com/do-lobsters-feel-pain/.

102   Corson, *The Secret Life of Lobsters*, 275.

103   Wallace, *Consider the Lobster*, 248.

104   Francesca Conte et al., "Humane Slaughter of Edible Decapod Crustaceans," *Animals* 11(4) (April 11, 2021), https://www.mdpi.com/2076-2615/11/4/1089.

105   Wallace, *Consider the Lobster*, 248.

106   "Nociception," *Science Direct*, https://www.sciencedirect.com/topics/neuro-science/nociception.

107   Conte et al., "Humane Slaughter of Edible Decapod Crustaceans," https://www.mdpi.com/2076-2615/11/4/1089.

108   Wallace, *Consider the Lobster*, 251.

109   Dina Spector, "Do Lobsters Feel Pain?" *Business Insider*, January 15, 2018, https://www.businessinsider.com/do-lobsters-feel-pain-2014-5.

110   Kim, "Do Lobsters Feel Pain? Here's What Scientists and Advocates Are Saying," https://sentientmedia.org/do-lobsters-feel-pain/.

111   Molly O'Neill, "What to Put in the Pot: Cooks Face Challenge Over Animal Rights," *New York Times*, August 8, 1990, https://www.nytimes.com/1990/08/08/garden/what-to-put-in-the-pot-cooks-face-challenge-over-animal-rights.html; "PETA protests Maine Lobster Festival in Rockland," WGME, August 3, 2016, https://wgme.com/news/local/peta-protests-maine-lobster-festival-in-rockland.

112   Wallace, *Consider the Lobster*, 253.

113   Corson, *The Secret Life of Lobsters*, 278.

114   O'Neill, "What to Put in the Pot," https://www.nytimes.com/1990/08/08/garden/what-to-put-in-the-pot-cooks-face-challenge-over-animal-rights.html.

115   Wallace, *Consider the Lobster*, 253.

116   Corson, *The Secret Life of Lobsters*, 129.

117   Linda Greenlaw, *The Lobster Chronicles: Life on a Very Small Island* (Hyperion, 2003), 5.

INTERNATIONAL CAMEL & OSTRICH RACES

118   Odie B. Faulk, *The U.S. Camel Corps* (Oxford University Press, 1976), 97; A. A. Gray et al., *Camels in Western America* (San Francisco California Historical Society, 1930), 7; John Shapard, "The United States Army Camel Corps 1856–66," *Military Review* (August 1975), https://www.armyupress.army.mil/Journals/Military-Review/Directors-Select-Articles/The-United-States-Army-Camel-Corps-1856-66/.

119   Faulk, *The U.S. Camel Corps*, 113.

120   Vince Hawkins, "The U.S. Army's 'Camel Corps' Experiment," The Army Historical Foundation (website), National Museum of the United States Army, https://armyhistory.org/the-u-s-armys-camel-corps-experiment/.

121   Shapard, "The United States Army Camel Corps 1856–66," https://www.armyupress.army.mil/Journals/Military-Review/Directors-Select-Articles/The-United-States-Army-Camel-Corps-1856-66/.

122   Faulk, *The U.S. Camel Corps*, 25, 35, 46–57.

123   Ibid., 112.

124   Ibid., 122–123.

125   Ken Thompson, *Where Do Camels Belong? Why Invasive Species Aren't All Bad* (Greystone, 2014), 1–2.

126   Emily Osterloff, "How do camels survive in deserts?" Natural History Museum, London, https://www.nhm.ac.uk/discover/how-do-camels-survive-in-deserts.html.

127   Gray et al., *Camels in Western America*, 12.

128   Joseph Warren Fabens, *The Uses of the Camel: Considered with a View to His Introduction into Our Western States and Territories* (Carleton, 1865), 14.

129   Faulk, *The U.S. Camel Corps*, 70–71, 74, 52.

130   Ibid., 87.

131   "Meet Aladdin," Mount Vernon (website), The Mount Vernon Ladies' Association, https://www.mountvernon.org/plan-your-visit/things-to-do/animals/aladdin/.

132   Faulk, *The U.S. Camel Corps*, 73.

133   Ibid., 155–157.

134   "Virginia City Historic District, Nevada," National Park Service, https://www.nps.gov/places/virginia-city-historic-district.htm.

135   Douglas McDonald, *Camels in Nevada* (Nevada Publications, 1983).

136   "The International Camel and Ostrich Races," Liquid Blue Events, https://liquidblueevents.com/international-camel-ostrich-races/.

137   "Hedrick's Camel & Ostrich Races," Hedrick's Promotions, https://www.hedricks.com/zooanimaldisplaysandraces.com/racingshows/camel-ostrich-zebr-araces.html.

138   "Camel & Ostrich Races at Ocean Downs (#1282 July 16, 2023)," posted August 22, 2023, by POST TIME with Heather Vitale, YouTube, 4 min., 37 sec., https://www.youtube.com/watch?v=3yLmRVgvlbM; "Extreme Day," Explore Minnesota, https://www.exploreminnesota.com/event/extreme-day/35288.

139   McDonald, *Camels in Nevada*.

140   Julia Ritchey, "Reporter Gets Schooled at Virginia City's Camel Races," KUNR, September 14, 2015, https://www.kunr.org/local-stories/2015-09-14/reporter-gets-schooled-at-virginia-citys-camel-races.

141   Ibid.

142   Molly Moser, "Epic Fall: The Story You Have All Been Waiting For," *Nevada Appeal*, September 10, 2016, https://www.nevadaappeal.com/news/2016/sep/10/epic-fall-the-story-you-have-all-been-waiting-for/.

143   Ibid.

144   Gregory Lawrence, "What is Slapstick Comedy? History, Examples, and Advice," *Backstage*, February 6, 2024, https://www.backstage.com/magazine/article/slapstick-comedy-definition-examples-76449/.

145   *Britannica*, "Slapstick," last updated September 4, 2024, https://www.britannica.com/art/slapstick-comedy.

146   *See* Lawrence, "What is Slapstick Comedy?" https://www.backstage.com/magazine/article/slapstick-comedy-definition-examples-76449/.

147   Robert Mankoff, "Killing a Frog," *New Yorker*, March 21, 2012, https://www.newyorker.com/cartoons/bob-mankoff/killing-a-frog.

148   Ben Healy, "What Makes Something Funny?" *The Atlantic*, March 2018, https://www.theatlantic.com/magazine/archive/2018/03/funny-how/550910/; Nina Shen Rastogi, "5 Leading Theories for Why We Laugh—and the Jokes That Prove Them Wrong," *Slate*, May 13, 2011, https://slate.com/culture/2011/05/5-leading-theories-for-why-we-laugh-and-the-jokes-that-prove-them-wrong.html.

149   Giovanni Sabato, "What's So Funny? The Science of Why We Laugh," *Scientific American*, June 26, 2019, https://www.scientificamerican.com/article/whats-so-funny-the-science-of-why-we-laugh/.

150   Rastogi, "5 Leading Theories for Why We Laugh," https://slate.com/culture/2011/05/5-leading-theories-for-why-we-laugh-and-the-jokes-that-prove-them-wrong.html.

151   Healy, "What Makes Something Funny?" https://www.theatlantic.com/magazine/archive/2018/03/funny-how/550910/.

152   "The Benign Violation Theory," Humor Research Lab at the University of Colorado, https://humorresearchlab.com/benign-violation-theory/.

153   Hilary Hanson, "If You Love Animals, Here Are 5 You Shouldn't Ride," *HuffPost*, July 9, 2015, https://www.huffpost.com/entry/animals-you-shouldnt-ride_n_7762286.

154   The Comedy Wildlife Photography Awards, https://www.comedywildlifephoto.com/.

155   Richard Varenchik, "Camels for Uncle Sam," *Desert* 44, no. 5 (June 1981), 27, https://www.yumpu.com/en/document/read/18004840/camels-for-uncle-sams-army-water-conservation-w-desert-.

156   Faulk, *The U.S. Camel Corps*, 155–157.

157   Kat Halsey, "Topsy the Camel," The Natural History Museum, Los Angeles County, https://nhm.org/stories/topsy-camel.

158   Cara Giaimo, "The Most Interesting Camel in the World," Atlas Obscura (website), April 4, 2017, https://www.atlasobscura.com/articles/old-topsy-camel-corps-griffith-park-zoo; Halsey, "Topsy the Camel," https://nhm.org/stories/topsy-camel.

JUMPING FROG JUBILEE

159   "Angels Camp," calaverashistory.org, Calaveras Heritage Council, calaverashistory.org/angels-camp.

160   "Calaveras County Fair & Jumping Frog Jubilee," Calaveras Visitors Bureau (website), https://www.gocalaveras.com/business/festivals-events/calaveras-county-fair-jumping-frog-jubilee/.

161   "Hop Up to Angels Camp: Famous frog jump & Calaveras County Fair Things are jumping in Angels Camp May 16 thru 19," *Escalon Times*, May 14, 2019, https://www.escalontimes.com/209-living/hop-angels-camp-famous-frog-jump-calaveras-county-fair-things-are-jumping-angels-camp-may-16-thru-19/.

162   Hennig Cohen, "Twain's Jumping Frog: Folktale to Literature to Folktale," *Western Folklore* 22, no. 1 (January 1963) 17–18.

163   *See, e.g.,* Gerd Hurm, "American Phonocentrism Revisited: The Hybrid Origins of Mark Twain's Celebrated Frog Tale," *AAA* 23, no. 1 (1998), 51–68; Edgar M. Branch, "'My Voice Is Still for Setchell': A Background Study of 'Jim Smiley and His Jumping Frog,'" *PMLA* 82, no. 7 (December 1967), 591–601.

164   Mark Twain, *The Celebrated Jumping Frog of Calaveras County* (Filter Press, 2012).

165   Roger Pen Cuff, "Mark Twain's Use of California Folklore in His Jumping Frog Story," *The Journal of American Folklore* 65, no. 256 (April–June 1952), 155–158.

166   *E.g.,* Branch, "My Voice is Still for Setchell," 591–601.

167   Lawrence R. Smith, "Mark Twain's 'Jumping Frog': Toward an American Heroic Ideal," *Mark Twain Journal* 20, no. 1 (Winter, 1979–1980), 15–18.

168   Randy Lewis, "Great Read: The Frog That Jump-Started Mark Twain's Career," *Los Angeles Times*, May 14, 2015, https://www.latimes.com/entertainment/great-reads/la-et-c1-mark-twain-california-20150514-story.html.

169   Randy Lewis, "Photo Gallery: The Frog That Jump-Started Mark Twain's Career," *Los Angeles Times*, https://www.latimes.com/entertainment/great-reads/la-et-mark-twain-california-pictures-photogallery.html.

170   "Calaveras County Fair & Jumping Frog Jubilee," Calaveras Visitors Bureau, https://www.gocalaveras.com/business/festivals-events/calaveras-county-fair-jumping-frog-jubilee/.

171   Pamphlet on view at Angels Camp Museum and Visitor Center recapping 1928 Jubilee.

172   Lewis, "The Frog That Jump-Started Mark Twain's Career," https://www.latimes.com/entertainment/great-reads/la-et-c1-mark-twain-california-20150514-story.html.

173   Jesse McKinley, "Celebrating, and Quarreling Over, Frogs," *New York Times*, May 20, 2007, https://www.nytimes.com/2007/05/20/us/20frog.html.

174   Lewis, "The Frog That Jump-Started Mark Twain's Career," https://www.latimes.com/entertainment/great-reads/la-et-c1-mark-twain-california-20150514-story.html.

175   Paul Baender, "The 'Jumping Frog' as a Comedian's First Virtue," *Modern Philology* 60, no. 3 (February 1963), 192–200.

176   Twain, *Jumping Frog*, 5.

177   McKinley, "Celebrating, and Quarreling Over, Frogs," https://www.nytimes.com/2007/05/20/us/20frog.html.

178   Walter Rose, "The Jumping Powers of Frogs," *Herpetologica* 10, no. 3 (December 4, 1954), 183.

179   *We Are the Champions*, episode 6, "Frog Jumping," written by Matthew-Lee Erlbach, directed by Brian Davis, featuring Rainn Wilson, aired November 17, 2020 on Netflix.

180   Sol Neelman, "Frog Jockeys Coax Amphibian Athletes to Great Lengths," *Wired,* May 24, 2012, https://www.wired.com/2012/05/jumping-frog-jubi-lee/.

181   Scott Harrison, "Frog in training for Calaveras County Jumping competition," *Los Angeles Times*, March 18, 2019, https://www.latimes.com/visuals/pho-tography/la-me-fw-archives-frog-training-for-calaveras-county-frog-jump-ing-competition-20190312-htmlstory.html.

182   McKinley, "Celebrating, and Quarreling Over, Frogs," https://www.nytimes.com/2007/05/20/us/20frog.html.

183   Mark Stein, "Goliaths Frogs Left in Dust in Hopping Derby," *Los Angeles Times*, May 21, 1990, https://www.latimes.com/archives/la-xpm-1990-05-21-mn-160-story.html.

184   *We Are the Champions.*

185   Justin Bookey, dir., *Jump: A Frogumentary*, Coolbellup Media, 2005. 36:00 ff.

186   Shelly Thorene, "Gustine team's 'Old Papa' wins 2022 Calaveras Frog Jump," *Union Democrat*, May 25, 2022, https://www.uniondemocrat.com/news/article_683e0c4e-dc61-11ec-97be-d798c0399571.html.

187   *We Are the Champions.*

188   Amina Khan, "Scientists get schooled at Calaveras County frog-jumping contest," *Los Angeles Times*, October 18, 2013, https://www.latimes.com/science/sciencenow/la-xpm-2013-oct-18-la-sci-sn-calaveras-county-frog-jumping-contest-breaks-record-20131018-story.html.

189   Ibid.

190   Ibid.

191   Joseph Stromberg, "The Science of Winning Leaps at the Calaveras County Frog Jumping Competition," *Smithsonian Magazine*, October 16, 2013, https://www.smithsonianmag.com/science-nature/the-science-of-winning-leaps-at-the-calaveras-county-frog-jumping-competition-2277694/.

192   McKinley, "Celebrating, and Quarreling Over, Frogs," https://www.nytimes.com/2007/05/20/us/20frog.html.

193   H. C. Astley et al., "Chasing maximal performance: a cautionary tale from the celebrated jumping frogs of Calaveras County," *The Journal of Experimental Biology* 216, 3947–3953, (2013).

194   Astley et al., "Chasing maximal performance," 3951–3952.

195   "Popular 'Jumping Frogs' Contest Angers Environmentalists, Animal Activ-ists," *VOA*, January 9, 2003, https://www.voanews.com/a/a-13-a-2003-01-09-36-popular-66298337/541847.html.

196   *Jump*, 45:40 ff.

197   Dan Thompson, "Jumping Frog Contest Poses Conundrum," *The Intelligencer*, January 1, 2003, https://www.theintelligencer.com/news/article/Jump-ing-Frog-Contest-Poses-Conundrum-10477814.php.

198   "Frog Welfare Policy," frogjump.org, https://www.frogjump.org/frog-jump-welfare-policy.

199   Kenneth Weiss, "Decision Saves Frog-Jumping Competition from Croaking,"

Los Angeles Times, February 6, 2003, https://www.latimes.com/archives/la-xpm-2003-feb-06-me-frogs6-story.html.

200   "California Red-Legged Frog," National Wildlife Federation (website), https://www.nwf.org/Educational-Resources/Wildlife-Guide/Amphibians/California-Red-Legged-Frog.

201   Don Thompson, "In Calaveras, No Hoppy Returns," *Washington Post*, January 19, 2003, https://www.washingtonpost.com/archive/politics/2003/01/19/in-calaveras-no-hoppy-returns/8e5012da-fe73-47d1-91f1-fa56c20829cb/.

202   "Saving the California Red-Legged Frog," Center for Biological Diversity (website), https://www.biologicaldiversity.org/species/amphibians/California_red-legged_frog/index.html.

203   "Goliaths of Frogdom Put Contest in Turmoil," *New York Times*, January 9, 1990, https://www.nytimes.com/1990/01/09/us/goliaths-of-frogdom-put-contest-in-turmoil.html.

204   Associated Press, "Fame Aside, Frog Finds No Habitat in Calaveras," *New York Times*, March 11, 2001, https://www.nytimes.com/2001/03/11/science/fame-aside-frog-finds-no-habitat-in-calaveras.html.

205   *See, e.g.,* Dirk Johnson, "Frogs' Best Friends: Students Who Won't Dissect Them," *New York Times*, May 29, 1997, https://www.nytimes.com/1997/05/29/us/frogs-best-friends-students-who-won-t-dissect-them.html.

206   *See, e.g.,* Arnold Arluke, "Animal Abuse as Dirty Play," *Symbolic Interaction* 25, no. 4 (2002), 405–430.

207   Jon Freeman, "Muppets on His Hands," *Saturday Evening Post*, November 1979, 51–52.

208   Nicola Stead, "Motivating your frogs, Calaveras county can help," *Journal of Experimental Biology*, vol. 216, issue 21 (November 1, 2013), https://journals.biologists.com/jeb/article/216/21/i/11657/motivating-your-frogs-calaveras-county-can-help.

209   Cuff, "Mark Twain's Use of California Folklore in His Jumping Frog Story," 158.

210   Mark Twain, "Private History of the 'Jumping Frog' Story," *The North American Review* 158, no. 449 (April 1894), 452–453; see also Gina Burkart, "The Jumping Frog Story—Both Old and New," *The North American Review* 293, no. 6 (November–December 2008), 40.

211   *Plutarch's Moralia*, vol. XII, trans. William Helmbold (Harvard University Press, 1947), 355.

GROUNDHOG DAY

212   Program from Annual Groundhog Club Banquet on Groundhog Day Eve.

213   Tristan Klinefelter and Aaron Marrie, "At 137 years old, Punxsutawney Phil has a secret to living forever," ABC27.com, January 31, 2023, https://www.abc27.com/pennsylvania/at-137-years-old-punxsutawney-phil-has-a-secret-to-living-forever/.

214   History.com Editors, "Imbolc," History.com, April 5, 2018, updated February 1, 2024, https://www.history.com/topics/holidays/imbolc.

215   Don Yoder, *Groundhog Day* (Stackpole, 2002), 51.

216   John Ray (1678), quoted in Stephen Winick, "Groundhog Day: Ancient Origins of a Modern Celebration," *Folklife Today* (blog), Library of Congress, https://blogs.loc.gov/folklife/2022/02/groundhog-day-ancient-origins-of-a-modern-celebration/.

217   *E.g.*, Jackie Wattles, "The animals you can count on to predict the weather, according to science," CNN.com, February 2, 2024, https://www.cnn.com/2024/02/02/world/can-groundhogs-predict-weather-scn/index.html; "8 Animals Thought to Predict the Weather," Weather Channel (website), February 18, 2013, https://weather.com/science/news/animals-predicting-weather-20130201; signs at the Punxsutawney Weather Discovery Center.

218   Yoder, *Groundhog Day*, 54.

219   Ibid., 1.

220   Emily DeLetter, "Did the groundhog see his shadow? See results of Punxsutawney Phil's 2024 winter forecast," *USA Today*, February 2, 2024, https://www.usatoday.com/story/news/nation/2024/02/02/groundhog-day-2024-shadow-results/72409638007/.

221   *E.g.*, Mark Scolforo, "The Origins of Groundhog Day and Punxsutawney Phil," Associated Press, January 31, 2024, https://apnews.com/article/groundhog-day-punxsutawney-pennsylvania-phil-winter-b037d58615f7b-5f0007a7153a888e263.

222   Yoder, *Groundhog Day*, 13–14; "History of Groundhog Day," Visit Pennsylvania (website), January 8, 2024, https://www.visitpa.com/article/history-groundhog-day.

223   *E.g.*, Andie Ioó, "How to Get Rid of Groundhogs," LawnLove (website), November 7, 2023, https://lawnlove.com/blog/how-to-get-rid-of-groundhogs/.

224   University of Michigan, "Tip Sheet: Mammal's hibernation interrupted by Groundhog Day," news release, January 26, 2001, https://news.umich.edu/tip-sheet-mammal-s-hibernation-interrupted-by-groundhog-day/.

225   "Nuisance Wildlife," Pennsylvania Game Commission (website), https://www.pgc.pa.gov/Wildlife/Pages/NuisanceWildlife.aspx; "2024–25 Seasons and Bag Limits," Pennsylvania Game Commission, https://www.pgc.pa.gov/HuntTrap/Law/Pages/SeasonsandBagLimits.aspx.

226   Joshua B. Johnson, *Pennsylvania Game Commission Bureau of Wildlife Management Annual Project Report* (Pennsylvania Game Commission, September 13, 2023), 6, https://www.pgc.pa.gov/InformationResources/MediaReportsSurveys/AnnualWildlifeManagementReports/Documents/11101-22.pdf.

227   Animal Legal Defense Fund, "In 2022, Wildlife Services intentionally killed 2,267 groundhogs and destroyed or removed 1,087 of their burrows," Facebook, https://www.facebook.com/reel/352777504190515.

228   Christopher Klein, "Groundhog was once on Punxsutawney's Menu," History.

com, January 30, 2019, https://www.history.com/news/groundhog-was-once-on-punxsutawneys-menu.

229   *See* "Groundhog Day Weather," National Weather Service, https://www.weather.gov/car/groundhogday; Yoder, *Groundhog Day*, 10–11.

230   Yoder, *Groundhog Day*, 12; Jennifer Latson, "The Original Groundhog Day Involved Eating the Groundhog," *Time* magazine, February 2, 2015, https://time.com/3685895/groundhog-day-history/.

231   Latson, "The Original Groundhog Day Involved Eating the Groundhog," https://time.com/3685895/groundhog-day-history/.

232   Elizabeth Wolfe and Jessica Moskowitz, "Texas Longhorn who snarled New Jersey trains service will spend his remaining days in an animal sanctuary," CNN.com, December 15, 2013, https://www.cnn.com/2023/12/14/us/new-jersey-bull-train-tracks-capture/index.html; "Cow Who Escaped New York Slaughterhouse Finds Sanctuary," *New York Times*, January 22, 2016, https://www.nytimes.com/2016/01/23/nyregion/cow-that-escaped-new-york-slaughterhouse-finds-sanctuary.html.

233   "Happy ever after for Butch and Sundance?" *BBC News*, January 16, 1998, http://news.bbc.co.uk/2/hi/uk_news/47671.stm.

234   Jason Horowitz, "A Famous Walrus Is Killed, and Norwegians Are Divided," *New York Times*, August 19, 2022, https://www.nytimes.com/2022/08/19/world/europe/norway-walrus-freya-killed.html.

235   Ed Shanahan, "The Year Flaco the Owl Roamed Free," *New York Times*, February 2, 2024, https://www.nytimes.com/2024/02/02/nyregion/flaco-owl-central-park-zoo.html.

236   Esme Mazzeo, "Owl Who Died After Escaping New York City Zoo Is Mourned by Busy Phillips and More Stars: 'I'm Devastated,'" *People*, February 25, 2024, https://people.com/owl-died-after-escaping-new-york-zoo-mourned-celebrities-including-busy-philipps-8599959.

237   Ed Shanahan, "New York Mourns Flaco, an Owl Who Inspired as He Made the City His Own," *New York Times*, February 26, 2024, https://www.nytimes.com/2024/02/24/nyregion/flaco-eurasian-eagle-owl-nyc.html.

238   *See* Emily Falk, "Why storytelling is an important tool for social change," *Los Angeles Times*, June 27, 2021, https://www.latimes.com/opinion/story/2021-06-27/stories-brain-science-memory-social-change.

239   Aline Lima-Nunes et al., "Justice seems not to be for all: Exploring the scope of justice," *The Inquisitive Mind* (2013), https://www.in-mind.org/article/justice-seems-not-to-be-for-all-exploring-the-scope-of-justice?page=2.

240   *See* "Here's Why You Should Boycott Groundhog Day," *Wholesome Culture* (blog), https://blog.wholesomeculture.com/heres-why-you-should-boycott-groundhog-day-this-year/.

241   Megan Brugger, "What does Punxsutawney Phil do the rest of the year?" ABC4, February 2, 2024, https://www.abc4.com/news/what-does-punxsutawney-phil-do-the-rest-of-the-year/.

242   *See* "Tip Sheet: Mammal's hibernation interrupted by Groundhog Day,"

https://news.umich.edu/tip-sheet-mammal-s-hibernation-interrupt-ed-by-groundhog-day/.

243 Holly Pretsky, "Remembering Staten Island Chuck 10 years later," *City & State New York*, February 1, 2024, https://www.cityandstateny.com/personal-ity/2024/02/remembering-staten-island-chuck-10-years-later/393823/.

244 Fernanda Santos, "Reclusive Staten Island Groundhog Bites Mayor," *New York Times*, February 2, 2009, https://www.nytimes.com/2009/02/03/nyregion/03groundhog.html; Matthew Lapierre, "Quebec groundhog wakes up to a snowstorm, predicts an early spring," CBC, February 2, 2024, https://www.cbc.ca/news/canada/montreal/fred-junior-early-spring-ground-hog-1.7102782.

245 Ingrid Newkirk, "Money Talks! PETA Offers Huge Coin to Let Punxsut-awney Phil Retire," news release, January 22, 2024, https://www.peta.org/media/news-releases/money-talks-peta-offers-huge-coin-to-let-punxsutaw-ney-phil-retire/.

246 Alyssa Bradford, "Is it time for Punxsutawney Phil to retire? PETA proposes a coin toss for Groundhog Day tradition," *Deseret News*, January 27, 2024, https://www.deseret.com/2024/1/27/24050610/peta-groundhog-day-coin-toss.

247 Nate Hambel, "Why Groundhogs Hit Snooze on Their Holiday," *Forest Preserve District of DuPage County* (blog), January 29, 2021, https://www.dupageforest.org/blog/groundhog-glory.

248 Kelly Bryant, "10 Famous Groundhogs Besides Punxsutawney Phil," *Reader's Digest*, January 30, 2024, https://www.rd.com/article/famous-ground-hogs-besides-punxsutawney-phil/; Ashley Williams, "Punxsutawney Phil isn't the only famous groundhog: At least 6 other states have their own weather prognosticators," AccuWeather (website), January 30, 2024, https://www.accuweather.com/en/weather-news/punxsutawney-phil-isnt-the-only-fa-mous-groundhog-at-least-6-other-states-have-their-own-weather-prognostica-tors/434145.

249 Fernanda Santos, "Reclusive Staten Island Groundhog Bites Mayor," *New York Times*, February 2, 2009, https://www.nytimes.com/2009/02/03/nyre-gion/03groundhog.html.

250 Gilles Gagné, "Fred, the Gaspé marmot, predicts a late spring," *le Soleil*, February 2, 2019, https://www.lesoleil.com/2019/02/02/fred-la-marmotte-gaspesienne-predit-un-printemps-tardif-16091c1c735d-1658d937e58859aab096/.

251 Alexandra Chomik, "Is Punxsutawney Phil a father and how old is the famed groundhog?" *The U.S. Sun*, March 28, 2024, https://www.the-sun.com-news/10911523/punxsutawney-phil-groundhog-day-father-babies/.

252 *See, e.g.*, "Teachable moment," USDA APHIS, Punxsutawney Groundhog Club (December 18, 2020); "Inspection Report," USDA APHIS, Punxsutaw-ney Groundhog Club (December 18, 2020).

253 Wayne Parry, "Punxsutawney Phil, the spring-predicting groundhog, and wife

Phyllis are parents of 2 babies," Associated Press, March 28, 2024, https://apnews.com/article/punxsutawney-phil-groundhog-babies-839fa23e87006f-75bc4eb716e55601e7.

254   "TIL: In the 1990s, Punxsutawney Phil died right before Groundhog Day because he was gifted a house that had toxic paint," Reddit.com, https://www.reddit.com/r/pittsburgh/comments/1ahhuky/til_in_the_1990s_punxsutawney_phil_died_right/.

255   Yoder, *Groundhog Day*, 83.

256   *See generally* William W. Donner, *Serious Nonsense: Groundhog Lodges, Versammlinge, and Pennsylvania German Heritage* (Pennsylvania University Press, 2016).

257   "History of Groundhog Day," Visit Pennsylvania (website), January 8, 2024, https://www.visitpa.com/article/history-groundhog-day.

258   Yoder, *Groundhog Day*, 13; Lisa Wardle, "Punxsutawney Phil the astronaut and sports analyst: What he does after Groundhog Day," *Penn Live*, January 31, 2017, https://www.pennlive.com/life/2017/01/punxsutawney_phil_astronaut_sports.html.

259   "History of Groundhog Day," https://www.visitpa.com/article/history-groundhog-day.

260   Yoder, *Groundhog Day*, 6, 14.

261   Dan Nephin, "'Terrible' Phil," *Ellwood City Ledger*, February 1, 2006, https://www.ellwoodcityledger.com/story/news/local/2006/02/02/terrible-phil/18602721007/.

262   Harold Ramis, dir., *Groundhog Day*, Columbia Pictures, 1993, ~58:44.

263   "Groundhog Day Forecasts and Climate History," National Oceanic and Atmospheric Administration, updated February 2, 2024, https://www.ncei.noaa.gov/news/groundhog-day-forecasts-and-climate-history.

264   Omega Ilijevich, "DC's Stuffed Groundhog Predicts an Early Spring," *Washingtonian*, February 2, 2024, https://www.washingtonian.com/2024/02/02/dcs-stuffed-groundhog-predicts-an-early-spring/.

265   Agence France-Press, "Canadian groundhog Fred la Marmotte found dead before planned prediction," *The Guardian*, February 2, 2023, https://www.theguardian.com/world/2023/feb/02/quebec-canada-dead-groundhog-spring-undetermined.

BUTTERFLY DAYS

266   Lucy Neely McLane, *A Piney Paradise* (Lawton Kennedy, 1952), 37.

267   *See* Dominick Sinicropi, Report, "Microclimate conditions at the Pacific Grove Monarch Sanctuary between October, 2021–April, 2022," https://friendsofthemonarchs.org/wp-content/uploads/2022/06/Microclimate-conditions-at-the-Pacific-Grove-Monarch-Sanctuary-2022.pdf.

268   John Steinbeck, *Sweet Thursday* (Viking, 1954), 250.

269   Lucia Shepardson, *The Butterfly Trees* (1914), quoted in Patricia Hamilton, *Monarchs in Butterfly Town, U.S.A.* (Pacific Grove Books, 2022), 1.

270   McLane, *A Piney Paradise*, 37.

271   John Detro, "Much Activity Planned this weekend to welcome the return of the Monarchs," *Pacific Grove Beacon* (October 7, 1994).

272   *2023 Butterfly Days Official Program*, letter from Mildred Gehringer (founder), 8; *History of the Butterfly Parade*, pamphlet from fiftieth anniversary of Butterfly Days.

273   Steinbeck, *Sweet Thursday*, 251.

274   Ibid., 251.

275   Steve Chawkins, "Anger flutters over 'Butterfly Town USA,'" *Los Angeles Times*, August 29, 2010, https://www.latimes.com/archives/la-xpm-2010-aug-29-la-me-butterflies-20100829-story.html.

276   Larry Parsons, "P.G.'s 'Butterfly Lady' dies," *Monterey Herald*, January 11, 2008, https://www.montereyherald.com/2008/01/11/pgs-butterfly-lady-dies/.

277   Ro Vacarro, "P.G. Butterflies and their human friends," *Sunday Herald*, November 21, 1994.

278   Boria Sax, *The Mythical Zoo* (Abrams Press, 2013), 349–350

279   "Monarchs and Día de Muertos in Mexico," *Monarch Joint Venture* (blog), November 2, 2020, https://monarchjointventure.org/blog/monarchs-and-dia-de-muertos-in-mexico.

280   Catherine Christopher, "Tales of Monarch Butterflies Date Back to Days of Serra," *Monterey Peninsula Herald*, November 5, 1954.

281   *E.g.*, "2020: A Metamorphosis," *Texas Butterfly Ranch*, October 29, 2020, https://www.youtube.com/watch?v=9BUITfH3q3E; Marilyn Kendrix, "Caterpillars to Butterflies," Southern New England Conference of United Church of Christ (website), May 26, 2020, https://www.sneucc.org/blogdetail/caterpillars-to-butterflies-14004471.

282   "Why are Butterfly Tattoos So Popular?" *HubPages*, February 2, 2024, https://discover.hubpages.com/style/butterflytattoos.

283   "The History and Meaning of the Butterfly," *Alex and Ani* (blog), March 18, 2022, https://www.alexandani.com/blogs/the-wire/symbol-meaning-butterfly.

284   Elizabeth Pennisi, "How the monarch butterfly evolved its resistance to toxic milkweed," *Science*, October 2, 2019, https://www.science.org/content/article/how-monarch-butterfly-evolved-its-resistance-toxic-milkweed.

285   Steve Rubenstein, "People seem to prefer things that flutter," *San Francisco Chronicle*, October 14, 1992.

286   "Monarch Butterfly Conservation," Xerces Society, https://www.xerces.org/monarchs.

287   "Western Monarch Conservation," Xerces Society, https://xerces.org/monarchs/western-monarch-conservation.

288   Jane Algeo Watson, *Mystery of the Monarchs* (The House of Advertising, 1959), chapter 2.

289   *Monarch Butterfly Migration*, handout from Monterey Public Library (October 16, 1950).

290   Pacific Grove, Cal. Municipal Code, § 11.48.010, Ordinance, https://www.codepublishing.com/CA/PacificGrove/html/PacificGrove11/PacificGrove1148.html.

291   Bonnie Gartshore, "Butterflies and Indians," *Monterey Peninsula Herald*, January 30, 1992.

292   McLane, *A Piney Paradise*, 38.

293   Ibid.

294   "Strict Law Protects Butterflies in P.G.," *Monterey Peninsula Herald*, June 21, 1956.

295   Dave Hoff, "'Butterfly Murder' Charged in Pacific Grove Dispute."

296   "Monarch butterflies appear to be recovering from last winter's devastating die-off," World Wildlife Fund, February 14, 2003, https://wwf.panda.org/wwf_news/?5881/Monarch-butterflies-appear-to-be-recovering-from-last-winters-devastating-die-off.

297   Steve Chawkins, "Anger flutters over 'Butterfly Town USA," *Los Angeles Times,* August 29, 2010, https://www.latimes.com/archives/la-xpm-2010-aug-29-la-me-butterflies-20100829-story.html.

298   "Petition to Protect the Monarch Butterfly (Danaus Plexippus Plexippus) Under the Endangered Species Act," Center for Biological Diversity, August 26, 2014, https://www.biologicaldiversity.org/species/invertebrates/pdfs/Monarch_ESA_Petition.pdf.

299   16 U.S.C. § 1532(19).

300   *Tenn. Valley Auth. v. Hill*, 437 U.S. 153 (1978).

301   "Migratory monarch butterfly now Endangered – IUCN Red List," IUCN, July 21, 2022, https://www.iucn.org/press-release/202207/migratory-monarch-butterfly-now-endangered-iucn-red-list.

302   85 Fed. Reg. 81813 (December 17, 2020), https://www.federalregister.gov/documents/2020/12/17/2020-27523/endangered-and-threatened-wildlife-and-plants-12-month-finding-for-the-monarch-butterfly.

303   Press Release: "Fish and Wildlife Service Proposes Endangered Species Act Protection for Monarch Butterfly; Urges Increased Public Engagement to Help Save the Species," U.S. Fish & Wildlife Service, December 10, 2024, https://www.fws.gov/press-release/2024-12/monarch-butterfly-proposed-endangered-species-act-protection.

304   Meghann Cuniff, "Swallows at San Juan Capistrano were driven away by development. But the birds are slowly coming back," *Los Angeles Times*, June 2, 2017, https://www.latimes.com/local/lanow/la-me-swallow-capistrano-20170602-htmlstory.html.

305   Ibid.

306   W. B. Yeats, "Tom O'Roughley," *The Wild Swans at Coole* (Macmillan, 1919), 26, line 12.

SCOPES TRIAL PLAY AND FESTIVAL

307 The Butler Act, HB no. 185, chapter 27 (1925), available at https://teva.contentdm.oclc.org/digital/collection/scopes/id/169.

308 Alfred Watterson McCann, *God—or Gorilla: How the Monkey Theory of Evolution Exposes Its Own Methods, Refutes Its Own Principles, Denies Its Own Inferences, Disproves Its Own Case* (Devin-Adair Company, 1925), vii.

309 *E.g.,* Edward J. Larson, *Summer for the Gods: The Scopes Trial and America's Continuing Debate over Science and Religion* (Basic Books, 1997), 69.

310 Original ACLU advertisement from the *Chattanooga Daily Times* appears in Randy Moore, *Evolution in the Courtroom* (ABC-CLIO, 2001), 9.

311 Marquis James, "Around Town at the Scopes Trial," *New Yorker*, July 4, 1925, https://www.newyorker.com/magazine/1925/07/11/dayton-tennessee.

312 Larson, *Summer for the Gods*, 84; Gregg Jarrett, *The Trial of the Century* (Threshold Editions, 2023), 55.

313 Ed Caudill email message to author, June 14, 2022.

314 John T. Scopes, *Center of the Storm: Memoirs of John T. Scopes* (Holt, Rinehart and Winston, 1967), 59.

315 Moore, *Evolution in the Courtroom*, 10.

316 "Monkey Trial: The Leopold and Loeb Trial," PBS, October 1, 2018, https://www.pbs.org/wgbh/americanexperience/features/monkeytrial-leopold-and-loeb-trial/.

317 Larson, *Summer for the Gods*, 72.

318 Ibid., 96–98.

319 Scopes, *Center of the Storm*, 77.

320 "WGN Radio Broadcasts the Trial," PBS, October 1, 2018, https://www.pbs.org/wgbh/americanexperience/features/monkeytrial-wgn-radio-broadcasts-trial/.

321 Larson, *Summer for the Gods*, 186.

322 *The World's Most Famous Court Trial: Tennessee Evolution Case* (Lawbook Exchange, 1925), 288.

323 Ibid., 284–285.

324 Ibid., 287–289.

325 Ibid., 304 (cleaned up).

326 Ibid., 305.

327 Ibid., 306.

328 Larson, *Summer for the Gods*, 191.

329 Ibid., 200–201.

330 Ibid., 225–234.

331 *See* ibid., 149.

332 Tom Davis, "The history of the Scopes play and festival," *Herald-News*, June 13, 2022, https://www.rheaheraldnews.com/news/article_481fff48-eb35-11ec-bb24-0387d8273306.html.

333 Larson, *Summer for the Gods*, 47.

334 Ibid., 8 (quoting *Chicago Tribune*, cleaned up).

335   Thomas Huxley, *Evidence as to Man's Place in Nature* (Cambridge University Press, 1863).

336   *The World's Most Famous Court Trial*, 174.

337   William Jennings Bryan, *The Prince of Peace* (Fleming H. Revell, 1914), 15–16.

338   Ibid., 13.

339   Phil Edwards, "The Scopes Monkey Trial was one of the greatest publicity stunts ever," *Vox*, July 21, 2015, https://www.vox.com/2015/7/21/9009713/scopes-trial-spectacle.

340   Larson, *Summer for the Gods*, 105.

341   Display at the Rhea County Heritage and Scopes Trial Museum in Dayton, TN, showing monkey doll and explaining that children played with them during the trial.

342   Larson, *Summer for the Gods*, 174–175.

343   L. Sprague de Camp, *The Great Monkey Trial* (Doubleday, 1968), 259–261. *See also* "Joe Mindy Performance," Volunteer Voices Collection at University of Tennessee, https://digital.lib.utk.edu/collections/islandora/object/vol-voices%3A2124.

344   Moore, *Evolution in the Courtroom*, 10; de camp, *The Great Monkey Trial*, 261.

345   de Camp, *The Great Monkey Trial*, 269.

346   William Jennings Bryan, "Man," reprinted in *Speeches of William Jennings Bryan*, vol. 2 (Funk & Wagnalls, 1911).

ACKNOWLEDGMENTS

I love seeing paintings where the artist sketched only a hand, or a face, on a blank canvas, conjuring a meaningful form out of the surrounding emptiness. Writing this book was a lot like that: pulling scene after scene into focus, one sentence, one festival at a time, concrete images emerging from the hazy space on the edge of the page. The book took shape from the void over months, at different places around the country, with so many people helping me along the way.

I am indebted to my agent, Malaga Baldi, whose support and excitement buoyed me through the entire publishing process. The group at Apollo Publishers, and especially my editor, Drew Anderla, have been eager and thoughtful partners in editing this book. It is a much stronger book for Drew's keen eye, and I will always be grateful for his careful contemplation and contributions.

Paying attention to animals, for me, was a learned skill. We are taught to ignore and use animals in our society, so recentering them required purposeful relearning. I cultivated this care for animals over years of studying and working with brilliant people such as Katherine Meyer, Jon Hanson, Justin Marceau, Kristen Stilt, Andy Stawasz, Rebecca Garverman, and more. Learning how to write is another learned skill, one I've worked on for decades, guided by countless teachers and mentors in high school, college, and beyond. Thank you all.

The stars of this book, of course, are the animals who slither and scuttle and trot and jump across the pages. I have tried to be a thoughtful, spiritual witness to their experiences. Though I could not stop any of the harm or prevent any of their deaths, I kept my eyes open. I watched as they fell and shook and squirmed. I'm grateful for every animal I crossed paths with, even if the path was cut short. Their lives mattered—to me, to this book project, and hopefully to anyone who reads about their unwitting roles in these events.

So many friends encouraged me while I wrote and researched, especially those from law school. I also had some strong cheerleaders in the Army Women's Soccer Team alumnae and NRDC's Litigation Team, for which I am humbled and grateful. And thank you to my Alpha Phi community, which has carried me through so much of my life and has always pushed me to be a better version of myself.

To my family, I am so grateful for your unwavering support. My grandmother's work is a legacy we have all equally inherited; thank you for trusting me to do this unfinished project justice. Mark, Steph, Maya, and Bryn, thank you for your thoughtful questions and good company. Jane and Tyler, your kindness, openness, and curiosity have been unmatched. And to my parents, thank you for your stalwart faith in me. I am who I am because of your love and encouragement in all things.

And finally: Molly. Thank you for everything. From traipsing around the country to eating dry bagels and sipping black coffee after red-eye flights so we could squeeze in a festival between two full work weeks to sharing endless dinner conversations about chapter structure, you've been my partner in this project every step of the way. When I first had the idea for this book, I was timid, scared by all I didn't know and all I hadn't done. But your belief in me is so deep, so unconditional, that it tamps down my own ever-present doubts and worries. To be loved and trusted like that is the greatest gift of my life.

Thank you, thank you.